# JasperReports for Java Developers

Create, Design, Format, and Export Reports with
the World's Most Popular Java Reporting Library

**David R. Heffelfinger**

PUBLISHING

BIRMINGHAM - MUMBAI

# JasperReports for Java Developers

## Create, Design, Format, and Export Reports with the World's Most Popular Java Reporting Library

First published: July 2006

Production Reference: 1180706

Published by Packt Publishing Ltd.
32 Lincoln Road
Olton
Birmingham, B27 6PA, UK.

ISBN 1-904811-90-6

www.packtpub.com

Cover Image by www.visionwt.com

# Credits

**Author**

David R. Heffelfinger

**Reviewers**

Thomas M. Ose

Meenakshi Singh

Sarosh Khateeb

**Development Editor**

Douglas Paterson

**Assistant Development Editor**

Nikhil Bangera

**Technical Editor**

Priyanka Baruah

**Project Manager**

Patricia Weir

**Editorial Manager**

Dipali Chittar

**Indexer**

Mithil Kulkarni

**Proofreader**

Chris Smith

**Production Coordinator**

Manjiri Nadkarni

**Layouts and Illustrations**

Shantanu Zagade

**Cover Designer**

Manjiri Nadkarni

# About the Author

**David R. Heffelfinger** has been developing software professionally since 1995; he has been using Java as his primary programming language since 1996. He has worked on many large-scale projects for several clients including Freddie Mac, Fannie Mae, and the US Department of Defense. He has a Masters degree in Software Engineering from Southern Methodist University. David is editor in chief of Ensode.net (`http://www.ensode.net`), a website about Java, Linux, and other technology topics.

I would like to thank everyone at Packt Publishing, particularly Douglas Paterson, Patricia Weir, Nikhil Bangera, and Priyanka Baruah, and the technical reviewer, Thomas Ose. This book wouldn't have been a reality without your help. I would especially like to thank my family for their support.

*A special dedication goes to my wife and daughter.*

# Table of Contents

# Preface

JasperReports was started by Teodor Danciu, in 2001, when he was faced with the task of evaluating reporting tools for a project he was working on. The existing solutions that he found were too expensive for his project's budget. Therefore, he decided to write his own reporting tool, JasperReports, which has now become immensely popular, and is currently one of the most popular (if not the most popular) Java reporting tool available.

JasperReports is an open-source Java class library designed to aid developers with the task of adding reporting capabilities to Java applications by providing an API to facilitate the ability to generate reports from any kind of Java application. Though primarily used to add reporting capabilities to web-based applications, it can also be used to create standalone desktop or command-line Java applications for report generation.

This book steers you through each point of report setup, to creating, designing, formatting, and exporting reports with data from a wide range of datasources, and integrating JasperReports with other Java frameworks.

## What This Book Covers

*Chapter 1* covers JasperReports' history, and its features and gives us an overview of the steps involved in generating reports using JasperReports.

*Chapter 2* shows us how to embed JasperReports into client and server-side Java applications. We will install JasperReports and learn how to identify and install required libraries. We will also see how to set up our development and execution environment to add reporting capabilities to Java applications.

In *Chapter 3*, we create our first static JasperReports both programmatically and by using the ANT tool. We will see how to work with JRXML and binary report templates to generate reports in JasperReports' native format. We will then learn how to view these reports.

In *Chapter 4*, we learn how to create dynamic reports. We will do this by embedding SQL queries in the JRXML report template, or by passing the database data to the compiled report via a datasource.

In *Chapter 5*, we cover how to use datasources other than databases to create reports. Specifically, we will learn to create reports from empty datasources, Java objects, TableModels, XML data, and also from our custom-created datasources.

In *Chapter 6*, we cover how to create elaborate layouts for our reports by adding background images or text to a report, logically grouping report data, conditionally printing report data, and creating subreports.

In *Chapter 7*, we cover how to take advantage of JasperReports' graphical features and create reports with graphical data like geometric shapes, images, and 2-D and 3-D charts.

*Chapter 8* discusses advanced JasperReports' features like creating crosstab (cross-tabulation) reports and adding anchors, hyperlinks, and bookmarks. We then see how to work with subdatasets and how to execute snippets of Java code by using scriptlets. This chapter also shows how to display report text in different languages.

In *Chapter 9*, we cover how to export our reports to all formats supported by JasperReports; these include PDF, RTF, Excel, HTML, CSV, XML, and plain text. We also see how to direct exported reports to a browser.

*Chapter 10* covers iReport, which is a report designer that can help us visually generate JRXML templates. This chapter shows how to install and get started with iReport. iReport can be used to do everything that we have covered so far in this book and this chapter shows us how.

*Chapter 11* covers the integration of JasperReports with three of the most popular Java web application frameworks around—Spring Web MVC, JavaServer Faces, and Struts. We shall also see how to generate reports with data obtained using Hibernate, which is a popular Java Object Relational Mapping tool.

## What You Need for This Book

To use this book, you will of course need JasperReports. This is freely downloadable from http://www.sourceforge.net/projects/jasperreports.

JasperReports has its own requirements for proper and successful functioning: Java Development Kit (JDK) 1.4 or newer (http://java.sun.com/javase/downloads/index.jsp), ANT 1.6 or newer (http://ant.apache.org/), iReport 1.2 or newer (http://ireport.sourceforge.net/). Any operating system supporting Java can be used (any modern version of Microsoft Windows, Mac OS X, Linux, or Solaris).

# Conventions

In this book, you will find a number of styles of text that distinguish between different kinds of information. Here are some examples of these styles, and an explanation of their meaning.

There are three styles for code. Code words in text are shown as follows: "All JRXML files contain a `<jasperReport>` root element that can contain many sub-elements."

A block of code will be set as follows:

```
package net.ensode.jasperbook;
import java.util.HashMap;
import net.sf.jasperreports.engine.JREmptyDataSource;
import net.sf.jasperreports.engine.JRException;
import net.sf.jasperreports.engine.JasperFillManager;
```

When we wish to draw your attention to a particular part of a code block, the relevant lines or items will be made bold:

```
<detail>
  <band height="20">
    <staticText>
      <reportElement x="20" y="0" width="200" height="20"/>
      <text><![CDATA[If you don't see this, it didn't work]]></text>
    </staticText>
  </band>
</detail>
```

Any command-line input and output is written as follows:

```
$ ant
```

**New terms** and **important words** are introduced in a bold-type font. Words that you see on the screen, in menus or dialog boxes for example, appear in our text like this: "clicking the **Next** button moves you to the next screen".

 Warnings or important notes appear in a box like this.

 Tips and tricks appear like this.

# Reader Feedback

Feedback from our readers is always welcome. Let us know what you think about this book, what you liked or may have disliked. Reader feedback is important for us to develop titles that you really get the most out of.

To send us general feedback, simply drop an email to feedback@packtpub.com, making sure to mention the book title in the subject of your message.

If there is a book that you need and would like to see us publish, please send us a note in the **SUGGEST A TITLE** form on www.packtpub.com or email suggest@packtpub.com.

If there is a topic that you have expertise in and you are interested in either writing or contributing to a book, see our author guide on www.packtpub.com/authors.

# Customer Support

Now that you are the proud owner of a Packt book, we have a number of things to help you to get the most from your purchase.

# Downloading the Example Code for the Book

Visit http://www.packtpub.com/support, and select this book from the list of titles to download any example code or extra resources for this book. The files available for download will then be displayed.

 The downloadable files contain instructions on how to use them.

# Errata

Although we have taken every care to ensure the accuracy of our contents, mistakes do happen. If you find a mistake in one of our books — maybe a mistake in text or code — we would be grateful if you would report this to us. By doing this you can save other readers from frustration, and help to improve subsequent versions of this book. If you find any errata, report them by visiting http://www.packtpub.com/support, selecting your book, clicking on the **Submit Errata** link, and entering the details of your errata. Once your errata have been verified, your submission will be accepted and the errata added to the list of existing errata. The existing errata can be viewed by selecting your title from http://www.packtpub.com/support.

# Questions

You can contact us at questions@packtpub.com if you are having a problem with some aspect of the book, and we will do our best to address it.

# 1
# An Overview of JasperReports

This chapter presents an overview of JasperReports and explains its capabilities and features. Here is a brief outline of the topics covered in this chapter:

- A brief history of JasperReports
- What JasperReports is, and what it can do for us
- A brief discussion of the JasperReports open-source license
- The features of JasperReports
- JasperReports' class library dependencies
- A brief overview of the steps required to generate reports with JasperReports
- Where to get support for JasperReports

## Brief History of JasperReports

JasperReports was started by Teodor Danciu, in 2001, when he was faced with the task of evaluating reporting tools for a project he was working on. The existing solutions that he found were too expensive for his project's budget. Therefore, he decided to write his own reporting tool. The project for which he was evaluating reporting tools got canceled; but, nevertheless, he started working on JasperReports in his spare time. He registered the project on `http://sourceforge.net` in September, 2001. Shortly after, he started getting emails from interested potential users even though he had not yet released any code.

JasperReports version 0.1.5 was released in November, 2001. Since then, JasperReports has become immensely popular, and is currently one of the most popular (if not the most popular) Java reporting tools available. As a testament to JasperReports' enormous popularity, a Google search for **java reporting tool** returns the JasperReports website as its first result.

Until recently, JasperReports was basically a one-man project, with Teodor working on it in his spare time. In April 2005, a company called **JasperSoft** was formally launched at the **MySQL User Conference** in California. JasperSoft sponsors JasperReports' development, allowing Teodor and other JasperSoft developers to work full-time on JasperReports. JasperSoft also provides commercial support and services for JasperReports and related products, including the **iReport Visual Designer** for JasperReports. In addition to providing support for JasperReports and iReport, JasperSoft sells commercial applications incorporating JasperReports.

JasperSoft has raised over 8 million dollars in venture capital funding, no small feat in these post-dotcom days. This investment is a clear indication that venture capitalists have confidence in the success of JasperSoft, and, by extension, in the success of JasperReports. According to JasperSoft, JasperReports has been downloaded over 300,000 times, and gets over 20,000 downloads a month. It has been deployed in over 10,000 companies and **Independent Software Vendors (ISVs)**.

# What is JasperReports?

JasperReports is an open-source Java class library designed to aid developers with the task of adding reporting capabilities to Java applications. Since it is not a standalone tool, it cannot be installed on its own. Instead, it is embedded into Java applications by including its library in the application's CLASSPATH. JasperReports is a Java class library, and is not meant for end users, but rather is targeted towards Java developers who need to add reporting capabilities to their applications.

Although JasperReports is primarily used to add reporting capabilities to web-based applications via the Servlet API, it has absolutely no dependencies on the Servlet API or any other Java EE library. It is, therefore, by no means limited to web applications. There is nothing stopping us from creating standalone desktop or command-line Java applications to generate reports with JasperReports. After all, JasperReports is nothing but a Java class library providing an API to facilitate the ability to generate reports from any kind of Java application.

JasperReports requires a **Java Development Kit (JDK) 1.3** or newer in order to successfully compile applications incorporating the JasperReports Java class library, and a **Java Runtime Environment 1.3** or newer to successfully execute these applications. Older versions of JasperReports required a JDK to successfully execute JasperReports applications (strictly speaking, JasperReports required `tools.jar` to be in the CLASSPATH, and `tools.jar` is included in the JDK, not the JRE). However, from version 0.6.4, JasperReports is bundled with the **Eclipse Java Development Tools (JDT)** compiler, and no longer needs a JDK to execute deployed applications. Examples in this book are developed using JDK 1.5, but should compile and execute successfully with any JDK or JRE supported by JasperReports.

# The JasperReports Open-Source License

JasperReports is licensed under the **Lesser GNU Public License (LGPL)**. This license was chosen for JasperReports since, unlike the GPL, it allows JasperReports to be used in both open-source and closed-source applications. Applications linking to the JasperReports Java class library do not need to be open-source. However, if you consider making modifications to the existing JasperReports source code, then your modifications will have to be released under the LGPL. See `http://jasperreports.sourceforge.net/license.html` for the complete license.

# Features of JasperReports

In addition to textual data, JasperReports is capable of generating professional reports including images, charts, and graphs. Some of the major JasperReports features include:

- It has flexible report layout.
- It is capable of presenting data textually or graphically.
- It allows developers to supply data in multiple ways.
- It can accept data from multiple datasources.
- It can generate watermarks.
- It can generate subreports.
- It is capable of exporting reports to a variety of formats.

Each of these features is briefly described in the next few sections.

# Flexible Report Layout

JasperReports allows us to separate data into optional report sections. These sections include:

- The report title, which will appear once at the top of the report.
- A page header, which will appear at the top of every page.
- A detail section, which typically contains the primary report data.
- A page footer, which will appear at the bottom of every page.
- A summary section, which will appear at the end of the report.

All of these and other report sections are discussed in detail in Chapter 6. In addition to allowing us to define report sections, JasperReports allows the creation of elaborate dynamic layouts based on the contents of the report. For example, depending on the value of a report field, data can be hidden or displayed in a report, or data can be grouped into logical sections. Say, we are creating a report about cars. JasperReports allows us to group the data by make, model, year, or a combination of these or any other piece of data displayed on the report. Data grouping allows us to better control the layout of the report. Data-group definitions can also be used to calculate subtotal values based on a subset of the report data. Groups are also used to define datasets for charts and graphs. Data grouping is discussed in detail in Chapter 6.

# Multiple Ways to Present Data

JasperReports provides the ability to display report data textually or graphically via charts. JasperReports allows us to use report expressions to generate reports that display dynamic data. That is, data that is not directly passed to the report or stored anywhere, but is calculated from the data contained in the datasource and/or report parameters.

# Multiple Ways to Supply Data

JasperReports allows developers to pass data to a report by passing it report parameters. Report parameters can be instances of any Java class.

Data can also be passed to a report by using special classes called datasources. Report parameters and datasources can be combined for maximum flexibility.

# Multiple Datasources

JasperReports can generate reports using any relational database system supported by JDBC. However, it is not limited to database reports only. It can generate reports from a number of datasources, including XML files, **Plain Old Java Objects (POJOs)**, any class implementing the `java.util.Map` interface, and any class implementing the `javax.swing.TableModel` interface.

JasperReports also supports empty datasources, which are used for simple reports that have no dynamic data displayed. If we need to create a report from a datasource, not directly supported by JasperReports, it allows us to create our own custom datasources. JDBC datasources are discussed in detail in Chapter 4. Other datasource types, including custom datasources, are discussed in detail in Chapter 5.

# Watermarks

JasperReports is capable of generating background images or text on the reports it generates. These background images can serve as a sort of 'watermark' for the report. A watermark is like a secondary image that is laid over the primary image.

Watermarks can be used for branding reports and for security purposes, since they make it difficult to forge reports. All report pages have the same watermark, which gives them a consistent look and feel.

# Subreports

Another feature of JasperReports is that it allows us to create subreports, or reports within reports. Subreports simplify report design significantly by allowing us to extract complex report sections into a separate report, and incorporating that separate report into a master report.

# Exporting Capabilities

Reports generated with JasperReports can be exported to a number of formats, including PDF (Portable Document Format), XLS (Excel), RTF (Rich Text Format, a format readable and editable by most word processors, including, but certainly not limited to, Microsoft Word, OpenOffice.org Writer, StarOffice Writer, and WordPerfect), HTML (HyperText Markup Language), XML (Extensible Markup Language), CSV (Comma-separated Values), and plain text. Exporting reports to these formats is discussed in detail in Chapter 9. There is also a third-party library to export JasperReports' reports to the **OpenDocument Format (ODF)**. The OpenDocument Format is a standard XML-based file format specification for office applications developed by the **Organization for the Advancement of Structured Information Standards (OASIS)**. OpenOffice.org version 2.0 uses ODF as its default format.

 The JasperReports OpenDocument Format exporter was developed in the summer of 2005, as a part of Google's Summer of Code program. More information about the JasperReports OpenDocument Format exporter can be found at http://netmoc.cpe.ucf.edu/Projects/jasper.html.

The screenshot overleaf demonstrates some of the features of JasperReports, including data grouping, adding images and watermarks to a report, and exporting to a PDF:

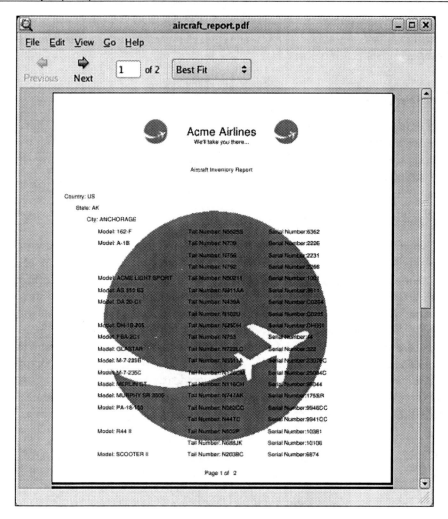

When creating the report given in the screenshot, we took advantage of the data-grouping capabilities of JasperReports to group data by country, state, and city. This grouping allowed us to display the data in a logical, easy-to-follow way. We also took advantage of JasperReports' ability to display images and added a watermark and a logo in the report heading. The report font was modified in the header section to display it in a bigger font and in bold. Text was laid out in an easy-to-follow format.

In the screenshot, the freely available **Evince document viewer** was used to display the PDF report. Of course, reports exported to PDF can be viewed with any PDF viewer, including Adobe Acrobat, Foxit, and xPDF.

# Class Library Dependencies

JasperReports leverages other open-source Java libraries to implement some of their functionality. Some of the libraries JasperReports builds on include:

- iText: iText is a PDF generation and manipulation library. It also has the ability to generate and manupulate RTF, XML, and HTML documents. JasperReports takes advantage of iText for exporting reports to PDF and RTF. More information about iText can be found at `http://www.lowagie.com/iText/`.

- JFreeChart: JFreeChart is a Java library for producing various charts, including pie charts, bar charts, line and area charts, and the like. JasperReports takes advantage of JFreeChart to implement its built-in charting functionality. More information about JFreeChart can be found at `http://www.jfree.org/jfreechart/index.php`.

- Jakarta POI: Jakarta POI is a Java class library to create and manipulate various Microsoft Office formats based on Microsoft's OLE 2 Compound Document format. JasperReports takes advantage of Jakarta POI for exporting reports to XLS (Microsoft Excel) format. More information about Jakarta POI can be found at `http://jakarta.apache.org/poi/`.

- JAXP: JAXP refers to the Java API for parsing and transforming XML documents. It is used by JasperReports to parse XML files and is included in Java SE 5.0. It has to be downloaded separately when using earlier versions of Java SE. More information about JAXP can be found at `http://java.sun.com/webservices/jaxp/index.jsp`.

- Jakarta Commons: Jakarta Commons is a collection of Java libraries providing a large number of reusable components. JasperReports takes advantage of the Digester, BeanUtils, and Logging components of Jakarta Commons to complement JAXP for XML parsing. More information about Jakarta Commons can be found at `http://jakarta.apache.org/commons/`.

 URLs are provided for informational purposes only. The JasperReports class library already includes the required JAR files listed here. There is no need for us to download them to take advantage of their functionality within JasperReports.

# Typical Workflow

The flow chart overleaf illustrates the typical workflow while creating reports with JasperReports:

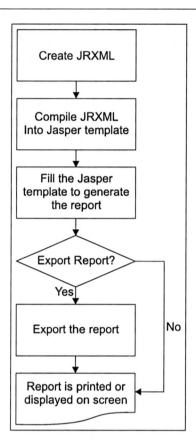

When working with JasperReports, the first step is to create a report template as an XML file. XML report templates can be hand-coded or generated by a graphical report designer. Even though JasperReports' report templates are XML files, template filenames are given an extension of `.jrxml`. JasperReports XML templates are commonly referred to as JRXML files, which is the term we will use for them in this book.

Here is what a typical JRXML file looks like. We will discuss JRXML files in detail in Chapter 4.

```
<?xml version="1.0" encoding="UTF-8"?>
<!DOCTYPE jasperReport PUBLIC "//JasperReports//DTD Report Design//EN"
  "http://jasperreports.sourceforge.net/dtds/jasperreport.dtd">
<jasperReport name="simple_template">
  <title>
    <band height="50">
    </band>
```

```
    </title>
    <pageHeader>
      <band height="50">
      </band>
    </pageHeader>
    <columnHeader>
      <band height="30">
      </band>
    </columnHeader>
    <detail>
      <band height="100">
      </band>
    </detail>
    <columnFooter>
      <band height="30">
      </band>
    </columnFooter>
    <pageFooter>
      <band height="50">
      </band>
    </pageFooter>
    <lastPageFooter>
      <band height="50">
      </band>
    </lastPageFooter>
    <summary>
      <band height="50">
      </band>
    </summary>
  </jasperReport>
```

The JRXML file here mostly illustrates the main elements of a JRXML file. All elements in the file are optional except for the root `<jasperReport>` element. The above JRXML file, when compiled and filled, will generate an empty report; not very useful in its own right, but it can be used as a template for creating more useful reports. As can be seen in the above example, each main element of the JRXML file contains a `<band>` element as its only child element. Bands contain the data that is displayed in the report. In the above example, all bands are empty. In *real* JRXML files, bands contain child elements that are used to position, format, and display the actual report data, both textual and graphical. There are commercial and open-source visual design tools that can aid in the development of JRXML files. iReport, the official JasperReports graphical report designer, is covered in detail in Chapter 10.

JRXML files are compiled into a JasperReports native binary template, either programmatically by calling the appropriate methods on the JasperReports class library (compileReportToFile()), or by using a custom ANT task (used to compile multiple XML report design files in a single operation, by specifying the root directory that contains those files or by selecting them using file patterns) provided by JasperReports. The resulting compiled template is commonly known as the **Jasper file**, and is typically saved to disk with a .jasper extension. The Jasper file is then used to generate the final report, by providing it with its required data. This process is known as *filling* the report. A JRXML file has to be compiled only once. The generated Jasper file can be filled as many times as necessary to create and display reports.

Filled reports can be saved to disk in a JasperReports native format. Reports saved in this format are known as JasperPrint files. JasperPrint file names have a .jrprint extension. JasperPrint files can only be viewed with a JasperReports-specific viewer. JasperPrint files can be exported to other formats so that they can be opened with commonly available tools like PDF viewers and word processors. Exporting to other formats is discussed in detail in Chapter 9.

# Where to Get Help?

JasperReports has official online forums and a mailing list where questions can be asked. Both the forums and the mailing list archives can be found at the JasperReports site at http://sourceforge.net/projects/jasperreports.

The JasperReports website contains tips, tricks, JavaDoc API documentation, and a quick reference for JRXML elements. We won't repeat this information in this book, since it is readily available online. The JasperReports website can be found at http://jasperreports.sourceforge.net.

Commercial support and training is offered by JasperSoft and other third-party companies.

# Summary

In this chapter we were introduced to JasperReports. We discussed the evolution of JasperReports from a small one-man project to a project backed and funded by a company that has raised millions of dollars in venture capital. We also had an overview of JasperReports, where we discussed that JasperReports is not a standalone reporting solution. Instead, it is a Java library that allows us to add reporting capabilities to our applications.

Next on the line was the JasperReports' open-source license (LGPL). The chapter provided us with a brief explanation of the features of JasperReports, including flexibility in report layout, the ability to display report data textually or graphically, and the ability to group report data. The JasperReports' class library dependencies were also discussed along with the typical workflow followed when designing reports. The chapter also provided us with the official online forums and mailing lists from where we can seek help.

# 2
# Adding Reporting Capabilities to Java Applications

We can easily add reporting capabilities to Java applications by taking advantage of the classes included in the JasperReports class library. JasperReports can be easily embedded into both client and server-side Java applications, simply by adding the required libraries to our CLASSPATH and calling the appropriate methods in the JasperReports API.

By the end of this chapter, we will be able to:

- Identify the purpose of the several downloads that can be found at the JasperReports website
- Identify required libraries for adding reporting capabilities to Java applications
- Identify optional libraries that can be used to enhance the reporting capabilities of Java applications
- Set up our development and execution environment to successfully add reporting capabilities to Java applications

## Downloading JasperReports

JasperReports can be downloaded from `http://www.sourceforge.net/projects/ jasperreports`. When visiting the JasperReports download page, you should see an image similar to the following around the middle of the page:

JasperReports can be downloaded by clicking on this image. Once you click on the image, you should see a window similar to the following on your browser:

| Package | Release (date) | Filename | Size (bytes) | Downloads | Architecture | Type |
|---|---|---|---|---|---|---|
| ⊟ **jasperreports** | | | | | | |
| Latest | ⊟ **JasperReports 1.2.2** [Notes] (2006-04-23 06:46) | | | | | |
| | | jasperreports-1.2.2-applet.jar | 190838 | 875 | Platform-Independent | .jar |
| | | jasperreports-1.2.2.jar | 1296402 | 2368 | Platform-Independent | .jar |
| | | jasperreports-1.2.2-project.zip | 24493918 | 308 | Any | Source .zip |
| | ⊞ **JasperReports 1.2.1** [Notes] (2006-04-07 04:59) | | | | | |
| | ⊞ **JasperReports 1.2.0** [Notes] (2006-02-06 10:50) | | | | | |
| | ⊞ **JasperReports 1.1.1** [Notes] (2005-11-28 03:55) | | | | | |
| | ⊞ **JasperReports 1.1.0** [Notes] (2005-10-21 08:57) | | | | | |
| | ⊞ **JasperReports 1.0.3** [Notes] (2005-10-12 01:07) | | | | | |
| | ⊞ **JasperReports 1.0.2** [Notes] (2005-09-07 08:15) | | | | | |
| | ⊞ **JasperReports 1.0.1** [Notes] (2005-08-26 08:24) | | | | | |
| | ⊞ **JasperReports 1.0.0** [Notes] (2005-07-20 11:58) | | | | | |
| | **View older releases in the jasperreports package »** | | | | | |
| **Totals:** | 9 | 27 | 206332398 | 194879 | | |

Clicking on the **JasperReports 1.2.2** link at the top left cell should take you to a page containing a tree displaying current and previous versions of JasperReports.

Each node in the tree contains three download links. It is not always clear what exactly is downloaded by clicking on these links. For this reason, a brief explanation for each link is given next.

The first link is to download a JAR file containing a subset of the JasperReports functionality. Specifically, it contains classes that can be used to display jrprint files, which are reports in JasperReports' native format. This file is offered as a separate download as a convenience for developers. It can be used for applications or applets that do not require full reporting capabilities, but which need to display generated reports. The file name has a suffix of **applet**. However, there is nothing preventing us from using it with standalone applications. This file is approximately 187 KB in size.

The second link is the complete JasperReports class library. It contains all the classes necessary to compile, fill, and export reports, but does not include any additional libraries JasperReports depends upon. This is the minimum file we need to add full reporting capabilities to our Java applications. This file is approximately 1.3 MB in size. If we choose to download this file, then we need to download JasperReports dependencies separately. These dependencies are listed in the following table:

| Dependency | Version | Download URL | Comments |
|---|---|---|---|
| Commons Logging | 1.0 or later | `http://jakarta.apache.org/commons/logging/` | Used for sending output to a log. |
| Commons Collections | 2.1 or later | `http://jakarta.apache.org/commons/collections/` | Used to manage collections of data. |
| Commons BeanUtils | 1.4 or later | `http://jakarta.apache.org/commons/beanutils/` | Used for JavaBeans introspection. |
| Commons Digester | 1.7 or later | `http://jakarta.apache.org/commons/digester/` | Used for XML parsing. |
| JFreeChart | 1.0 or later | `http://www.jfree.org/jfreechart/` | Only required when the report contains charts. |
| iText | 1.01 or later | `http://www.lowagie.com/iText/` | Only required when exporting reports to PDF or RTF. |
| Jakarta POI | 2.0 or later | `http://jakarta.apache.org/poi/` | Only required when exporting reports to Excel format. |
| JExcelApi | 2.5.7 or later | `http://jexcelapi.sourceforge.net/` | Only required when exporting reports to Excel format. |
| Hibernate | 3.0 or later | `http://www.hibernate.org/` | Only required when writing report queries using the Hibernate Query Language (HQL). |

The third and the last link is a ZIP file containing the complete JasperReports class library along with all the required and optional libraries. The ZIP file also includes the JasperReports source code, as well as a lot of source code providing examples demonstrating JasperReports' functionality. This file is approximately 24 MB in size. Unless internet connectivity speed is an issue, downloading this file is recommended since it includes everything we need to create reports with JasperReports. Moreover, the included examples are a great way to learn how to implement the different JasperReports features. All of the examples in the file come with an ANT build file containing targets to compile and execute. We will refer to this file as the JasperReports project file, or, more succinctly, as the project ZIP file.

 Detailed instructions on installing ANT can be found in the online ANT manual at `http://ant.apache.org/manual/index.html`.

Once we have downloaded the appropriate file for our purpose, we need to set up our environment to be able to start creating reports. In the next section, we discuss how to do this, assuming that the project ZIP file was downloaded.

# Setting Up Our Environment

To set up our environment to get ready to start creating reports, we need to extract the JasperReports project ZIP file to a location of our choice. Once we extract the project ZIP file, we should see a `jasperreports-1.2.2` directory containing the following files and directories:

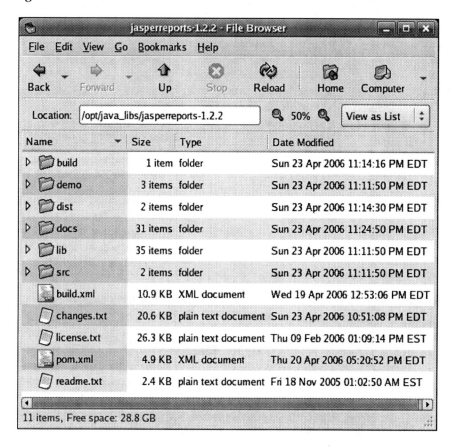

- `build`: A directory containing the compiled JasperReports class files.
- `build.xml`: An ANT build file to build the JasperReports source code. If we don't intend to modify JasperReports, we don't need to use this file since JasperReports is distributed in compiled form.
- `changes.txt`: A text document explaining the differences between the current and previous versions of the JasperReports class library.
- `demo`: A directory containing various examples demonstrating several aspects of JasperReports functionality.

- `dist`: A directory containing a JAR file that contains the JasperReports library. We should add this JAR file to our CLASSPATH to take advantage of JasperReports.

- `docs`: A directory that contains a local copy of the JasperReports website.

- `lgpl.txt`: A text document that contains the full text of the LGPL license.

- `lib`: A directory containing all libraries needed, both to build JasperReports and to use it in our applications.

- `readme.txt`: A text document containing instructions on how to build and execute the supplied examples.

- `src`: A directory containing the JasperReports source code.

**Getting Up and Running Quickly**

To get up and running quickly, the files to be added to the CLASSPATH are the JasperReports JAR file (its file name should be `jasperreports-1.2.2.jar` or similar, depending on the exact JasperReports version) which can be found under the `dist` subdirectory of the directory created while extracting the project ZIP file, or downloaded directly as described above, and all the JAR files under the `lib` subdirectory of the directory created while extracting the project ZIP file. By adding these files to the CLASSPATH, we don't have to worry about the CLASSPATH when implementing additional functionality (e.g. exporting to PDF or producing charts).

# JasperReports Class Library

JasperReports is distributed as a JAR file that needs to be added to the CLASSPATH of any application for which we wish to add reporting capabilities. The JasperReports library requires a Java Runtime Environment (JRE) 1.3 or newer. For all JasperReports -related tasks, we need to add the JasperReports library to our CLASSPATH. The JasperReports library can be found under the `dist` subdirectory of the directory created while extracting the project ZIP file. It is named `jasperreports-1.2.2.jar`. The exact file name will vary depending on the version of JasperReports we are working with.

# Required Libraries for Report Compilation

The project ZIP file, described in the previous section, contains all the required supporting libraries. If that file is downloaded, all the required libraries can be found under the `lib` subdirectory of the directory created when extracting the ZIP file. JasperReports uses these required files for XML parsing. Therefore, they are needed when compiling JRXML files. However, programmatically they are not needed for filling or displaying reports. JRXML files can be compiled via a custom ANT task provided by JasperReports. If we choose to compile our JRXML files via this custom ANT target, these required libraries need to be added to the CLASSPATH variable of the ANT build file. There are build file examples included in the project file as well as in this book's website: `http://www.packtpub.com/jasper_reports/book/`.

# Jakarta Commons

Jakarta Commons is a collection of Java libraries developed and distributed by the **Apache Software Foundation**. Jakarta Commons includes libraries and utility classes that provide commonly used functionality, freeing developers from the task of re-implementing them. Before implementing a piece of functionality that is frequently needed, we should make sure there isn't a Jakarta Commons library that implements it. Jakarta Commons includes libraries for logging, XML parsing, sending and receiving email, I/O, network utility classes, and many others. For more information, visit the Jakarta Commons website at `http://jakarta.apache.org/commons/`. The following list of libraries highlights the fact that JasperReports makes extensive use of Jakarta Commons.

## Jakarta Commons Digester

The **Commons Digester** library includes utility classes used to initialize Java objects from XML files. JasperReports takes advantage of the Digester component of the Jakarta Commons repository to implement its XML parsing functionality. Version 1.2.2 of the JasperReports project ZIP file includes version 1.7 of Commons Digester. The file name is `commons-digester-1.7.jar` and it must be on your CLASSPATH for your JasperReports application to work correctly.

If you download the bare JasperReports class library, you will need to download Commons Digester separately from `http://jakarta.apache.org/commons/digester/`.

## Jakarta Commons Collections

Another component of the Jakarta Commons suite is **Commons Collections**. This component provides the functionality to complement and augment the Java Collections Framework. JasperReports takes advantage of the Collections component to implement some of its functionality. Like all other required libraries, the Commons Collections library can be found under the `lib` subdirectory of the directory created when extracting the project ZIP file. The JasperReports project file, version 1.2.2, includes version 2.1 of Commons Collections, distributed as a JAR file named `commons-collections-2.1.jar`.

If you download the bare JasperReports class library, you will need to download Commons Collections separately from `http://jakarta.apache.org/commons/collections/`.

## Jakarta Commons Logging

The **Commons Logging** library includes components that aid developers with sending data to log files. JasperReports takes advantage of this component, which can be found under the `lib` subdirectory of the directory created when extracting the project ZIP file. The version included with JasperReports version 1.2.2 is version 1.0.2. The file to be added to your CLASSPATH is `commons-logging-1.0.2.jar`.

If you download the bare JasperReports class library, you will need to download Commons Logging separately from `http://jakarta.apache.org/commons/logging/`.

## Jakarta Commons BeanUtils

The last library that JasperReports requires for compiling reports is **Commons BeanUtils**. BeanUtils is a library that provides easy-to-use wrappers around the Java reflection and introspection APIs. Version 1.2.2 of the JasperReports project ZIP file includes BeanUtils version 1.5. The file to be added to your CLASSPATH is `commons-beanutils-1.5.jar`.

If you download the bare JasperReports class library, you will need to download Commons BeanUtils separately from `http://jakarta.apache.org/commons/beanutils/`.

# Optional Libraries and Tools

There are a number of libraries that are required only if we wish to take advantage of some of JasperReports' features. These optional libraries and their uses are listed next.

# Apache ANT

JasperReports comes bundled with some custom ANT targets for previewing report designs and for viewing reports serialized in JasperReports' native format. Although not mandatory, it is very helpful to have ANT available to take advantage of these custom targets.

Throughout this book, we will be using JasperReports-specific ANT targets. Therefore, ANT is required when following the examples. ANT can be downloaded from `http://ant.apache.org/`.

# JDT Compiler

JDT stands for Java Development Tools. The **JDT compiler** is the Java compiler included with the Eclipse IDE (Integrated Development Environment). The JDT compiler is needed only when the JasperReports application is running under a Java Runtime Environment (JRE), and not under a full JDK.

When compiling reports, JasperReports creates temporary Java files and compiles them. When using a JDK, JasperReports takes advantage of `tools.jar` for this functionality. Since a JRE does not include `tools.jar`, the JDT compiler is needed. The JasperReports project ZIP file version 1.2.2 includes the JDT compiler. It can be found under the `lib` subdirectory of the directory created when extracting the project ZIP file. The file to be added to your CLASSPATH is `jdt-compiler.jar`.

This file cannot be downloaded separately. Therefore, if we need to execute our code under a JRE, we need to download the JasperReports project ZIP file, since it includes the file, which is needed for report compilation.

JasperReports requires either `tools.jar` or the JDT when compiling JRXML templates into binary JasperReports templates. A JRE is sufficient if our Java application does not compile reports.

# JDBC Driver

When using a JDBC datasource, the appropriate **JDBC driver** for our specific RDBMS is needed. The following table lists popular relational database systems and the required JAR files to be added to the CLASSPATH (exact file names may vary depending on the version). The names shown in the table reflect the latest stable versions at the time of writing:

| RDBMS | Driver JAR Files |
|---|---|
| Firebird | `firebirdsql-full.jar` |
| HSQLDB | `hsqldb.jar` |
| MySQL | `mysql-connector-java-3.1.10-bin.jar` |
| Oracle | `classes12dms.jar` |
| DB2 | `db2java.zip` |
| PostgreSQL | `postgresql-8.0-312.jdbc3.jar` |
| SQL Server | `mssqlserver.jar`<br>`msbase.jar`<br>`msutil.jar` |
| Sybase | `jconn3.jar` |

The JasperReports project ZIP file includes the JDBC driver for HSQLDB. Consult your RDBMS documentation for information on where to download the appropriate JDBC driver for your RDBMS.

# iText

**iText** is an open-source library for creation and manipulation of PDF files. iText is needed only if you want to export your reports to PDF or RTF format. Version 1.2.2 of the JasperReports project ZIP file includes iText version 1.3.1. The file to be added to your CLASSPATH is `itext-1.3.1.jar`.

iText can be downloaded separately from `http://www.lowagie.com/iText/`.

# JFreeChart

**JFreeChart** is an open-source library for creating professional-looking charts including, but not limited to 2-D and 3-D pie charts, 2-D and 3-D bar charts, and line charts. JFreeChart is needed in our CLASSPATH only if you intend to add charts to your reports. JFreeChart version 1.0 RC1 can be found in the `lib` directory inside the JasperReports project ZIP file version 1.1. The file to be added to the CLASSPATH is `jfreechart-1.0.0-rc1.jar`.

JFreeChart can be downloaded separately from `http://www.jfree.org/jfreechart/`.

# Jakarta POI

**Jakarta POI** is a Java library that allows Java applications to read and write Microsoft Office files. We need POI in our CLASSPATH only if we need to export our reports to XLS format. Version 1.1 of the JasperReports project ZIP file includes POI version 2.0. To add XLS exporting capabilities to your reports, the file you need to add to your CLASSPATH is `poi-2.0-final-20040126.jar`.

POI can be downloaded separately from `http://jakarta.apache.org/poi/`.

# Summary

This chapter covered the required and optional libraries needed to add reporting capabilities to Java applications. All the libraries covered in this chapter are needed both at compile time and at run time.

The chapter provided an explanation of the different files available for download on JasperReports' website and in which conditions it is appropriate to use them. We saw which libraries are required for report compilation under a Java Development Kit as well as which additional libraries are required when compiling JRXML templates under a Java Runtime Environment (JRE). Besides, the chapter also covered which libraries are required when using JDBC datasources for our reports, and finally the libraries required when exporting our reports to several formats.

Now that we have seen the libraries needed to work with JasperReports, we are ready to create our first report, which is what the next chapter is based on.

# 3

# Creating Your First Report

In this chapter, you will create, compile, and preview your first report. At the end of this chapter, you will be able to:

- Create a simple JRXML report template
- Generate Jasper binary report templates by compiling JRXML files
- Preview report templates by using JasperReports custom ANT targets
- Write code that will generate a report from a JasperReport template
- View generated reports in JasperReports' native format using the tools provided by JasperReports
- Generate reports that can be viewed in a web browser
- Identify the JRXML elements corresponding to the different report sections

## Creating a JRXML Report Template

The first step when creating a report is to create a JRXML template. As mentioned in Chapter 1, JasperReports JRXML templates are standard XML files. However, by convention, they have an extension of `.jrxml`, and are referred to as JRXML files or JRXML templates. All JRXML files contain a `<jasperReport>` root element that can contain many sub-elements. All of these sub-elements are optional. Since our goal for this chapter is to get a feel of how to design a report, we will obviate most of the `<jasperReport>` sub-elements. We will use only one sub-element, namely the `<detail>` sub-element.

Our first report will display a static String. Its JRXML follows:

```
<?xml version="1.0"?>

<!DOCTYPE jasperReport
  PUBLIC "-//JasperReports//DTD Report Design//EN"
  "http://jasperreports.sourceforge.net/dtds/jasperreport.dtd">
<jasperReport name="FirstReport">
  <detail>
    <band height="20">
      <staticText>
        <reportElement x="20" y="0" width="200" height="20"/>
        <text><![CDATA[If you don't see this, it didn't work]]></text>
      </staticText>
    </band>
  </detail>
</jasperReport>
```

There are some elements in this JRXML file that we haven't seen before:

- `<staticText>` defines static text that does not depend on any datasources, variables, parameters, or report expressions.

- `<reportElement>` defines the position and width of the `<staticText>` element.

- `<text>` defines the actual static text that is displayed on the report.

We have seen the `<band>` element in previous examples. The `<detail>` element can contain only a single `<band>` element as its only sub-element. The `<band>` element can contain many different elements that can be used to display text, charts, images, or geometric figures. In this example, it contains a single `<staticText>` element.

`<reportElement>` is a required element not only of the `<staticText>` element, but also of all sub-elements of the `<band>` element. The x and y coordinates defined in `<reportElement>` are relative to the `<band>` element, which contains its parent element (`<staticText>` in this example).

# Previewing the XML Report Template

JasperReports includes a utility that can be used to preview report designs. This utility makes designing reports much faster, since we can immediately preview a report design without having to compile or fill it.

The utility is a standalone Java application included in the JasperReports JAR file. The class that needs to be executed is net.sf.jasperreports.view.JasperDesignViewer. The easiest way to execute this class is to use an ANT target, including all the required libraries in the CLASSPATH. This is the approach that is used in the JasperReports samples, included in the project ZIP file, and by us as well. The following ANT build file will launch the **JasperDesignViewer** to preview our report:

```
<project name="FirstReport XML Design Preview" default="viewDesignXML"
        basedir=".">
  <description>Previews our First Report XML Design</description>
  <property name="file.name" value="FirstReport"/>
  <!-- Directory where the JasperReports project file was extracted
        needs to be changed to match the local environment -->
  <property name="jasper.dir"
              value="/usr/local/share/java/jasperreports-1.1.0"/>
  <property name="classes.dir" value="${jasper.dir}/build/classes"/>
  <property name="lib.dir" value="${jasper.dir}/lib"/>
  <path id="classpath">
    <pathelement location="./"/>
    <pathelement location="${classes.dir}"/>
    <fileset dir="${lib.dir}">
      <include name="**/*.jar"/>
    </fileset>
  </path>
  <target name="viewDesignXML"
          description="Launches the design viewer to preview the XML
                      report design.">
    <java classname="net.sf.jasperreports.view.JasperDesignViewer"
          fork="true">
      <arg value="-XML"/>
      <arg value="-F${file.name}.jrxml"/>
      <classpath refid="classpath"/>
    </java>
  </target>
</project>
```

This ANT build file must be saved in the same directory as our JRXML file. It is recommended that the JRXML file be saved with the report name as its file name. The report name is defined in the <jasperReport> root element. In the JRXML file, we chose to use FirstReport as the report name. Therefore, the recommended file name for this report template is FirstReport.jrxml.

If we save our ANT build file with the standard name of `build.xml`, there is no need to specify the build file name in the command line. The build file, in this example, has one `<target>` element named `viewDesignXML`. Since this target is the default target, there is no need to specify it in the command line; just typing `ant` in the command line will execute the default target and a preview of our report will be displayed.

```
$ ant
Buildfile: previewReportDesignXML.xml

viewDesignXML:
```

After executing the `viewDesignXML` target, we should see a window labeled **JasperDesignViewer** displaying our report template preview.

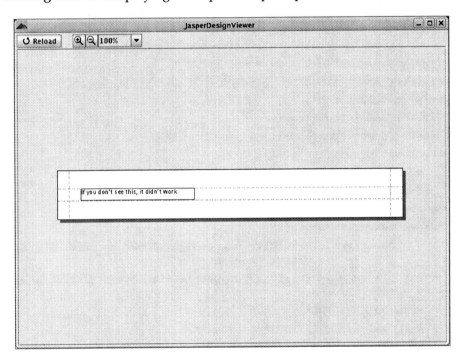

The **JasperDesignViewer** can be safely terminated by closing the window or by hitting *Ctrl-c* in the command-line window.

In this particular case we can see all the text in the preview, since this report contains only static text. For reports displaying data coming from datasources or report parameters, the actual text won't be displayed in the report. Instead, report expressions for obtaining the data are displayed. This is because **JasperDesignViewer** does not have access to the actual datasource or report parameters.

# Creating a Binary Report Template

JRXML files cannot be used directly to generate reports. They need to be compiled into JasperReports' native binary format. Compiled report templates are called **Jasper files**. There are two ways to compile a JRXML file into a Jasper file. We can either do it programmatically, or we can do it through a custom ANT task provided by JasperReports.

## Compiling a JRXML Template Programmatically

A JRXML template can be compiled into a Jasper file and saved to disk by calling the `compileReportToFile()` method on the `net.sf.jasperreports.engine.JasperCompileManager` class. There are three overloaded versions of the `JasperCompileManager.compileReportToFile()` method, listed below:

- `JasperCompileManager.compileReportToFile(String sourceFileName)`.

- `JasperCompileManager.compileReportToFile(String sourceFileName, String destFileName)`.

- `JasperCompileManager.compileReportToFile(JasperDesign jasperDesign, String destFileName)`.

The following table illustrates the parameters used in these methods:

| Parameter | Description |
| --- | --- |
| `String sourceFileName` | This contains the location of the JRXML template to be used to generate the compiled report template. It can be an absolute or a relative path. The generated compiled report template is saved using the same name and location as the supplied JRXML file, substituting the file extension with `.jasper`. |
| `String destFileName` | This is used to determine the file name used to save the compiled report template in the file system. It can contain an absolute or a relative path. |
| `JasperDesign jasperDesign` | This contains an in-memory representation of the report design. `net.sf.jasperreports.engine.design.JasperDesign` instances can be created by calling one of the several methods in the `net.sf.jasperreports.engine.xml.JRXmlLoader` class. |

The following code fragment demonstrates the use of the `JasperCompileManager.`
`compileReportToFile()` method:

```
package net.ensode.jasperbook;

import net.sf.jasperreports.engine.JRException;
import net.sf.jasperreports.engine.JasperCompileManager;

public class FirstReportCompile
{
  public static void main(String[] args)
  {
    try
    {
      System.out.println("Compiling report...");
      JasperCompileManager.compileReportToFile(
                              "reports/FirstReport.jrxml");
      System.out.println("Done!");
    }
    catch (JRException e)
    {
      e.printStackTrace();
    }
  }
}
```

After compiling and executing the code, we should see a file called `FirstReport.`
`jasper` in the file system. This file is the compiled template in JasperReports'
native format. For this example, we chose to use the first version of the
`JasperCompileManager.compileReportToFile()` method we discussed, since by
default the root file name is used for the compiled report, and we did not have an
in-memory representation of the JRXML template. If we had wished to use a
different root file name for the compiled report template, we should have used the
second version of the `JasperCompileManager.compileReportToFile()` method
and specified the desired file name as the second parameter.

## Previewing the Compiled Report Template

The `net.sf.jasperreports.view.JasperDesignViewer` discussed previously can
be used to preview compiled report templates as well as JRXML templates. Again the
easiest way to execute this utility is to wrap a call to it into an ANT target. Let us add
a second ANT target to our `build.xml` file. We will call this new target `viewDesign`,
as it will let us preview the compiled report.

```xml
<project name="FirstReport XML Design Preview" default="viewDesignXML"
        basedir=".">
  <description>Previews our First Report Design</description>
  <property name="file.name" value="FirstReport"/>
  <!-- Directory where the JasperReports project file was extracted,
       needs to be changed to match the local environment -->
  <property name="jasper.dir"
            value="/usr/local/share/java/jasperreports-1.1.0"/>
  <property name="classes.dir" value="${jasper.dir}/build/classes"/>
  <property name="lib.dir" value="${jasper.dir}/lib"/>
  <path id="classpath">
    <pathelement location="./"/>
    <pathelement location="${classes.dir}"/>
    <fileset dir="${lib.dir}">
      <include name="**/*.jar"/>
    </fileset>
  </path>
  <target name="viewDesignXML"
      description="Launches the design viewer to preview the XML
                  report design.">
    <java classname="net.sf.jasperreports.view.JasperDesignViewer"
          fork="true">
      <arg value="-XML"/>
      <arg value="-F${file.name}.jrxml"/>
      <classpath refid="classpath"/>
    </java>
  </target>
  <target name="viewDesign"
        description="Launches the design viewer to preview the
                    compiled report design.">
    <java classname="net.sf.jasperreports.view.JasperDesignViewer"
          fork="true">
      <arg value="-F${file.name}.jasper"/>
      <classpath refid="classpath"/>
    </java>
  </target>
</project>
```

We can invoke the new target from the command line as follows:

```
ant viewDesign
```

After invoking the target, we should see a window very similar to the one we saw when previewing the JRXML template.

## Compiling a JRXML Template through ANT

JasperReports includes a custom ANT task that can be used to compile report templates. Since we don't have to write code to perform the compilation, compiling reports in this manner is very convenient. However, for certain applications we need to compile a report programmatically, for example, in situations where the JRXML file is created at run time. The custom ANT task included by JasperReports is called JRC. It is defined in the net.sf.jasperreports.ant.JRAntCompileTask class. Let us add a third target to our build.xml file to invoke the JRC task.

```xml
<project name="FirstReport XML Design Preview" default="viewDesignXML"
            basedir=".">
  <description>Previews and compiles our First Report</description>
  <property name="file.name" value="FirstReport"/>
      <!-- Directory where the JasperReports project file was extracted,
      needs to be changed to match the local environment -->
  <property name="jasper.dir"
          value="/usr/local/share/java/jasperreports-1.1.0"/>
  <property name="classes.dir" value="${jasper.dir}/build/classes"/>
  <property name="lib.dir" value="${jasper.dir}/lib"/>
  <path id="classpath">
      <pathelement location="./"/>
      <pathelement location="${classes.dir}"/>
      <fileset dir="${lib.dir}">
        <include name="**/*.jar"/>
      </fileset>
  </path>
  <target name="viewDesignXML"
          description="Launches the design viewer to preview the XML
                      report design.">
    <java classname="net.sf.jasperreports.view.JasperDesignViewer"
          fork="true">
      <arg value="-XML"/>
      <arg value="-F${file.name}.jrxml"/>
      <classpath refid="classpath"/>
    </java>
```

```
    </target>
    <target name="viewDesign"
            description="Launches the design viewer to preview the
                         compiled report design.">
      <java classname="net.sf.jasperreports.view.JasperDesignViewer"
            fork="true">
        <arg value="-F${file.name}.jasper"/>
        <classpath refid="classpath"/>
      </java>
    </target>
    <target name="compile"
            description="Compiles the XML report design and produces the
                         .jasper file.">
      <taskdef name="jrc"
               classname="net.sf.jasperreports.ant.JRAntCompileTask">
        <classpath refid="classpath"/>
      </taskdef>
      <jrc destdir=".">
        <src>
          <fileset dir=".">
            <include name="**/*.jrxml"/>
          </fileset>
        </src>
        <classpath refid="classpath"/>
      </jrc>
    </target>
  </project>
```

The new target can be invoked from the command line as:

```
ant compile
```

The compile target produces the following output:

```
Buildfile: build.xml
compile:
     [jrc] Compiling 1 report design files.
     [jrc] log4j:WARN No appenders could be found for logger
(org.apache.commons.digester.Digester.sax).
     [jrc] log4j:WARN Please initialize the log4j system properly.
     [jrc] File : /home/heffel/personal_workspace/JasperBookExamples/
reports/FirstReport.jrxml ... OK.
BUILD SUCCESSFUL
Total time: 4 seconds
```

After successful execution of the compile target, we should have a
`FirstReport.jasper` file in the file system. This file is identical to the one
generated programmatically by calling the `net.sf.jasperreports.engine.`
`JasperCompileManager.compileReportToFile()`.

 As can be seen in the output above, the JRC target will generate
a `log4j` warning. This warning can be safely ignored.

As explained in the previous section, we can preview the generated Jasper file by
using the JasperDesign utility included by JasperReports. The output will be identical.

# Generating the Report

In JasperReports lingo, the process of generating a report from a report template,
or Jasper file, is known as *filling* the report. Reports are filled programmatically, by
calling the `fillReportToFile()` method in the `net.sf.jasperreports.engine.`
`JasperFillManager` class. The `fillReportToFile()` method fills a report and saves
it to disk.

There are six overloaded versions of the `fillReportToFile()` method, which are
listed below:

- `JasperFillManager.fillReportToFile(JasperReport jasperReport,`
  `String destFileName, Map parameters, Connection connection)`

- `JasperFillManager.fillReportToFile(JasperReport jasperReport,`
  `String destFileName, Map parameters, JRDataSource datasource)`

- `JasperFillManager.fillReportToFile(String sourceFileName, Map`
  `parameters, Connection connection)`

- `JasperFillManager.fillReportToFile(String sourceFileName, Map`
  `parameters, JRDatasource dataSource)`

- `JasperFillManager.fillReportToFile(String sourceFileName, String`
  `destFileName, Map parameters, Connection connection)`

- `JasperFillManager.fillReportToFile(String sourceFileName, String`
  `destFileName, Map parameters, JRDataSource dataSource)`

The following table illustrates the parameters used in these methods:

| Parameter | Description |
|---|---|
| JasperReport jasper-Report | This is used as the report template. Instances of net.sf.jasperreports.engine.JasperReport are in-memory representations of compiled report templates. |
| String destFileName | This is used to define the name of the destination file to which to save the report. |
| Map parameters | This is an instance of a class implementing the java.util.Map interface. It is used to initialize all report parameters defined in the report template. |
| Connection connection | This is used to connect to a database, in order to execute an SQL query defined in the report template. |
| JRDataSource dataSource | This is an instance of a class implementing the net.sf.jasperreports.engine.JRDataSource interface. JasperReports provides several implementations of the JRDataSource interface. Moreover, we are also free to create our own custom implementations. |
| String sourceFileName | This is used to indicate the file system location of the compiled report template. The generated report is saved using the same name and location as the given compiled report, substituting the .jasper extension with .jrprint. |

As can be seen above, in most cases, we pass data for filling reports via an instance of a class implementing the net.sf.jasperreports.engine.JRDataSource interface. Report templates can have embedded SQL queries. These SQL queries are defined inside the <queryString> element in the JRXML file. For reports that contain an SQL query, instead of passing a JRDataSource, we pass an instance of a class implementing the java.sql.Connection interface. JasperReports then uses this Connection object to execute the query and obtain the report data from the database.

Our report contains only static text; there is no dynamic data displayed in the report. There is no way to fill a report without passing either a JRDataSource or a Connection. JasperReports provides an implementation of the JRDataSource containing no data. The class is named, appropriately enough, JREmptyDataSource. Since our report takes no parameters, passing an empty instance of java.util.HashMap will be enough for our purposes. We will follow the recommended approach of naming our report using the same name as the one used for the report template (except for the extension). Given all of these facts, the most appropriate version of fillReportToFile() for our report is the fourth version. Here is its signature again:

```
JasperFillManager.fillReportToFile(String sourceFileName, Map parameters,
JRDataSource dataSource)
```

The following Java class fills the report and saves it to disk:

```
package net.ensode.jasperbook;

import java.util.HashMap;

import net.sf.jasperreports.engine.JREmptyDataSource;
import net.sf.jasperreports.engine.JRException;
import net.sf.jasperreports.engine.JasperFillManager;

public class FirstReportFill
{
  public static void main(String[] args)
  {
    try
    {
      System.out.println("Filling report...");
      JasperFillManager.fillReportToFile("reports/FirstReport.jasper",
                             new HashMap(), new JREmptyDataSource());
      System.out.println("Done!");
    }
    catch (JRException e)
    {
      e.printStackTrace();
    }
  }
}
```

After executing the above class, we should have a file named `FirstReport.JRprint` in the same location as our compiled report template, which was named `FirstReport.jasper`.

# Viewing the Report

JasperReports includes a utility class, `net.sf.jasperreports.view.JasperViewer`, that we can use to view generated reports. As with the tool to preview designs, the easiest way to use it is to wrap it into an ANT target. Again, this is the approach taken by the samples included with JasperReports, and the approach taken by us as well. Let us add a new target to our ANT build file. Following the conventions established by the JasperReports samples, we will name this target `view`.

```xml
<project name="FirstReport XML Design Preview" default="viewDesignXML"
        basedir=".">
  <description>Previews and compiles our First Report</description>
  <property name="file.name" value="FirstReport"/>
<!-- Directory where the JasperReports project file was extracted,
     needs to be changed to match the local environment -->
  <property name="jasper.dir"
            value="/usr/local/share/java/jasperreports-1.1.0"/>
  <property name="classes.dir" value="${jasper.dir}/build/classes"/>
  <property name="lib.dir" value="${jasper.dir}/lib"/>
  <path id="classpath">
    <pathelement location="./"/>
    <pathelement location="${classes.dir}"/>
    <fileset dir="${lib.dir}">
      <include name="**/*.jar"/>
    </fileset>
  </path>
  <target name="viewDesignXML"
          description="Launches the design viewer to preview the XML
                       report design.">
    <java classname="net.sf.jasperreports.view.JasperDesignViewer"
          fork="true">
      <arg value="-XML"/>
      <arg value="-F${file.name}.jrxml"/>
      <classpath refid="classpath"/>
    </java>
  </target>
  <target name="viewDesign"
          description="Launches the design viewer to preview the
                       compiled report design.">
    <java classname="net.sf.jasperreports.view.JasperDesignViewer"
          fork="true">
      <arg value="-F${file.name}.jasper"/>
      <classpath refid="classpath"/>
    </java>
  </target>
  <target name="compile"
          description="Compiles the XML report design and produces the
                       .jasper file.">
    <taskdef name="jrc"
             classname="net.sf.jasperreports.ant.JRAntCompileTask">
```

```
            <classpath refid="classpath"/>
      </taskdef>
      <jrc destdir=".">
        <src>
          <fileset dir=".">
            <include name="**/*.jrxml"/>
          </fileset>
        </src>
        <classpath refid="classpath"/>
      <jrc>
    </target>
    <target name="view"
            description="Launches the report viewer to preview the
                         report stored in the .JRprint file.">
      <java classname="net.sf.jasperreports.view.JasperViewer"
            fork="true">
        <arg value="-F${file.name}.JRprint"/>
        <classpath refid="classpath"/>
        </java>
    </target>
</project>
```

After executing the new `view` ANT target, we should see a window like the following:

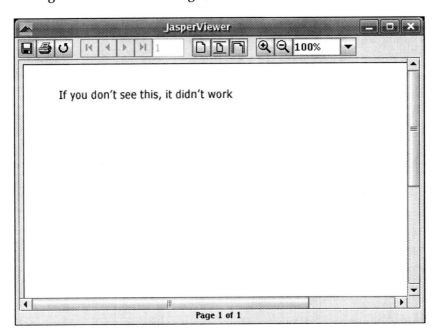

That's it! We have successfully created our first report.

# Displaying Reports on a Web Browser

In the previous section, we discussed how to create a report and save it to disk in JasperReports' native format. In this section, we will explain how to display a report in a web browser with the help of the Servlet API. The following example demonstrates how to accomplish this:

```
package net.ensode.jasperbook;

import java.io.IOException;
import java.io.InputStream;
import java.io.PrintWriter;
import java.io.StringWriter;
import java.util.HashMap;

import javax.servlet.ServletException;
import javax.servlet.ServletOutputStream;
import javax.servlet.http.HttpServlet;
import javax.servlet.http.HttpServletRequest;
import javax.servlet.http.HttpServletResponse;

import net.sf.jasperreports.engine.JREmptyDataSource;
import net.sf.jasperreports.engine.JRException;
import net.sf.jasperreports.engine.JasperRunManager;

public class FirstReportSendToBrowserServlet extends HttpServlet
{

  protected void doGet(HttpServletRequest request, HttpServletResponse
                       response) throws ServletException, IOException
  {
    ServletOutputStream servletOutputStream =
                                      response.getOutputStream();
    InputStream reportStream = getServletConfig().getServletContext()
    .getResourceAsStream("/reports/FirstReport.jasper");

    try
    {
      JasperRunManager.runReportToPdfStream(reportStream,
        servletOutputStream, new HashMap(), new JREmptyDataSource());
```

```
         response.setContentType("application/pdf");
         servletOutputStream.flush();
         servletOutputStream.close();
      }
      catch (JRException e)
      {
         // display stack trace in the browser
         StringWriter stringWriter = new StringWriter();
         PrintWriter printWriter = new PrintWriter(stringWriter);
         e.printStackTrace(printWriter);
         response.setContentType("text/plain");
         response.getOutputStream().print(stringWriter.toString());
      }
   }
}
```

Since web browsers are incapable of displaying reports in JasperReports' native format (at least without the help of an applet), we must export the report to a format that the browser can understand. JasperReports allows us to export reports to PDF and many other formats. Since the PDF format is widely used, we chose to export to this format in this example.

The servlet in the above example calls the static `JasperRunManager.` `runReportToPdfStream()` method. The signature for this method is:

```
runReportToPdfStream(java.io.InputStream inputStream,
                     java.io.OutputStream outputStream,
                     java.util.Map parameters,
                     JRDataSource dataSource)
```

To display the report on the browser, we need to pass the binary report template, or Jasper file, in the form of a stream, as the first argument of this method. We can accomplish this by calling the `javax.servlet.ServletContext.` `getResourceAsStream()` method, passing a `String` containing the location of the Jasper file as a parameter. This method will return an instance of `java.` `io.InputStream` that we can use as the first argument for the `JasperRunManager.` `runReportToPDFStream()` method.

The `JasperRunManager.runReportToPDFStream()` method needs an instance of `java.io.OutputStream()` to write the compiled report. We can simply use the default output stream for the servlet, which can be obtained by calling the `javax.` `servlet.http.HttpServletResponse.getOutputStream()` method.

The next two arguments for the `JasperRunManager.runReportToPDFStream()` method are `java.util.Map` and `JRDataSource`. The former is used to pass any parameters to the report, the latter to pass data in the form of a `net.sf.jasperreports.engine.JRDataSource`. Since we are not passing any parameters or data to this simple report, an empty `HashMap` and `JREmptyDataSource` suffice.

To make sure the browser displays the report properly, we must set the content type to `application/pdf`. We can accomplish this by calling the `javax.servlet.http.HttpServletResponse.setContentType()` method.

The resulting code for this example needs to be deployed to a servlet container. An ANT script to automate this process can be found at this book's website. The following screenshot shows the report being displayed as a PDF on a browser:

# Elements of a JRXML Report Template

In the previous example, we used the `<detail>` element of the JRXML report template to generate a report displaying some static text. The `<detail>` element is used to display the main section of the report. However, JRXML templates can contain many other elements that allow us to display secondary data on the report, or allow us to do some other tasks like importing Java packages, or setting the report font. Unless stated otherwise, each element can be used any number of times in the template. The following sections outline all the sub-elements of the `<jasperReport>` root element.

# \<property\>

This element is used to put arbitrary information in the report template.

```
<property name="someproperty"
          value="somevalue"/>
```

Properties can be retrieved by a Java application loading the report by invoking the `JasperReport.getProperty()` method.

A JRXML template can contain zero or more `<property>` elements.

# \<import\>

This element is used to import individual Java classes or complete packages.

```
<import value="java.util.HashMap"/>
```

A JRXML template can contain zero or more `<import>` elements.

# \<reportFont\>

This element is used to define one or more fonts that can be used on the text displayed on the report.

```
<reportFont name="Arial"
            isDefault="true"
            fontName="Arial" size="12"
            isBold="true" isItalic="false"
            isUnderline="false"
            isStrikeThrough="false"
            pdfFontName="Helvetica"
            pdfEncoding="CP1252"
            isPdfEmbedded="false"/>
```

A JRXML template can contain zero or more `<reportFont>` elements.

# \<parameter\>

This element is used to define report parameters. Parameter values are supplied via a `java.util.Map` by calling the appropriate methods in the JasperReports API.

```
<parameter name="SomeParameter"
          class="java.lang.String"/>
```

A JRXML template can contain zero or more `<parameter>` elements.

# \<queryString\>

This element is used to define an SQL query to obtain data from a database.

```
<queryString>
  <![CDATA[SELECT column_name FROM table_name]]>
</queryString>
```

A JRXML template can contain zero or one `<queryString>` element. This element is required if we wish to embed an SQL query into the report template.

# \<field\>

This element is used to map data from datasources or queries into report templates. Fields can be combined in report expressions to obtain the necessary output.

```
<field name="FieldName" class="java.lang.String"/>
```

A JRXML template can contain zero or more `<field>` elements.

# \<variable\>

Report expressions, used several times in a report, can be assigned to variables to simplify the template.

```
<variable name="VariableName"
          class="java.lang.Double"
          calculation="Sum">
    <variableExpression>
      $F{FieldName}
    </variableExpression>
</variable>
```

A JRXML template can contain zero or more `<variable>` elements.

# \<group>

This element is used to group consecutive records in a datasource sharing some common characteristics.

```
<group name="GroupName">
  <groupExpression>
    <![CDATA[$F{FieldName}]]>
  </groupExpression>
</group>
```

A JRXML template can contain zero or more \<group> elements.

# \<background>

This element is used to define the page background for all pages in the report. It can be used to display images or text and also to display watermarks.

```
<background>
  <band height="745">
    <image scaleImage="Clip" hAlign="Left" vAlign="Bottom">
      <reportElement x="0" y="0" width="160" height="745"/>
      <imageExpression>"image.gif"
      </imageExpression>
    </image>
  </band>
</background>
```

A JRXML template can contain zero or one \<background> element.

# \<title>

This is the report title and appears only once, at the beginning of the report.

```
<title>
  <band height="50">
    <staticText>
      <reportElement x="180" y="0" width="200" height="20"/>
      <text>
```

```
        <![CDATA[Title]]>
      </text>
    </staticText>
  </band>
</title>
```

A JRXML template can contain zero or one `<title>` element.

# <pageHeader>

This element defines a page header that is printed at the beginning of every page in the report.

```
<pageHeader>
  <band height="20">
    <staticText>
      <reportElement x="180" y="30" width="200" height="20"/>
      <text>
        <![CDATA[Page Header]]>
      </text>
    </staticText>
  </band>
</pageHeader>
```

A JRXML template can contain zero or one `<pageHeader>` element.

# <columnHeader>

This element is ignored if the report has a single column.

```
<columnHeader>
  <band height="20">
    <staticText>
      <reportElement x="180" y="50" width="200" height="20"/>
      <text>
        <![CDATA[Column Header]]>
      </text>
    </staticText>
  </band>
</columnHeader>
```

A JRXML template can contain zero or more `<columnHeader>` elements. If present, the number of `<columnHeader>` elements in the template must match the number of columns.

# <detail>

This element defines the detail section of the report and is repeated for each record in the report's datasource.

```
<detail>
  <band height="20">
    <textField>
      <reportElement x="10" y="0" width="600" height="20"/>
      <textFieldExpression class="java.lang.String">
        <![CDATA[$F{FieldName}]]>
      </textFieldExpression>
    </textField>
  </band>
</detail>
```

A JRXML template can contain zero or one `<detail>` elements. Most report templates contain a `<detail>` element since typically this is where the main data in the report is displayed.

# <columnFooter>

This element is ignored if the report has a single column.

```
<columnFooter>
  <band height="20">
    <staticText>
      <reportElement x="0" y="0" width="200" height="20"/>
      <text>
        <![CDATA[Column Footer]]>
      </text>
    </staticText>
  </band>
</columnFooter>
```

A JRXML template can contain zero or more `<columnFooter>` elements. If present, the number of `<columnFooter>` elements in the template must match the number of columns.

# <pageFooter>

This element defines a page footer that is printed at the bottom of every page in the report.

```
<pageFooter>
  <band height="20">
    <staticText>
      <reportElement  x="0" y="5" width="200" height="20"/>
      <text>
        <![CDATA[Page Footer]]>
      </text>
    </staticText>
  </band>
</pageFooter>
```

A JRXML template can contain zero or one `<pageFooter>` element.

# <lastPageFooter>

Data defined in this element is displayed as the page footer of the last page, instead of the footer defined in the `<pageFooter>` element.

```
<lastPageFooter>
  <band height="20">
    <staticText>
      <reportElement  x="0" y="5"
        width="200" height="20"/>
      <text>
        <![CDATA[Last Page Footer]]>
      </text>
    </staticText>
  </band>
</lastPageFooter>
```

A JRXML template can contain zero or one `<lastPageFooter>` element.

# &lt;summary&gt;

This is printed once at the end of the report.

```
<summary>
  <band height="20">
    <staticText>
      <reportElement  x="0" y="5" width="200" height="20"/>
      <text>
        <![CDATA[Summary]]>
      </text>
    </staticText>
  </band>
</summary>
```

A JRXML template can contain zero or one `<summary>` element.

Just like the `<detail>` element, every element discussed previously contains a single `<band>` element as its child element. We will discuss the specific sub-elements of the `<band>` element in the appropriate chapters.

In the following screenshot, we can see a report that can help us visualize the relative position of report sections:

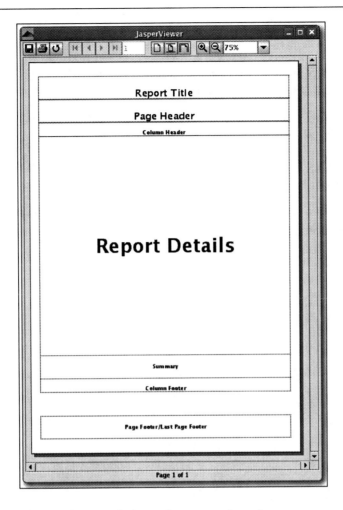

There are some things to be noted about the screenshot. As you can see, the page footer is labeled **Page Footer/Last Page Footer**. If the JRXML template for the report contains a `<lastPageFooter>` element, it will be displayed in the last page of the report instead of the `<pagefooter>` element being displayed. It is worth mentioning that, if your report has only one page and the report template contains both a `<pageFooter>` and a `<lastPageFooter>` element, then the contents of `<lastPageFooter>` will be displayed as the footer of the first (and the only) page. The `<pageFooter>` element will never be displayed in this case.

Moreover, the `<columnHeader>` and `<columnFooter>` elements will only be displayed on the report if it has more than one column. Adding columns to a report is discussed in detail in Chapter 6.

# Summary

In this chapter, we learned to create a JRXML report template by editing an XML file and preview the template by using tools supplied by JasperReports. We also learned to compile a JRXML template programmatically and via a custom ANT task.

After the successful compilation of the report, we filled the report template with data by calling the appropriate methods supplied by the `JasperFillManager` class and viewed the generated reports in native JasperReports format by using the JasperViewer utility. The chapter also took us through the different report sections in a JRXML template.

Finally, we created web-based reports by displaying generated reports in a web browser. We are now ready to move on to the next chapter.

# 4

# Creating Dynamic Database Reports

In the previous chapter, we learned how to create our first report. The simple report in the previous chapter contained no dynamic data. In this chapter, we will explore how to create a report from data obtained from a database.

In this chapter, we will cover the following topics:

- How to embed SQL queries into a report definition
- How to pass rows returned by an SQL query to a report via a datasource
- How to use report fields to display data obtained from a database in a report
- How to display data from a database in a report by using the `<textField>` element of the JRXML template

**Datasources: Definition**

A datasource is what JasperReports uses to obtain data to generate a report. Data can be obtained from databases, XML files, arrays of objects, collections of objects, and XML files.

This chapter focuses on using databases as a datasource. The next chapter discusses other types of datasources.

## Database for Our Reports

In this chapter, we will use a MySQL database to obtain data for our reports. The database is a subset of public domain data that can be downloaded from `http://dl.flightstats.us`. The original download is 1.3GB. However, we deleted most of the tables and a lot of the data to trim the download size considerably.

A MySQL dump of the modified database can be found at this book's website: `http://www.packtpub.com/support`.

The database contains the following tables: **aircraft, aircraft_models, aircraft_types, aircraft_engines,** and **aircraft_engine_types.** The database structure can be seen in the following diagram:

```
aircraft
tail_num char(6) NOT NULL (PK)
aircraft_serial char(20) NOT NULL
aircraft_model_code char(7) NOT NULL
aircraft_engine_code char(5) NOT NULL
year_built year(4) NOT NULL
aircraft_type_id tinyint unsigned(3) NOT NULL
registrant_type_id tinyint unsigned(3) NOT NULL
name char(5) NOT NULL
address1 char(33) NOT NULL
address2 char(33) NOT NULL
city char(18) NOT NULL
state char(2) NOT NULL
zip char(10) NOT NULL
region char(1) NOT NULL
country char(3) NOT NULL
country char(2) NOT NULL
certification char(10) NOT NULL
status_code char(1) NOT NULL
mode_s_code char(8) NOT NULL
fract_owner char(1) NOT NULL
last_action_date date(10) NOT NULL
cert_issue_date date(10) NOT NULL
air_worth_date date(10) NOT NULL
```

```
aircraft_types
aircraft_type_id tinyint unsigned(3) NOT NULL (PK)
description char(30) NOT NULL
```

```
aircraft_models
aircraft_model_code char(7) NOT NULL (PK)
manufacturer char(3) NOT NULL
model char(20) NOT NULL
aircraft_type_id tinyint unsigned(3) NOT NULL
aircraft_engine_type_id tinyint unsigned(3) NOT NULL
aircraft_category_id tinyint unsigned(3) NOT NULL
amateur tinyint unsigned(3) NOT NULL
engines tinyint(4) NOT NULL
seats smallint(6) NOT NULL
weight int(11) NOT NULL
speed smallint(6) NOT NULL
```

```
aircraft_engines
aircraft_engine_code char(5) NOT NULL (PK)
manufacturer char(10) NOT NULL
model char(13) NOT NULL
aircraft_engine_type_id tinyint unsigned(3) NOT NULL
horsepower mediumint unsigned(8) NOT NULL
thrust mediumint unsigned(8) NOT NULL
fuel_consumed decimal(10,2) NOT NULL
```

```
aircraft_engine_types
aircraft_engine_type_id tinyint unsigned(3) NOT NULL (PK)
description char(30) NOT NULL
```

The FlightStats database uses the default MyISAM MySQL engine, which does not support referential integrity (foreign keys). That is the reason for which we don't see any arrows in the diagram indicating dependencies between the tables.

Let us create a report that will show the most powerful aircraft in the database, say, those with a horsepower of 1000 or above. The report will show the aircraft tail number, aircraft serial number, the aircraft model, and the aircraft's engine model. The following query will give us these results:

```
select a.tail_num, a.aircraft_serial, am.model as aircraft_model,
ae.model as engine_model

from aircraft a, aircraft_models am, aircraft_engines ae

where a.aircraft_engine_code in ( select aircraft_engine_code
                                  from aircraft_engines
```

```
                            where horsepower >= 1000)
and am.aircraft_model_code = a.aircraft_model_code
and ae.aircraft_engine_code = a.aircraft_engine_code
```

# Generating Database Reports

There are two ways to generate database reports. It can either be done by embedding SQL queries into the JRXML report template, or by passing data from the database to the compiled report via a datasource. We will discuss both of these techniques.

We will first create the report by embedding the query into the JRXML template. We will then generate the same report by passing it a datasource containing the database data.

# Embedding SQL Queries into a Report Template

JasperReports allows us to embed database queries into a report template. This can be achieved by using the `<queryString>` element of the JRXML file. The following example demonstrates this technique:

```xml
<?xml version="1.0" encoding="UTF-8"?>
<!DOCTYPE jasperReport PUBLIC "//JasperReports//DTD Report Design//EN"
 "http://jasperreports.sourceforge.net/dtds/jasperreport.dtd">
<jasperReport name="DbReport">
  <queryString>
     <![CDATA[select a.tail_num,
                   a.aircraft_serial,
                   am.model as aircraft_model,
                   ae.model as engine_model
             from aircraft a,
                   aircraft_models am,
                   aircraft_engines ae
             where a.aircraft_engine_code in ( select
                                             aircraft_engine_code
                                             from aircraft_engines
                                             where horsepower >= 1000)
             and am.aircraft_model_code = a.aircraft_model_code
             and ae.aircraft_engine_code = a.aircraft_engine_code]]>
  </queryString>
  <field name="tail_num" class="java.lang.String"/>
  <field name="aircraft_serial" class="java.lang.String"/>
  <field name="aircraft_model" class="java.lang.String"/>
  <field name="engine_model" class="java.lang.String"/>
```

```xml
<pageHeader>
  <band height="30">
    <staticText>
      <reportElement x="0" y="0" width="69" height="24"/>
      <textElement verticalAlignment="Bottom"/>
      <text>
        <![CDATA[Tail Number: ]]>
      </text>
    </staticText>
    <staticText>
      <reportElement x="140" y="0" width="79" height="24"/>
      <text>
        <![CDATA[Serial Number: ]]>
      </text>
    </staticText>
    <staticText>
      <reportElement x="280" y="0" width="69" height="24"/>
      <text>
        <![CDATA[Model: ]]>
      </text>
    </staticText>
    <staticText>
      <reportElement x="420" y="0" width="69" height="24"/>
      <text>
        <![CDATA[Engine: ]]>
      </text>
    </staticText>
  </band>
</pageHeader>
<detail>
  <band height="30">
    <textField>
      <reportElement x="0" y="0" width="69" height="24"/>
      <textFieldExpression class="java.lang.String">
        <![CDATA[$F{tail_num}]]>
      </textFieldExpression>
    </textField>
    <textField>
      <reportElement x="140" y="0" width="69" height="24"/>
      <textFieldExpression class="java.lang.String">
        <![CDATA[$F{aircraft_serial}]]>
      </textFieldExpression>
    </textField>
```

```
          </textField>
          <textField>
            <reportElement x="280" y="0" width="69" height="24"/>
            <textFieldExpression   class="java.lang.String">
              <![CDATA[$F{aircraft_model}]]>
            </textFieldExpression>
          </textField>
          <textField>
            <reportElement x="420" y="0" width="69" height="24"/>
            <textFieldExpression   class="java.lang.String">
              <![CDATA[$F{engine_model}]]>
            </textFieldExpression>
          </textField>
        </band>
      </detail>
    </jasperReport>
```

There are a few JRXML elements in this example we haven't seen before.

As we mentioned, the `<queryString>` element is used to embed a database query into the report template. As we can see in the example, the `<queryString>` element contains the query to be executed, wrapped in a CDATA block. The `<queryString>` element has no attributes or sub-elements other than the CDATA block containing the query.

> Text wrapped inside an XML CDATA block is ignored by the XML parser. As we can see in the example, our query contains the > character, which would invalidate the XML if it wasn't inside a CDATA block. A CDATA block is optional, if the data inside it does not break the XML structure. However, for consistency and maintainability, we have used it wherever it is allowed, in the given example.

The `<field>` element defines fields that are populated at run time when the report is filled. Field names must match the column name or alias of the corresponding column in the SQL query. The `class` attribute of the `<field>` element is optional. Its default value is `java.lang.String`. Even though all of our fields are Strings, we still added the `class` attribute for clarity. As can be seen in the example above, the syntax to obtain the value of a report field is `$F{field_name}`, where `field_name` is the name of the field as defined in its definition.

The next attribute that we haven't discussed before is the `<textField>` attribute. Text fields are used to display dynamic textual data in reports. In this case, we are using them to display the value of the fields. Like all sub-elements of `<band>`, `<textField>` must contain a `<reportElement>` sub-element indicating the text field's `height`, `width`, and `x`, `y` coordinates within the band. The data that is displayed in text fields is defined by the `<textFieldExpression>` sub-element of `<textField>`. The

`<textFieldExpresson>` has a single sub-element, which is the report expression that will be displayed by the text field, wrapped in an XML CDATA block. In this example, each text field is displaying the value of a field. Therefore, the expression inside `<textFieldExpression>` uses the `<field>` syntax explained previously.

Compiling a report containing a query is no different from compiling a report without a query. It can be done either programmatically or through the custom JasperReports JRC ANT task. We covered compiling reports in Chapter 3.

## Generating the Report

As mentioned previously, in JasperReports terminology, the action of generating a report from a binary report template is called *filling* the report. To fill a report containing an embedded database query, we must pass a database connection object to the report. The following example illustrates this process:

```
package net.ensode.jasperbook;

import java.sql.Connection;
import java.sql.DriverManager;
import java.sql.SQLException;
import java.util.HashMap;

import net.sf.jasperreports.engine.JRException;
import net.sf.jasperreports.engine.JasperFillManager;

public class DbReportFill
{
  Connection connection;

  public void generateReport()
  {
    try
    {
      Class.forName("com.mysql.jdbc.Driver");

      connection = DriverManager.getConnection ("jdbc:mysql://
              localhost:3306/flightstats?user=user&password=secret");

      System.out.println("Filling report...");
      JasperFillManager.fillReportToFile("reports/DbReport.jasper",
                                  new HashMap(), connection);
      System.out.println("Done!");
```

```
            connection.close();
    }
    catch (JRException e)
    {
        e.printStackTrace();
    }
    catch (ClassNotFoundException e)
    {
        e.printStackTrace();
    }
    catch (SQLException e)
    {
        e.printStackTrace();
    }
    }

    public static void main(String[] args)
    {
        new DbReportFill().generateReport();
    }
}
```

As can be seen in this example, a database connection is passed to the report in the form of a `java.sql.Connection` object as the last parameter of the static `JasperFillManager.fillReportToFile()` method. The first two parameters are of type `String`, used to indicate the location of the binary report template, or Jasper file, and an instance of a class implementing the `java.util.Map` interface, used to pass additional parameters to the report. Since for this report we don't need to pass any additional parameters, we used an empty `HashMap`.

There are six overloaded versions of the `JasperFillManager.fillReportToFile()` method. Three of them take a `Connection` object as a parameter. Refer to Chapter 3 for a description of the other versions of this method that take a `Connection` object as a parameter.

 For simplicity, our examples open and close database connections every time they are executed. It is usually a better idea to use a connection pool, since connection pools increase performance considerably. Most Java EE application servers come with connection pooling functionality. The `Commons-dbcp` component of Jakarta Commons includes utility classes for adding connection pooling capabilities to applications that do not make use of an application server.

After executing the preceding example, a new report, or jrprint file, is saved to disk. We can view it by using the **JasperViewer** utility included with JasperReports.

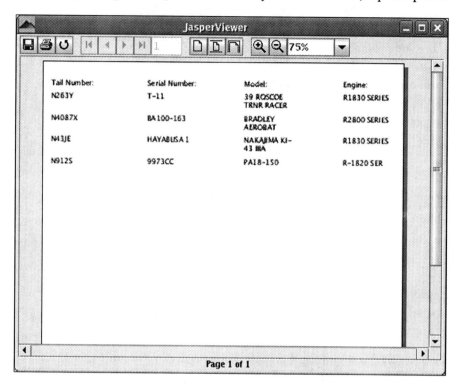

The **JasperViewer** utility is discussed in detail in Chapter 3.

In this example, we created the report and immediately saved it to disk. The JasperFillManager class also contains methods to send a report to an output stream, or to store it in memory in the form of a JasperPrint object. Storing the compiled report in a JasperPrint object allows us to further manipulate the report. We could, for example, export it to PDF or another format.

The method used to store a report into a JasperPrint object is JasperFillManager. fillReport(). The method used to send the report to an output stream is JasperFillManager.fillReportToStream(). These two methods accept the same parameters as JasperFillManager.fillReportToFile(), and are trivial to use once we are familiar with this method. Refer to the JasperReports API for details.

In the next example, we will fill our report and immediately export it to PDF by taking advantage of the net.sf.jasperreports.engine.JasperRunManager. runReportToPDFStream() method.

```
package net.ensode.jasperbook;

import java.io.IOException;
import java.io.InputStream;
import java.io.PrintWriter;
import java.io.StringWriter;
import java.sql.Connection;
import java.sql.DriverManager;
import java.util.HashMap;

import javax.servlet.ServletException;
import javax.servlet.ServletOutputStream;
import javax.servlet.http.HttpServlet;
import javax.servlet.http.HttpServletRequest;
import javax.servlet.http.HttpServletResponse;

import net.sf.jasperreports.engine.JasperRunManager;

public class DbReportServlet extends HttpServlet
{

  protected void doGet(HttpServletRequest request, HttpServletResponse
                       response) throws ServletException, IOException
  {
    Connection connection;
    ServletOutputStream servletOutputStream =
                       response.getOutputStream();
    InputStream reportStream =
           getServletConfig().getServletContext().getResourceAsStream
                                        ("/reports/DbReport.jasper");

    try
    {
      Class.forName("com.mysql.jdbc.Driver");

      connection = DriverManager.getConnection ("jdbc:mysql://
            localhost:3306/flightstats?user=dbuser&password=secret");

      JasperRunManager.runReportToPdfStream(reportStream,
          servletOutputStream, new HashMap(), connection);

      connection.close();
```

```
      response.setContentType("application/pdf");
      servletOutputStream.flush();
      servletOutputStream.close();
    }
    catch (Exception e)
    {
      // display stack trace in the browser
      StringWriter stringWriter = new StringWriter();
      PrintWriter printWriter = new PrintWriter(stringWriter);
      e.printStackTrace(printWriter);
      response.setContentType("text/plain");
      response.getOutputStream().print(stringWriter.toString());
    }
  }
}
```

We had already discussed this technique in the previous chapter. The only difference, here, is that we are passing a connection to the report to generate a database report. After deploying this servlet and pointing the browser to its URL, we should see a screen like the following:

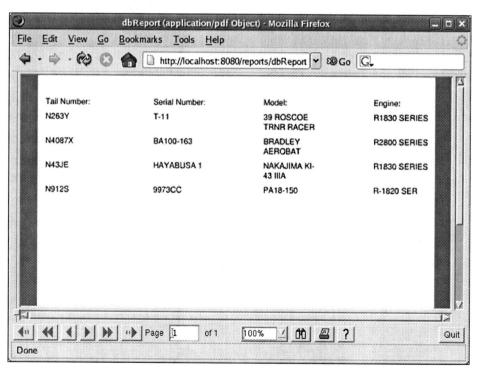

Although not directly related to database reporting, one more thing worth mentioning is that we used the <pageHeader> element of the JRXML template for laying out the report labels. If our report had more than one page, these labels would have appeared at the top of every page.

# Modifying a Report Query via Report Parameters

Embedding a database query into a report template is the simplest way to generate a database report. However, it is not very flexible. If we need to modify the report query, it is also necessary to modify the report's JRXML template.

The sample JRXML template, discussed in the previous section, generates a report that displays all aircraft in the database with a horsepower equal to or greater than 1000. If we wanted to generate a report to display all aircraft with a horsepower greater than or equal to 750, we would have to modify the JRXML and recompile it. That's a lot of work for such a small change. Fortunately, JasperReports allows us to modify an embedded database query easily, by using report parameters. The following JRXML template is a new version of the one we saw in the previous section, modified to take advantage of report parameters.

```xml
<?xml version="1.0" encoding="UTF-8"?>
<!DOCTYPE jasperReport PUBLIC "//JasperReports//DTD Report Design//EN"
 "http://jasperreports.sourceforge.net/dtds/jasperreport.dtd">
<jasperReport name="DbReportParam">
<parameter name="hp" class="java.lang.Integer"/>
<queryString>
  <![CDATA[select a.tail_num,
               a.aircraft_serial,
               am.model as aircraft_model,
               ae.model as engine_model
         from aircraft a,
              aircraft_models am,
              aircraft_engines ae
         where a.aircraft_engine_code in (
                                    select aircraft_engine_code
                                    from aircraft_engines
                                    where horsepower >= $P{hp})
         and am.aircraft_model_code = a.aircraft_model_code
         and ae.aircraft_engine_code = a.aircraft_engine_code]]>
</queryString>
<field name="tail_num" class="java.lang.String"/>
<field name="aircraft_serial" class="java.lang.String"/>
<field name="aircraft_model" class="java.lang.String"/>
<field name="engine_model" class="java.lang.String"/>
```

```
<pageHeader>
  <band height="30">
    <staticText>
      <reportElement x="0" y="0" width="69" height="24"/>
      <textElement verticalAlignment="Bottom"/>
      <text>
        <![CDATA[Tail Number: ]]>
      </text>
    </staticText>
    <staticText>
      <reportElement x="140" y="0" width="79" height="24"/>
      <text>
        <![CDATA[Serial Number: ]]>
      </text>
    </staticText>
    <staticText>
      <reportElement x="280" y="0" width="69" height="24"/>
      <text>
        <![CDATA[Model: ]]>
      </text>
    </staticText>
    <staticText>
      <reportElement x="420" y="0" width="69" height="24"/>
      <text>
        <![CDATA[Engine: ]]>
      </text>
    </staticText>
  </band>
</pageHeader>
<detail>
  <band height="30">
    <textField>
      <reportElement x="0" y="0" width="69" height="24"/>
      <textFieldExpression class="java.lang.String">
        <![CDATA[$F{tail_num}]]>
      </textFieldExpression>
    </textField>
    <textField>
      <reportElement x="140" y="0" width="69" height="24"/>
```

```
      <textFieldExpression class="java.lang.String">
        <![CDATA[$F{aircraft_serial}]]>
      </textFieldExpression>
    </textField>
    <textField>
      <reportElement x="280" y="0" width="69" height="24"/>
      <textFieldExpression class="java.lang.String">
        <![CDATA[$F{aircraft_model}]]>
      </textFieldExpression>
    </textField>
    <textField>
      <reportElement x="420" y="0" width="69" height="24"/>
      <textFieldExpression class="java.lang.String">
        <![CDATA[$F{engine_model}]]>
      </textFieldExpression>
    </textField>
  </band>
</detail>
</jasperReport>
```

The only difference between this JRXML template and the previous one is that we declared a report parameter in the following line:

```
<parameter name="hp" class="java.lang.Integer"/>
```

We then used the declared parameter to dynamically retrieve the horsepower in the where clause of the report query. As can be seen in the example above, the value of a report parameter can be retrieved by using the syntax $P{paramName}, where paramName is the parameter name as defined in its declaration (hp in the example above).

Passing a parameter to a report from Java code is very simple. In most of the examples we have seen so far, we have been passing an empty HashMap to report templates when we fill them. The purpose of that HashMap is to pass parameters to the report template. The following servlet is a new version of the one we saw in the previous section, modified to send a report parameter to the report template:

```
package net.ensode.jasperbook;

import java.io.IOException;
import java.io.InputStream;
import java.io.PrintWriter;
import java.io.StringWriter;
import java.sql.Connection;
```

```
import java.sql.DriverManager;
import java.util.HashMap;

import javax.servlet.ServletException;
import javax.servlet.ServletOutputStream;
import javax.servlet.http.HttpServlet;
import javax.servlet.http.HttpServletRequest;
import javax.servlet.http.HttpServletResponse;

import net.sf.jasperreports.engine.JasperRunManager;

public class DbReportParamServlet extends HttpServlet
{

  protected void doGet(HttpServletRequest request, HttpServletResponse
                       response)
     throws ServletException, IOException
  {

    Connection connection;
    ServletOutputStream servletOutputStream =
                        response.getOutputStream();
    InputStream reportStream =
        getServletConfig().getServletContext().getResourceAsStream(
                                  "/reports/DbReportParam.jasper");
    HashMap parameterMap = new HashMap();

    parameterMap.put("hp", new Integer(750));

    try
    {
      Class.forName("com.mysql.jdbc.Driver");

      connection = DriverManager.getConnection ("jdbc:mysql://
          localhost:3306/flightstats?user=dbuser&password=secret");

      JasperRunManager.runReportToPdfStream(reportStream,
          servletOutputStream, parameterMap, connection);

      connection.close();

      response.setContentType("application/pdf");
      servletOutputStream.flush();
      servletOutputStream.close();
```

```
      }
      catch (Exception e)
      {
         // display stack trace in the browser
         StringWriter stringWriter = new StringWriter();
         PrintWriter printWriter = new PrintWriter(stringWriter);
         e.printStackTrace(printWriter);
         response.setContentType("text/plain");
         response.getOutputStream().print(stringWriter.toString());
      }
   }
}
```

The only difference between this servlet and the one in the previous section is that we declare a HashMap and populate it with the report parameters. Notice how the HashMap key must match the report parameter name.

After deploying the servlet and directing the browser to its URL, we should see a report like the following:

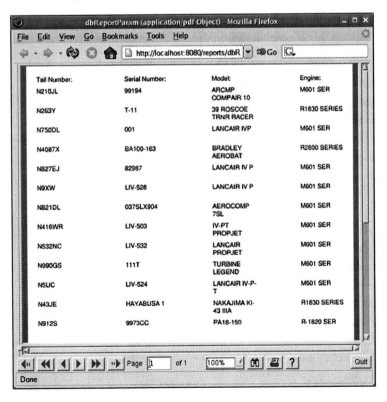

Dynamically modifying report queries is only one of the many possible uses of report parameters. Report parameters are discussed in more detail in the next chapter.

# Database Reporting via a Datasource

Another way to generate reports based on database data is by using a datasource. In JasperReports terminology, a datasource is a class implementing the `net.sf.jasperreports.engine.JRDataSource` interface.

To use a database as a datasource, the JasperReports API provides the `net.sf.jasperreports.engine.JRResultSetDataSource` class. This class implements `JRDataSource` and has a single public constructor that takes `java.sql.ResultSet` as its only parameter. `JRResultSetDataSource` provides no public methods or variables. To use it, all we need to do is provide a result set to its constructor and pass it to the report via the `JasperFillManager` class.

Let us modify the above JRXML template so that it uses a `JRResultSetDataSource` to obtain database data.

The only change we need to make on the JRXML template is to remove the `<queryString>` element.

```
<?xml version="1.0" encoding="UTF-8"?>
<!DOCTYPE jasperReport PUBLIC "//JasperReports//DTD Report Design//EN"
  "http://jasperreports.sourceforge.net/dtds/jasperreport.dtd">
<jasperReport name="DbReportDS">
<field name="tail_num" class="java.lang.String"/>
<field name="aircraft_serial" class="java.lang.String"/>
<field name="aircraft_model" class="java.lang.String"/>
<field name="engine_model" class="java.lang.String"/>
<pageHeader>
  <band height="30">
    <staticText>
      <reportElement x="0" y="0" width="69" height="24"/>
      <textElement verticalAlignment="Bottom"/>
      <text>
        <![CDATA[Tail Number: ]]>
      </text>
    </staticText>
    <staticText>
      <reportElement x="140" y="0" width="69" height="24"/>
      <text>
```

```
        <![CDATA[Serial Number: ]]>
      </text>
    </staticText>
    <staticText>
      <reportElement x="280" y="0" width="69" height="24"/>
      <text>
        <![CDATA[Model: ]]>
      </text>
    </staticText>
    <staticText>
      <reportElement x="420" y="0" width="69" height="24"/>
      <text>
        <![CDATA[Engine: ]]>
      </text>
    </staticText>
  </band>
</pageHeader>
<detail>
  <band height="30">
    <textField>
      <reportElement x="0" y="0" width="69" height="24"/>
      <textFieldExpression class="java.lang.String">
        <![CDATA[$F{tail_num}]]>
      </textFieldExpression>
    </textField>
    <textField>
      <reportElement x="140" y="0" width="69" height="24"/>
      <textFieldExpression class="java.lang.String">
        <![CDATA[$F{aircraft_serial}]]>
      </textFieldExpression>
    </textField>
    <textField>
      <reportElement x="280" y="0" width="69" height="24"/>
      <textFieldExpression class="java.lang.String">
        <![CDATA[$F{aircraft_model}]]>
      </textFieldExpression>
    </textField>
    <textField>
      <reportElement x="420" y="0" width="69" height="24"/>
      <textFieldExpression class="java.lang.String">
```

```
          <![CDATA[$F{engine_model}]]>
        </textFieldExpression>
      </textField>
    </band>
  </detail>
</jasperReport>
```

The procedure for compiling a database report, by using `JRResultSetDataSource`, is no different from what we have already seen. To fill the report, we need to execute a database query in our Java code, and pass the query results to the report in a datasource, as can be seen in the following example:

```java
package net.ensode.jasperbook;

import java.sql.Connection;
import java.sql.DriverManager;
import java.sql.ResultSet;
import java.sql.SQLException;
import java.sql.Statement;
import java.util.HashMap;

import net.sf.jasperreports.engine.JRException;
import net.sf.jasperreports.engine.JRResultSetDataSource;
import net.sf.jasperreports.engine.JasperFillManager;

public class DbReportDSFill
{
  Connection connection;
  Statement statement;
  ResultSet resultSet;

  public void generateReport()
  {
    try
    {
      String query = "select a.tail_num, a.aircraft_serial, "
        + "am.model as aircraft_model, ae.model as engine_model from
          aircraft a, "
        + "aircraft_models am, aircraft_engines ae where a.aircraft_
          engine_code in ("
        + "select aircraft_engine_code from aircraft_engines "
        + "where horsepower >= 1000) and am.aircraft_model_code =
          a.aircraft_model_code "
```

```
        + "and ae.aircraft_engine_code = a.aircraft_engine_code";

    Class.forName("com.mysql.jdbc.Driver");

    connection = DriverManager.getConnection ("jdbc:mysql://
            localhost:3306/flightstats?user=user&password=secret");
    statement = connection.createStatement();
    resultSet = statement.executeQuery(query);

    JRResultSetDataSource resultSetDataSource = new
                            JRResultSetDataSource(resultSet);

    System.out.println("Filling report...");
    JasperFillManager.fillReportToFile("reports/DbReportDS.jasper",
                            new HashMap(), resultSetDataSource);
    System.out.println("Done!");

    resultSet.close();
    statement.close();
    connection.close();
  }
  catch (JRException e)
  {
    e.printStackTrace();
  }
  catch (ClassNotFoundException e)
  {
    e.printStackTrace();
  }
  catch (SQLException e)
  {
    e.printStackTrace();
  }
}

public static void main(String[] args)
{
  new DbReportDSFill().generateReport();
}
}
```

As can be seen in this example, to provide a report with database data, by using `JRResultSetDataSource`, we must execute the database query from the Java code, and wrap the resulting `resultSet` object into an instance of `JRResultSetDataSource`, by passing it to its constructor. The instance of `JRResultSetDataSource` must then be passed to the `JasperFillManager.fillReportToFile()` method. Strictly speaking, any method that takes an instance of a class implementing `JRDataSource` can be called. In this example, we wish to save the report to a file. Therefore, we chose to use the `fillReportToFile()` method. This method fills the report with data from the datasource and saves it to a file in the file system. It has the potential of throwing a `JRException`, if there is something wrong. Therefore, this exception must either be caught, or declared in the `throws` clause.

After executing this code, a report, identical to the first one we saw in the previous section, is generated. The following example demonstrates how a web-based report can be created by using a database datasource:

```
package net.ensode.jasperbook;

import java.io.IOException;
import java.io.InputStream;
import java.io.PrintWriter;
import java.io.StringWriter;
import java.sql.Connection;
import java.sql.DriverManager;
import java.sql.ResultSet;
import java.sql.Statement;
import java.util.HashMap;

import javax.servlet.ServletException;
import javax.servlet.ServletOutputStream;
import javax.servlet.http.HttpServlet;
import javax.servlet.http.HttpServletRequest;
import javax.servlet.http.HttpServletResponse;

import net.sf.jasperreports.engine.JRResultSetDataSource;
import net.sf.jasperreports.engine.JasperRunManager;

public class DbDSReportServlet extends HttpServlet
{

    protected void doGet(HttpServletRequest request, HttpServletResponse
                        response) throws ServletException, IOException
```

```
{
  Connection connection;
  Statement statement;
  ResultSet resultSet;

  ServletOutputStream servletOutputStream =
                                  response.getOutputStream();
  InputStream reportStream = getServletConfig().getServletContext().
              getResourceAsStream("/reports/DbReportDS.jasper");

  try
  {
    String query = "select a.tail_num, a.aircraft_serial, "
      + "am.model as aircraft_model, ae.model as engine_model from
        aircraft a, "
      + "aircraft_models am, aircraft_engines ae where a.aircraft_
        engine_code in ("
      + "select aircraft_engine_code from aircraft_engines "
      + "where horsepower >= 1000) and am.aircraft_model_code =
        a.aircraft_model_code "
      + "and ae.aircraft_engine_code = a.aircraft_engine_code";

    Class.forName("com.mysql.jdbc.Driver");

    connection = DriverManager.getConnection ("jdbc:mysql://
        localhost:3306/flightstats?user=dbuser&password=secret");
    statement = connection.createStatement();
    resultSet = statement.executeQuery(query);

    JRResultSetDataSource resultSetDataSource = new
                                JRResultSetDataSource(resultSet);

    JasperRunManager.runReportToPdfStream(reportStream,
        servletOutputStream, new HashMap(), resultSetDataSource);

    resultSet.close();
    statement.close();
    connection.close();

    response.setContentType("application/pdf");
    servletOutputStream.flush();
    servletOutputStream.close();
```

```
    }
    catch (Exception e)
    {
      // display stack trace in the browser
      StringWriter stringWriter = new StringWriter();
      PrintWriter printWriter = new PrintWriter(stringWriter);
      e.printStackTrace(printWriter);
      response.setContentType("text/plain");
      response.getOutputStream().print(stringWriter.toString());
    }
  }
}
```

This code is very similar to the previous examples. It executes an SQL query via JDBC and wraps the resulting result set in an instance of `JRResultSetDataSource`. This instance of `JRResultSetDataSource` is then passed to the `JasperRunManager.runReportToPdfStream()` method to export the report to PDF format and stream it to the browser window.

All the examples in this chapter use simple SQL `select` queries to obtain report data. It is also possible to obtain report data from the database by calling stored procedures or functions (if supported by the RDBMS and JDBC driver we are using).

# Database Report Methods Compared

Although embedding a database query into a report template is a simple way to create database reports with JasperReports, it is also the least flexible. Using a `JRResultSetDataSource` involves writing some more code, but results in more flexible reports, since the same report template can be used for different datasources.

Depending on our needs, we choose the appropriate method. If we are sure we will always be using a database as a datasource for our report, and that the database query is unlikely to change much, then embedding the database query into the JRXML template at design time is the most straightforward solution. If the query is likely to change, or if we need to use datasources other than a database for our reports, then using a `JRResultSetDataSource` provides the required flexibility.

Some report design tools will only generate database reports by embedding a database query into the report template. If we are using one of these tools, then we have little choice but to use this method. We are free to remove the `<queryString>` element from the JRXML after we are done designing the report and pass the `JRResultSetDataSource` at run time. However, if we do this, we lose the ability to modify the report template from the report designer.

# Summary

In this chapter, we covered the different ways through which we can create database reports. We learned to embed SQL queries in a report template by using the `<queryString>` JRXML element as well as to populate an instance of `JRResultSetDataSource` with data from a result set and use it to fill a report.

The chapter also dealt with the procedure to declare report fields to access data from individual columns in the result set of the query used to fill the report. Towards the end of the chapter, we generated reports that are displayed in the user's web browser in PDF format.

# 5
# Working with Other Datasources

In the previous chapter, we mentioned that JasperReports allows us to use not only databases, but also many other sources of data to generate reports. In this chapter, we will cover how to use datasources, other than databases, to create our reports.Since creating web-based reports is by far the most common use of JasperReports, most examples in this chapter will use the technique, described in Chapter 3, to stream a PDF report to a web browser via the `JasperFillManager.fillReportToStream()` method.

By the end of the chapter, you will be able to:

- Use empty datasources for reports that don't require an external datasource
- Use any implementation of `java.util.Map` as a datasource
- Use arrays or collections of Java objects as datasources
- Use TableModels as a datasource
- Use an XML as a datasource
- Create your own custom datasources

All JasperReports datasources implement the `net.sf.jasperreports.engine.JRDataSource` interface. Reports are generated, or *filled*, by calling one of several static methods in the `net.sf.jasperreports.JasperFillManager` class. The `JasperFillManager` class contains several overloaded versions of the following three methods:

- `JasperFillManager.fillReport()`: The `JasperFillManager.fillReport()` method creates a report and stores it in a `net.sf.jasperreports.engine.JasperPrint()` object.

- JasperFillManager.fillReportToFile(): The JasperFillManager. fillReportToFile() method creates a report and stores it in the file system as a JRprint file, JasperReports' native report format.

- JasperFillmanager.fillReportToStream(): The JasperFillManager. fillReportToStream() method generates a report and streams it through a java.io.OutputStream object.

Each of these methods takes an instance of a net.sf.jasperreports.engine. JRDataSource object as one of its arguments, or an instance of java.sql.Connection to connect directly to the database. In the previous chapter, we saw how we can pass either a connection object or an instance of JRResultSetDataSource to a report template to generate a report from database data. Report templates don't need to change at all if we decide to change the type of datasource we will use to populate them. For most examples in this chapter, we will use a slightly modified version of the report template we used in the previous chapter, populating it with different types of datasources. As a matter of fact, the only example that will not use the template from the previous chapter is the one illustrating empty datasources, which we discuss next.

# Empty Datasources

The first type of datasource we will discuss in this chapter is empty datasources. There is no way to create a report without using either a database connection or a datasource. If we need to create simple reports that require no external datasources, we can use an empty datasource to accomplish this. JasperReports provides the net.sf.jasperreports.engine.JREmptyDataSource class that we can use for these situations. Let us create a simple report template containing only static data to illustrate this process.

```xml
<?xml version="1.0"?>
<!DOCTYPE jasperReport
 PUBLIC "-//JasperReports//DTD Report Design//EN"
 "http://jasperreports.sourceforge.net/dtds/jasperreport.dtd">
<jasperReport name="EmptyDataSourceReport">
  <detail>
    <band height="20">
      <staticText>
        <reportElement x="20" y="0" width="200" height="20"/>
        <text><![CDATA[This simple report contains only static
              data.]]></text>
      </staticText>
    </band>
  </detail>
</jasperReport>
```

As we can see, the preceding JRXML template contains no fields nor any kind of dynamic data. It simply generates some static text on the final report.

> In the given JRXML template, we chose to add an XML CDATA section between the `<text>` and `</text>` tags. Although not strictly necessary in this case, doing so allows us to easily modify the text between those tags to include text that would prevent the XML from parsing successfully.

After compiling this report, the binary template `EmptyDataSource.jasper` is created in the file system. We can use the following servlet code to fill the report, and stream it as a PDF to the web browser:

```
package net.ensode.jasperbook;
import java.io.IOException;
import java.io.InputStream;
import java.io.PrintWriter;
import java.io.StringWriter;
import java.util.HashMap;

import javax.servlet.ServletException;
import javax.servlet.ServletOutputStream;
import javax.servlet.http.HttpServlet;
import javax.servlet.http.HttpServletRequest;
import javax.servlet.http.HttpServletResponse;

import net.sf.jasperreports.engine.JREmptyDataSource;
import net.sf.jasperreports.engine.JRException;
import net.sf.jasperreports.engine.JasperRunManager;
public class EmptyDSReportServlet extends HttpServlet
{

  protected void doGet(HttpServletRequest request,HttpServletResponse
                        response) throws ServletException, IOException
  {
    ServletOutputStream servletOutputStream =
                                       response.getOutputStream();
    InputStream reportStream = getServletConfig().getServletContext()
      .getResourceAsStream("/reports/EmptyDataSourceReport.jasper");
    try
    {
      JasperRunManager.runReportToPdfStream(reportStream,
        servletOutputStream, new HashMap(), new JREmptyDataSource());
      response.setContentType("application/pdf");
```

```
      servletOutputStream.flush();
      servletOutputStream.close();
    }
    catch (JRException e)
    {
      // display stack trace in the browser
      StringWriter stringWriter = new StringWriter();
      PrintWriter printWriter = new PrintWriter(stringWriter);
      e.printStackTrace(printWriter);
      response.setContentType("text/plain");
      response.getOutputStream().print(stringWriter.toString());
    }
  }
}
```

After deploying this servlet and directing the browser to its URL, our browser will display the report as a PDF, as can be seen in the following screenshot:

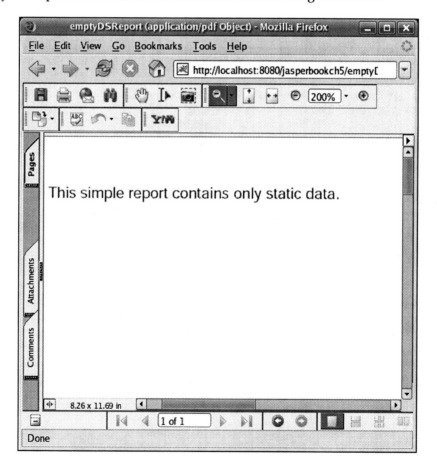

If empty datasources could only be used to generate reports with static data, they wouldn't be very useful. We might as well type the report with our favorite word processor. JasperReports allows us to pass *parameters* to a report. We can send some dynamic data to the report by sending it some parameters.

The following JRXML file demonstrates how parameters are retrieved in a report:

```
<?xml version="1.0"?>
<!DOCTYPE jasperReport
  PUBLIC "-//JasperReports//DTD Report Design//EN"
  "http://jasperreports.sourceforge.net/dtds/jasperreport.dtd">
<jasperReport name="ParameterReport">
  <parameter name="paramName" class="java.lang.String"/>
  <detail>
    <band height="35">
      <staticText>
        <reportElement x="20" y="0" width="115" height="30"/>
        <text>
          <![CDATA[Parameter Value:]]>
        </text>
      </staticText>
      <textField>
        <reportElement x="135" y="11" width="100" height="19"/>
        <textFieldExpression>
          <![CDATA[$P{paramName}]]>
        </textFieldExpression>
      </textField>
    </band>
  </detail>
</jasperReport>
```

As can be seen from the example, report parameters need to be declared at the beginning of the JRXML template, just like report fields. The `class` attribute defaults to `java.lang.String`. Even though our report parameter is a `String`, we included it in the JRXML template for clarity. The value of the parameter can be retrieved by using the syntax `$P{name}`, where `name` is the name of the parameter as declared in the JRXML template.

Every method in the `net.sf.jasperreports.engine.JasperFillManager` class contains a `java.util.Map` object as one of its arguments. The purpose of this argument is to allow us to send some parameters to the report. So far we have been using an empty `HashMap` in the reports we have created, since none of them required any parameters. In the following example, we will send a parameter to the report template created by the above JRXML file:

```java
package net.ensode.jasperbook;
import java.io.IOException;
import java.io.InputStream;
import java.io.PrintWriter;
import java.io.StringWriter;
import java.util.HashMap;

import javax.servlet.ServletException;
import javax.servlet.ServletOutputStream;
import javax.servlet.http.HttpServlet;
import javax.servlet.http.HttpServletRequest;
import javax.servlet.http.HttpServletResponse;

import net.sf.jasperreports.engine.JREmptyDataSource;
import net.sf.jasperreports.engine.JRException;
import net.sf.jasperreports.engine.JasperRunManager;
public class ParameterReportServlet extends HttpServlet
{

  protected void doGet(HttpServletRequest request,HttpServletResponse
                       response) throws ServletException, IOException
  {
    ServletOutputStream servletOutputStream =
                                        response.getOutputStream();
    InputStream reportStream = getServletConfig().getServletContext()
          .getResourceAsStream("/reports/ParameterReport.jasper");
    HashMap parameterMap = new HashMap();
    parameterMap.put("paramName", "paramValue");
    try
    {

      JasperRunManager.runReportToPdfStream(reportStream,
          servletOutputStream, parameterMap, new JREmptyDataSource());
      response.setContentType("application/pdf");
      servletOutputStream.flush();
      servletOutputStream.close();
    }
    catch (JRException e)
    {
      // display stack trace in the browser
      StringWriter stringWriter = new StringWriter();
      PrintWriter printWriter = new PrintWriter(stringWriter);
      e.printStackTrace(printWriter);
      response.setContentType("text/plain");
```

```
        response.getOutputStream().print(stringWriter.toString());
    }
  }
}
```

In this servlet, we populate a key/value pair with an instance of `java.util.`
`HashMap` and pass that `HashMap` to the report template via the `JasperRunManager.`
`runReportToPdfStream()` method. As can be seen in the code, the `Map`'s key must
match the parameter name in the JRXML template. After deploying the servlet and
browsing the appropriate URL, we should see a PDF report being rendered in the
browser, as demonstrated in the following screenshot:

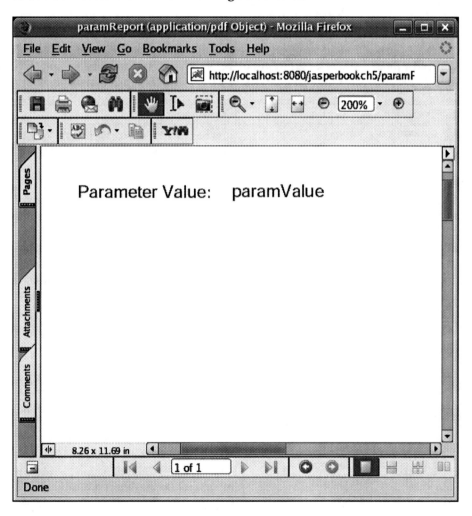

As we can see, the value we used for the `paramName` parameter in the servlet is displayed in the report.

Report parameters can be assigned values in the report template. That way we can assign a default value to any parameter that contains a null value. The syntax to assign a default value to a report parameter is demonstrated in the following JRXML snippet:

```
<parameter name="someParam" class="java.lang.String">
  <defaultValueExpression>
  new java.lang.String("default parameter value");
  </defaultValueExpression>
</parameter>
```

In addition to allowing us to send report parameters, all JasperReports reports have a number of built-in parameters that are always present, without us having to pass them explicitly. The following table lists all of the built-in report parameters:

| Built-in Parameter | Description |
|---|---|
| REPORT_PARAMETERS_MAP | Can be used to obtain a reference to the instance of `java.util.Map` containing the parameters for the report. |
| REPORT_DATA_SOURCE | Can be used to obtain a reference to the instance of `net.sf.jasperreports. engine.JRDataSource` containing the fields for the report. |
| REPORT_CONNECTION | Can be used to obtain a reference to the `java.sql.Connection` passed to the report to connect to the database. If no database connection was passed to the report, it returns `null`. |
| IS_IGNORE_PAGINATION | JasperReports allows reports to be exported to several formats. Some of these formats are not page oriented, for example, HTML. Setting the value of `IS_IGNORE_PAGINATION` to `Boolean.TRUE` makes JasperReports ignore all page-breaking settings in the report and generates a report containing a single (and, in the case of reports with a lot of data, very long) page. |
| REPORT_LOCALE | Determines the language used to generate reports when the report is localized. |
| REPORT_RESOURCE_BUNDLE | Indicates the `java.util.ResourceBundle` instance used to localize the report. |

| Built-in Parameter | Description |
|---|---|
| REPORT_MAX_COUNT | Indicates the maximum number of records that will be processed by the report. |
| REPORT_SCRIPTLET | When a report uses a scriptlet, this parameter returns a reference to it. If the report does not use a scriptlet, this parameter returns an instance of net.sf.jasperreports. engine.JRDefaultScriptlet. |
| REPORT_VIRTUALIZER | Very large reports some times are too large to be handled by the available memory. Setting this parameter to an instance of a class implementing net.sf.jasperreports. engine.JRVirtualizer, will allow JasperReports to store temporary data in serialized form in order to reduce the amount of memory required to fill the report. |

Some of the built-in parameters might not make sense yet. They will make more sense as we discuss some more JasperReports features in future chapters. The primary use of the REPORT_CONNECTION and REPORT_DATA_SOURCE built-in parameters is for passing them to subreports, which are discussed in detail in the next chapter. Report localization and report scriptlets will be covered in Chapter 8.

# Map Datasources

JasperReports allows us to use instances of any class implementing the java.util. Map interface as a datasource. We can use either an array or a collection of Map objects to generate a report. Each Map in the collection or array is a record that will be used to generate the data for each row inside the <detail> tag of the report. The JasperReports API provides an implementation of net.sf.jasperreports. engine.JRDataSource called net.sf.jasperreports.engine.data. JRMapArrayDataSource that will enable us to use an array of Map objects as a datasource. The following example demonstrates this class in action:

```
package net.ensode.jasperbook;
import java.io.IOException;
import java.io.InputStream;
import java.io.PrintWriter;
import java.io.StringWriter;
import java.util.HashMap;
import java.util.Map;
```

```java
import javax.servlet.ServletException;
import javax.servlet.ServletOutputStream;
import javax.servlet.http.HttpServlet;
import javax.servlet.http.HttpServletRequest;
import javax.servlet.http.HttpServletResponse;

import net.sf.jasperreports.engine.JRDataSource;
import net.sf.jasperreports.engine.JasperRunManager;
import net.sf.jasperreports.engine.data.JRMapArrayDataSource;
public class MapArrayDSReportServlet extends HttpServlet
{
  private JRDataSource createReportDataSource()
  {
    JRMapArrayDataSource dataSource;
    Map[] reportRows = initializeMapArray();
    dataSource = new JRMapArrayDataSource(reportRows);
    return dataSource;
  }

  private Map[] initializeMapArray()
  {
    HashMap[] reportRows = new HashMap[4];
    HashMap row1Map = new HashMap();
    HashMap row2Map = new HashMap();
    HashMap row3Map = new HashMap();
    HashMap row4Map = new HashMap();

    row1Map.put("tail_num", "N263Y");
    row1Map.put("aircraft_serial", "T-11");
    row1Map.put("aircraft_model", "39 ROSCOE TRNR RACER");
    row1Map.put("engine_model", "R1830 SERIES");
    row2Map.put("tail_num", "N4087X");
    row2Map.put("aircraft_serial", "BA100-163");
    row2Map.put("aircraft_model", "BRADLEY AEROBAT");
    row2Map.put("engine_model", "R2800 SERIES");
    row3Map.put("tail_num", "N43JE");
    row3Map.put("aircraft_serial", "HAYABUSA 1");
    row3Map.put("aircraft_model", "NAKAJIMA KI-43 IIIA");
    row3Map.put("engine_model", "R1830 SERIES");
    row4Map.put("tail_num", "N912S");
    row4Map.put("aircraft_serial", "9973CC");
    row4Map.put("aircraft_model", "PA18-150");
    row4Map.put("engine_model", "R-1820 SER");
    reportRows[0] = row1Map;
    reportRows[1] = row2Map;
    reportRows[2] = row3Map;
    reportRows[3] = row4Map;
```

```
        return reportRows;
    }

    protected void doGet(HttpServletRequest request, HttpServletResponse
                      response) throws ServletException, IOException
    {
        ServletOutputStream servletOutputStream = response
                                            getOutputStream();
        InputStream reportStream = getServletConfig().getServletContext()
              .getResourceAsStream("/reports/AircraftReport.jasper");
        try
        {

            JRDataSource dataSource = createReportDataSource();
            JasperRunManager.runReportToPdfStream(reportStream,
                        servletOutputStream, new HashMap(), dataSource);
            response.setContentType("application/pdf");
            servletOutputStream.flush();
            servletOutputStream.close();
        }
        catch (Exception e)
        {
            // display stack trace in the browser
            StringWriter stringWriter = new StringWriter();
            PrintWriter printWriter = new PrintWriter(stringWriter);
            e.printStackTrace(printWriter);
            response.setContentType("text/plain");
            response.getOutputStream().print(stringWriter.toString());
        }
    }
}
```

The JRMapArrayDataSource class has a single public constructor. This constructor
takes an array of Map objects as its only argument. The array must already
contain the maps to be used to populate the report before we pass it to the
JRMapArrayDataSource object. Map keys must map field names in the report
template. This way the JasperReports engine knows what values to use to populate
the report template's fields.

In addition to allowing us to use arrays of maps as datasources, JasperReports also
allows us to use a Collection of Map objects as a datasource. JasperReports provides
an implementation of JRDataSource that we can use for this purpose. It is called
net.sf.jasperreports.engine.data.JRMapCollectionDataSource. Using this

class is very similar to using JRMapArrayDataSource. The only difference is that we pass a Collection of Map objects to its constructor, instead of an array. The following example illustrates this:

```java
package net.ensode.jasperbook;
import java.io.IOException;
import java.io.InputStream;
import java.io.PrintWriter;
import java.io.StringWriter;
import java.util.ArrayList;
import java.util.Collection;
import java.util.HashMap;

import javax.servlet.ServletException;
import javax.servlet.ServletOutputStream;
import javax.servlet.http.HttpServlet;
import javax.servlet.http.HttpServletRequest;
import javax.servlet.http.HttpServletResponse;

import net.sf.jasperreports.engine.JRDataSource;
import net.sf.jasperreports.engine.JasperRunManager;
import net.sf.jasperreports.engine.data.JRMapCollectionDataSource;
public class MapCollectionDSReportServlet extends HttpServlet
{
  private JRDataSource createReportDataSource()
  {
    JRMapCollectionDataSource dataSource;
    Collection reportRows = initializeMapCollection();
    dataSource = new JRMapCollectionDataSource(reportRows);
    return dataSource;
  }

  private Collection initializeMapCollection()
  {
    ArrayList reportRows = new ArrayList();
    HashMap row1Map = new HashMap();
    HashMap row2Map = new HashMap();
    HashMap row3Map = new HashMap();
    HashMap row4Map = new HashMap();

    row1Map.put("tail_num", "N263Y");
    row1Map.put("aircraft_serial", "T-11");
    row1Map.put("aircraft_model", "39 ROSCOE TRNR RACER");
    row1Map.put("engine_model", "R1830 SERIES");
    row2Map.put("tail_num", "N4087X");
    row2Map.put("aircraft_serial", "BA100-163");
```

```
      row2Map.put("aircraft_model", "BRADLEY AEROBAT");
      row2Map.put("engine_model", "R2800 SERIES");
      row3Map.put("tail_num", "N43JE");
      row3Map.put("aircraft_serial", "HAYABUSA 1");
      row3Map.put("aircraft_model", "NAKAJIMA KI-43 IIIA");
      row3Map.put("engine_model", "R1830 SERIES");
      row4Map.put("tail_num", "N912S");
      row4Map.put("aircraft_serial", "9973CC");
      row4Map.put("aircraft_model", "PA18-150");
      row4Map.put("engine_model", "R-1820 SER");
      reportRows.add(row1Map);
      reportRows.add(row2Map);
      reportRows.add(row3Map);
      reportRows.add(row4Map);

      return reportRows;
   }

   protected void doGet(HttpServletRequest request, HttpServletResponse
                        response) throws ServletException, IOException
   {
      ServletOutputStream servletOutputStream = response
                                            getOutputStream();
      InputStream reportStream = getServletConfig().getServletContext()
              .getResourceAsStream("/reports/AircraftReport.jasper");
      try
      {

         JRDataSource dataSource = createReportDataSource();
         JasperRunManager.runReportToPdfStream(reportStream,
                     servletOutputStream, new HashMap(), dataSource);
         response.setContentType("application/pdf");
         servletOutputStream.flush();
         servletOutputStream.close();
      }
      catch (Exception e)
      {
         // display stack trace in the browser
         StringWriter stringWriter = new StringWriter();
         PrintWriter printWriter = new PrintWriter(stringWriter);
         e.printStackTrace(printWriter);
         response.setContentType("text/plain");
         response.getOutputStream().print(stringWriter.toString());
      }
   }
}
```

This example is very similar to the previous example. The only difference is that we use a `Collection` of `Map` objects instead of an array, and pass that to the constructor of `JRMapCollectionDataSource` so that the `Map` objects can be used to populate the report. It is worth noting that, even though we use `java.util.ArrayList` to group the `Map` objects, this does not have to be the case. Any class implementing the `java.util.Collection` interface will work just as well.

# Java Objects as Datasources

In addition to databases and maps, JasperReports allows us to use **Plain Old Java Objects (POJOs)** as datasources. We can use any Java object that adheres to the JavaBeans specification as a datasource. The only requirements for an object to adhere to the JavaBeans specification are that it must have no public properties, it must have a no-argument constructor, and it must provide *getter* and *setter* methods to access its private and protected properties. Let us create a Java object that can be used as a datasource for our next example:

```
package net.ensode.jasperbook;
public class AircraftData
{

  public AircraftData(String tail, String serial, String model,
                      String engine)
  {
    setTailNum(tail);
    setAircraftSerial(serial);
    setAircraftModel(model);
    setEngineModel(engine);
  }

  public AircraftData()
  {
  }

  private String tailNum;
  private String aircraftSerial;
  private String aircraftModel;
  private String engineModel;

  public String getAircraftModel()
  {
    return aircraftModel;
  }

  public void setAircraftModel(String aircraftModel)
```

```
  {
    this.aircraftModel = aircraftModel;
  }

  public String getAircraftSerial()
  {
    return aircraftSerial;
  }

  public void setAircraftSerial(String aircraftSerial)
  {
    this.aircraftSerial = aircraftSerial;
  }

  public String getEngineModel()
  {
    return engineModel;
  }

  public void setEngineModel(String engineModel)
  {
    this.engineModel = engineModel;
  }

  public String getTailNum()
  {
    return tailNum;
  }

  public void setTailNum(String tailNum)
  {
    this.tailNum = tailNum;
  }
}
```

This type of object is called a **Data Object**, a **Data Transfer Object (DTO)**, or a **Value Object (VO)**. Since one of the requirements of the JavaBeans specification is to have a no-argument constructor, we included one in our bean. We also included another convenient constructor that initializes all the properties in it. It is always a good idea to follow standard naming conventions, a practice we followed in the preceding code. Since this object's properties don't match the report template's field names, we need to modify the report template. The modified JRXML template looks like this:

```
<?xml version="1.0" encoding="UTF-8"?>
<!DOCTYPE jasperReport PUBLIC "//JasperReports//DTD Report Design//EN"
    "http://jasperreports.sourceforge.net/dtds/jasperreport.dtd">
```

```
<jasperReport name="AircraftReport">
  <field name="tailNum" class="java.lang.String"/>
  <field name="aircraftSerial" class="java.lang.String"/>
  <field name="aircraftModel" class="java.lang.String"/>
  <field name="engineModel" class="java.lang.String"/>
  <pageHeader>
    <band height="30">
      <staticText>
        <reportElement x="0" y="0" width="69" height="24"/>
        <textElement verticalAlignment="Bottom"/>
        <text>
          <![CDATA[Tail Number: ]]>
        </text>
      </staticText>
      <staticText>
        <reportElement x="140" y="0" width="69" height="24"/>
        <text>
        <![CDATA[Serial Number: ]]>
        </text>
      </staticText>
      <staticText>
        <reportElement x="280" y="0" width="69" height="24"/>
        <text>
          <![CDATA[Model: ]]>
        </text>
      </staticText>
      <staticText>
        <reportElement x="420" y="0" width="69" height="24"/>
        <text>
          <![CDATA[Engine: ]]>
        </text>
      </staticText>
    </band>
  </pageHeader>
  <detail>
    <band height="30">
      <textField>
        <reportElement x="0" y="0" width="69" height="24"/>
        <textFieldExpression class="java.lang.String">
          <![CDATA[$F{tailNum}]]>
        </textFieldExpression>
      </textField>
      <textField>
        <reportElement x="140" y="0" width="69" height="24"/>
```

```
          <textFieldExpression class="java.lang.String">
            <![CDATA[$F{aircraftSerial}]]>
          </textFieldExpression>
        </textField>
        <textField>
          <reportElement x="280" y="0" width="69" height="24"/>
          <textFieldExpression class="java.lang.String">
            <![CDATA[$F{aircraftModel}]]>
          </textFieldExpression>
        </textField>
        <textField>
          <reportElement x="420" y="0" width="69" height="24"/>
          <textFieldExpression class="java.lang.String">
            <![CDATA[$F{engineModel}]]>
          </textFieldExpression>
        </textField>
      </band>
    </detail>
  </jasperReport>
```

The only difference between this JRXML template and the one we've been using so far is in the field names. Previously, they were mapping to database columns and, since we are now using a Java bean to populate the report, they now map to the corresponding fields in the bean.

Just as with Map objects, JasperReports allows us to group Java beans in either a Collection or an array. The JRDataSource implementation used to pass an array of Java beans to a report template is called net.sf.jasperreports.engine. JRBeanArrayDataSource. The following example demonstrates how to use it:

```
package net.ensode.jasperbook;
import java.io.IOException;
import java.io.InputStream;
import java.io.PrintWriter;
import java.io.StringWriter;
import java.util.HashMap;

import javax.servlet.ServletException;
import javax.servlet.ServletOutputStream;
import javax.servlet.http.HttpServlet;
import javax.servlet.http.HttpServletRequest;
import javax.servlet.http.HttpServletResponse;

import net.sf.jasperreports.engine.JRDataSource;
import net.sf.jasperreports.engine.JasperRunManager;
```

```java
import net.sf.jasperreports.engine.data.JRBeanArrayDataSource;
public class BeanArrayDSReportServlet extends HttpServlet
{

  private JRDataSource createReportDataSource()
  {
    JRBeanArrayDataSource dataSource;
    AircraftData[] reportRows = initializeBeanArray();
    dataSource = new JRBeanArrayDataSource(reportRows);
    return dataSource;
  }

  private AircraftData[] initializeBeanArray()
  {

    AircraftData[] reportRows = new AircraftData[4];
    reportRows[0] = new AircraftData("N263Y", "T-11", "39 ROSCOE TRNR
                                RACER", "R1830 SERIES");
    reportRows[1] = new AircraftData("N4087X", "BA100-163", "BRADLEY
                                AEROBAT", "R2800 SERIES");
    reportRows[2] = new AircraftData("N43JE", "HAYABUSA 1", "NAKAJIMA
                                KI-43 IIIA", "R1830 SERIES");
    reportRows[3] = new AircraftData("N912S", "9973CC", "PA18-150",
                                "R-1820 SER");

    return reportRows;
  }


  protected void doGet(HttpServletRequest request, HttpServletResponse
                   response) throws ServletException, IOException
  {
    ServletOutputStream servletOutputStream = response
                                            getOutputStream();
    InputStream reportStream = getServletConfig().getServletContext()
            .getResourceAsStream("/reports/BeanDSReport.jasper");
    try
    {

      JRDataSource dataSource = createReportDataSource();
      JasperRunManager.runReportToPdfStream(reportStream,
                  servletOutputStream, new HashMap(), dataSource);
      response.setContentType("application/pdf");
      servletOutputStream.flush();
      servletOutputStream.close();
    }
    catch (Exception e)
    {
      // display stack trace in the browser
```

```
            StringWriter stringWriter = new StringWriter();
            PrintWriter printWriter = new PrintWriter(stringWriter);
            e.printStackTrace(printWriter);
            response.setContentType("text/plain");
            response.getOutputStream().print(stringWriter.toString());
        }
    }
}
```

In this example, we populate an array with `AircraftData` objects, which
contain the data to be displayed in the report. We then pass this array to the
constructor of `JRBeanArrayDataSource`. Finally, we pass the new instance of
`JRBeanArrayDataSource` to the `JasperRunManager.runReportToPdfStream()`
method, which generates the report and exports it to PDF format on the fly. The
generated report is then displayed on the browser.

If we need to group our Beans in a Collection instead of an array, JasperReports provides
the `net.sf.jasperreports.engine.data.JRBeanCollectionDataSource()` class.
This class has only one public constructor, which takes a `java.util.Collection`
object as its only parameter. It expects this collection to be populated with JavaBeans
that can be used to populate the report. The following example demonstrates how to
use `JRBeanCollectionDataSource` to populate our reports:

```
package net.ensode.jasperbook;
import java.io.IOException;
import java.io.InputStream;
import java.io.PrintWriter;
import java.io.StringWriter;
import java.util.ArrayList;
import java.util.Collection;
import java.util.HashMap;

import javax.servlet.ServletException;
import javax.servlet.ServletOutputStream;
import javax.servlet.http.HttpServlet;
import javax.servlet.http.HttpServletRequest;
import javax.servlet.http.HttpServletResponse;

import net.sf.jasperreports.engine.JRDataSource;
import net.sf.jasperreports.engine.JasperRunManager;
import net.sf.jasperreports.engine.data.JRBeanCollectionDataSource;
public class BeanCollectionDSReportServlet extends HttpServlet
{
    private JRDataSource createReportDataSource()
    {
```

```
  JRBeanCollectionDataSource dataSource;
  Collection reportRows = initializeBeanCollection();
  dataSource = new JRBeanCollectionDataSource(reportRows);
  return dataSource;
}

private Collection initializeBeanCollection()
{
  ArrayList reportRows = new ArrayList();
  reportRows.add(new AircraftData("N263Y", "T-11", "39 ROSCOE TRNR
                              RACER", "R1830 SERIES"));
  reportRows.add(new AircraftData("N4087X", "BA100-163", "BRADLEY
                              AEROBAT", "R2800 SERIES"));
  reportRows.add(new AircraftData("N43JE", "HAYABUSA 1", "NAKAJIMA
                              KI-43 IIIA", "R1830 SERIES"));
  reportRows.add(
      new AircraftData("N912S", "9973CC", "PA18-150",
                      "R-1820 SER"));
  return reportRows;
}

protected void doGet(HttpServletRequest request, HttpServletResponse
                    response) throws ServletException, IOException
{
  ServletOutputStream servletOutputStream = response
                                        getOutputStream();
  InputStream reportStream = getServletConfig().getServletContext()
            .getResourceAsStream("/reports/BeanDSReport.jasper");
  try
  {

    JRDataSource dataSource = createReportDataSource();
    JasperRunManager.runReportToPdfStream(reportStream,
                  servletOutputStream, new HashMap(), dataSource);
    response.setContentType("application/pdf");
    servletOutputStream.flush();
    servletOutputStream.close();
  }
  catch (Exception e)
  {
    // display stack trace in the browser
    StringWriter stringWriter = new StringWriter();
    PrintWriter printWriter = new PrintWriter(stringWriter);
    e.printStackTrace(printWriter);
    response.setContentType("text/plain");
```

```
        response.getOutputStream().print(stringWriter.toString());
    }
  }
}
```

The main difference between this example and the previous one is that here we are grouping our data objects in a `java.util.ArrayList` instead of an array. When using `JRBeanCollectionDataSource` to populate our reports, we do not necessarily need to use an `ArrayList` to populate our beans. Any class implementing `java.util.Collection` will work just as well. `JRBeanCollectionDataSource` works like the previous `JRDataSource` implementations we have seen; that is, it has a single public constructor that takes a `Collection` of objects as its only argument. We can then use the initialized `JRBeanCollectionDataSource` to fill the report. This is accomplished by the call to `JasperRunManager.runReportToPDFStream()` from the `doGet()` method in the preceding example.

# TableModels as Datasources

In many client-side applications, data is displayed in tabular format. A common requirement in many applications is to allow the user to print this tabular format as a report.

JasperReports provides an implementation of the `JRDataSource` interface that makes the task of generating reports from tabular format trivial for Swing applications. The class in question is the `net.sf.jasperreports.engine.data.JRTableModelDataSource`. This class takes a `javax.swing.table.TableModel` as its only parameter. Since tables in Swing are populated via `TableModels`, all we need to do to generate a report from a table is to pass the appropriate table's `TableModel` as a parameter. The following example is a simple but complete Swing application demonstrating this process:

```
package net.ensode.jasperbook;
import java.awt.BorderLayout;
import java.awt.event.ActionEvent;
import java.awt.event.ActionListener;
import java.util.HashMap;

import javax.swing.JButton;
import javax.swing.JFrame;
import javax.swing.JLabel;
import javax.swing.JTable;
import javax.swing.table.DefaultTableModel;

import net.sf.jasperreports.engine.JRException;
```

```java
import net.sf.jasperreports.engine.JasperFillManager;
import net.sf.jasperreports.engine.JasperPrint;
import net.sf.jasperreports.engine.data.JRTableModelDataSource;
import net.sf.jasperreports.view.JasperViewer;
public class TableModelReport
{
  JFrame mainFrame;
  BorderLayout borderLayout;
  DefaultTableModel tableModel;
  JTable table = new JTable();
  JButton generateReportButton = new JButton("Generate Report");

  public TableModelReport()
  {
    mainFrame = new JFrame("Aircraft Data");
    borderLayout = new BorderLayout();
    generateReportButton.addActionListener(new ReportGenerator());

    populateTableModel();
    mainFrame.setSize(640, 150);
    mainFrame.setVisible(true);
    mainFrame.getContentPane().setLayout(borderLayout);
    mainFrame.add(new JLabel("Aircraft Data"), BorderLayout.NORTH);
    table.setModel(tableModel);
    mainFrame.getContentPane().add(table, BorderLayout.CENTER);
    mainFrame.getContentPane().add(generateReportButton, BorderLayout.
                                 SOUTH); mainFrame.setVisible(true);
  }

  private void populateTableModel()
  {
  String[] columnNames =
  { "tail_num", "aircraft_serial", "aircraft_model", "engine_model" };
  String[][] data =
  {{ "N263Y", "T-11", " 39 ROSCOE TRNR RACER", "R1830 SERIES" },
  { "N4087X", "BA100-163", "BRADLEY AEROBAT", "R2800 SERIES" },
  { "N43JE", "HAYABUSA 1", "NAKAJIMA KI-43 IIIA", "R1830 SERIES" },
  { "N912S", "9973CC", "PA18-150", "R-1820 SER" }};
  tableModel = new DefaultTableModel(data, columnNames);
  }

  private void displayReport()
  {
```

```
      JasperPrint jasperPrint = generateReport();
      JasperViewer jasperViewer = new JasperViewer(jasperPrint);
      jasperViewer.setVisible(true);
   }

   private JasperPrint generateReport()
   {
      JasperPrint jasperPrint = null;
      try
      {
         jasperPrint = JasperFillManager.fillReport(
             "reports/AircraftReport.jasper", new HashMap(),
             new JRTableModelDataSource(tableModel));
      }
      catch (JRException e)
      {
         e.printStackTrace();
      }

      return jasperPrint;
   }

   private class ReportGenerator implements ActionListener
   {
      public void actionPerformed(ActionEvent e)
      {
         displayReport();
      }
   }

   /**
    * @param args
    */
   public static void main(String[] args)
   {
      new TableModelReport();
   }
}
```

This example, when executed, will display a window on the screen displaying a table
containing the **Aircraft Data** we have been using for most of the examples in this
chapter, along with a **Generate Report** button at the bottom.

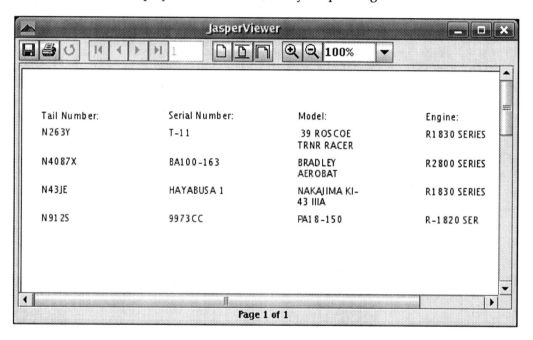

Clicking on the **Generate Report** button will generate the report in JasperReports'
native format, and display it on the screen, ready for printing.

This window should look familiar. What we are seeing here is the same application
we used before to view reports in JasperReports' native format. The only difference
is that instead of invoking the application from an ANT script, we invoked it
programmatically from our code. The class in question is net.sf.jasperreports.
view.JasperViewer. Its constructor takes a JasperPrint object as its only
parameter. A JasperPrint object is an in-memory representation of a report
in JasperReports' native format. JasperViewer extends javax.swing.JFrame;
therefore, to make it visible, all we need to do is call its setVisible() method,
passing the Boolean value true as a parameter. The displayReport() method in the
preceding example illustrates this procedure.

Of course, before we can display the report, we need to generate it by filling the report template. As we mentioned earlier, when generating reports from a `TableModel`, report filling is done by passing the `TableModel` as a parameter to the constructor of `JRTableModelDataSource`, as can be seen in the `generateReport()` method in the example.

Normally, when generating reports from a `TableModel`, report fields must match the `TableModel`'s column names, as can be seen from the example. Sometimes it is impractical to use the column names as report fields. JasperReports provides a way to generate reports from `TableModel`s without having to map the table columns to the report fields. We can name our report fields `COLUMN_X`, where `X` is the column index, starting with 0. The following JRXML template illustrates this. It will generate a report identical to the one in the previous screenshot.

```xml
<?xml version="1.0" encoding="UTF-8"?>
<!DOCTYPE jasperReport PUBLIC "//JasperReports//DTD Report Design//EN"
  "http://jasperreports.sourceforge.net/dtds/jasperreport.dtd">
<jasperReport name="AircraftReportColumnIndex">
  <field name="COLUMN_0" class="java.lang.String"/>
  <field name="COLUMN_1" class="java.lang.String"/>
  <field name="COLUMN_2" class="java.lang.String"/>
  <field name="COLUMN_3" class="java.lang.String"/>
  <pageHeader>
    <band height="30">
      <staticText>
        <reportElement x="0" y="0" width="69" height="24"/>
        <textElement verticalAlignment="Bottom"/>
        <text>
          <![CDATA[Tail Number: ]]>
        </text>
      </staticText>
      <staticText>
        <reportElement x="140" y="0" width="69" height="24"/>
        <text>
          <![CDATA[Serial Number: ]]>
        </text>
      </staticText>
      <staticText>
        <reportElement x="280" y="0" width="69" height="24"/>
        <text>
          <![CDATA[Model: ]]>
        </text>
      </staticText>
      <staticText>
```

```
          <reportElement x="420" y="0" width="69" height="24"/>
          <text>
            <![CDATA[Engine: ]]>
          </text>
        </staticText>
      </band>
  </pageHeader>
  <detail>
    <band height="30">
      <textField>
        <reportElement x="0" y="0" width="69" height="24"/>
        <textFieldExpression class="java.lang.String">
          <![CDATA[$F{COLUMN_0}]]>
        </textFieldExpression>
      </textField>
      <textField>
        <reportElement x="140" y="0" width="69" height="24"/>
        <textFieldExpression class="java.lang.String">
          <![CDATA[$F{COLUMN_1}]]>
        </textFieldExpression>
      </textField>
      <textField>
        <reportElement x="280" y="0" width="69" height="24"/>
        <textFieldExpression class="java.lang.String">
          <![CDATA[$F{COLUMN_2}]]>
        </textFieldExpression>
      </textField>
      <textField>
        <reportElement x="420" y="0" width="69" height="24"/>
       <textFieldExpression class="java.lang.String">
          <![CDATA[$F{COLUMN_3}]]>
        </textFieldExpression>
      </textField>
    </band>
  </detail>
</jasperReport>
```

Since we changed the report name, we need to change a single line in the previous example to make it work with this report template.

```
jasperPrint = JasperFillManager.fillReport( "reports/AircraftReport.
    jasper", new HashMap(), new JRTableModelDataSource(tableModel));
```

Needs to be changed to:

```
jasperPrint = JasperFillManager.fillReport("reports/
AircraftReportColumnIndex.jasper", new HashMap(),
        new JRTableModelDataSource(tableModel));
```

If we hadn't changed the report name, then the code in the example would have worked without modification with the new report template.

# XML as Datasource

JasperReports allows us to use any well-formatted XML document as a datasource. JasperReports uses **XPath** expressions to traverse the XML documents and extract the data for the report.

XPath is a language used to navigate through an XML document's attributes and elements. More information about XPath can be found at http://www.w3.org/TR/xpath.

For our next example, we are going to need an XML file to read data from. The following XML document will serve this purpose:

```xml
<?xml version="1.0" encoding="UTF-8"?>
<AircraftData>
  <aircraft>
    <tail_num>N263Y</tail_num>
    <aircraft_serial>T-11</aircraft_serial>
    <aircraft_model>39 ROSCOE TRNR RACER</aircraft_model>
    <engine_model>R1830 SERIES</engine_model>
  </aircraft>
  <aircraft>
    <tail_num>N4087X</tail_num>
    <aircraft_serial>BA100-163</aircraft_serial>
    <aircraft_model>BRADLEY AEROBAT</aircraft_model>
    <engine_model>R2800 SERIES</engine_model>
  </aircraft>
  <aircraft>
    <tail_num>N43JE</tail_num>
    <aircraft_serial>HAYABUSA 1</aircraft_serial>
    <aircraft_model>NAKAJIMA KI-43 IIIA</aircraft_model>
    <engine_model>R1830 SERIES</engine_model>
```

```
    </aircraft>
    <aircraft>
      <tail_num>N912S</tail_num>
      <aircraft_serial>9973CC</aircraft_serial>
      <aircraft_model>PA18-150</aircraft_model>
      <engine_model>R-1820 SER</engine_model>
    </aircraft>
  </AircraftData>
```

We need to make a slight modification to the JRXML template to be able to successfully create a report from an XML datasource. We need to add a `<fieldDescription>` element inside each `<field>` element. The following JRXML template illustrates this:

```
<?xml version="1.0" encoding="UTF-8"?>
<!DOCTYPE jasperReport PUBLIC "//JasperReports//DTD Report Design//EN"
 "http://jasperreports.sourceforge.net/dtds/jasperreport.dtd">
<jasperReport name="AircraftReport">
  <field name="tail_num" class="java.lang.String">
    <fieldDescription>
      <![CDATA[tail_num]]>
    </fieldDescription>
  </field>
  <field name="aircraft_serial" class="java.lang.String">
    <fieldDescription>
      <![CDATA[aircraft_serial]]>
    </fieldDescription>
  </field>
  <field name="aircraft_model" class="java.lang.String">
    <fieldDescription>
      <![CDATA[aircraft_model]]>
    </fieldDescription>
  </field>
  <field name="engine_model" class="java.lang.String">
    <fieldDescription>
      <![CDATA[engine_model]]>
    </fieldDescription>
  </field>
  <pageHeader>
    <band height="30">
      <staticText>
        <reportElement x="0" y="0" width="69" height="24"/>
        <textElement verticalAlignment="Bottom"/>
        <text>
          <![CDATA[Tail Number: ]]>
        </text>
      </text>
    </staticText>
```

```xml
<staticText>
  <reportElement x="140" y="0" width="79" height="24"/>
  <text>
    <![CDATA[Serial Number: ]]>
  </text>
</staticText>
<staticText>
  <reportElement x="280" y="0" width="69" height="24"/>
  <text>
    <![CDATA[Model: ]]>
  </text>
</staticText>
<staticText>
  <reportElement x="420" y="0" width="69" height="24"/>
  <text>
    <![CDATA[Engine: ]]>
  </text>
</staticText>
</band>
</pageHeader>
<detail>
  <band height="30">
    <textField>
      <reportElement x="0" y="0" width="69" height="24"/>
      <textFieldExpression class="java.lang.String">
        <![CDATA[$F{tail_num}]]>
      </textFieldExpression>
    </textField>
    <textField>
      <reportElement x="140" y="0" width="69" height="24"/>
      <textFieldExpression class="java.lang.String">
        <![CDATA[$F{aircraft_serial}]]>
      </textFieldExpression>
    </textField>
    <textField>
      <reportElement x="280" y="0" width="69" height="24"/>
      <textFieldExpression class="java.lang.String">
        <![CDATA[$F{aircraft_model}]]>
      </textFieldExpression>
    </textField>
    <textField>
      <reportElement x="420" y="0" width="69" height="24"/>
      <textFieldExpression class="java.lang.String">
        <![CDATA[$F{engine_model}]]>
```

```
        </textFieldExpression>
      </textField>
    </band>
  </detail>
</jasperReport>
```

The main difference between this JRXML template and the one we've been using for most of our examples is the addition of the `<fieldDescription>` element for each field. The purpose of the `<fieldDescription>` element is to map the field name with the appropriate element in the XML file. In this particular example, field names match the corresponding XML elements. However, this is not always the case, and so `<fieldDescription>` elements are required for XML datasources.

The JRDataSource implementation we need to use to create reports from XML files is called net.sf.jasperreports.engine.data.JRXmlDataSource. The following example demonstrates how to use it:

```java
package net.ensode.jasperbook;
import java.io.BufferedInputStream;
import java.io.IOException;
import java.io.InputStream;
import java.io.PrintWriter;
import java.io.StringWriter;
import java.util.HashMap;

import javax.servlet.ServletException;
import javax.servlet.ServletOutputStream;
import javax.servlet.http.HttpServlet;
import javax.servlet.http.HttpServletRequest;
import javax.servlet.http.HttpServletResponse;

import net.sf.jasperreports.engine.JasperRunManager;
import net.sf.jasperreports.engine.data.JRXmlDataSource;
public class XmlDSReportServlet extends HttpServlet
{

  protected void doGet(HttpServletRequest request, HttpServletResponse
                       response) throws ServletException, IOException
  {
    ServletOutputStream servletOutputStream = response
                                          getOutputStream();
    InputStream reportStream = getServletConfig().getServletContext()
       .getResourceAsStream("/reports/XmlAircraftReport.jasper");
    try
    {
```

```
JRXmlDataSource xmlDataSource = new JRXmlDataSource(
    new BufferedInputStream(getServletConfig().getServletContext()
        .getResourceAsStream("/reports/AircraftData.xml")),
                            "/AircraftData/aircraft");
JasperRunManager.runReportToPdfStream(reportStream,
            servletOutputStream, new HashMap(), xmlDataSource);
response.setContentType("application/pdf");
servletOutputStream.flush();
servletOutputStream.close();
}
catch (Exception e)
{
    // display stack trace in the browser
    StringWriter stringWriter = new StringWriter();
    PrintWriter printWriter = new PrintWriter(stringWriter);
    e.printStackTrace(printWriter);
    response.setContentType("text/plain");
    response.getOutputStream().print(stringWriter.toString());
}
}
}
```

As can be seen in the example above, we need to pass the XML document and an XPath expression to the constructor of JRXmlDataSource. The example assumes that we saved the XML file, shown in the beginning of this section, as AircraftData. xml. In this particular case, we chose to pass the XML document as an input stream. JRXmlDataSource contains other constructors that allow us to send the XML document as an org.w3c.dom document, as a java.io file, or as a String containing a **Uniform Resource Identifier (URI)**. Passing an XPath expression is optional. If we don't pass one, the datasource will be created from all the sub-elements of the root element in the XML file. However, if we do pass one, then the datasource will be created from all the elements inside the XPath expression.

# Custom Datasources

So far we've seen all of the JRDataSource implementations provided by JasperReports. If we need to extract data from a type of datasource not directly supported by JasperReports, we can create a class implementing JRDataSource to meet our needs. In this section, we will create a CsvDataSource class, which will allow us to create reports from **Comma Separated Value (CSV)** files.

To aid us in CSV parsing, we will use Glen Smith's excellent **OpenCsv** library. OpenCsv contains utility classes to ease the task of working with CSV files. OpenCsv is licensed under the Apache 2.0 license. It can be downloaded from `http://opencsv.sourceforge.net/`.

# Writing a Custom JRDataSource Implementation

As we have seen from previous examples, all JasperReports datasources implement the `JRDataSource` interface. JasperReports also includes the `net.sf.jasperreports.engine.JRRewindableDataSource` interface. This interface extends `JRDatasource`, adding a single method called `moveFirst()`. The `moveFirst()` method is intended to move the cursor to the first element in the datasource. Our `CsvDataSource` will implement `JRRewindableDataSource`. Let us take a look at the source code of the `CsvDataSource` class.

```
package net.ensode.jasperbook;
import java.io.FileNotFoundException;
import java.io.IOException;
import java.io.Reader;
import java.util.List;

import net.sf.jasperreports.engine.JRException;
import net.sf.jasperreports.engine.JRField;
import net.sf.jasperreports.engine.JRRewindableDataSource;
import au.com.bytecode.opencsv.CSVReader;
public class CsvDataSource implements JRRewindableDataSource
{
  private CSVReader csvReader;
  private List rows;
  private int currentRowIndex = -1;
  private int currentColIndex = 0;
  private int totalRows;

  public CsvDataSource(Reader reader)
  {
    try
    {
      csvReader = new CSVReader(reader);
      rows = csvReader.readAll();
      totalRows = rows.size();
    }
```

```
      catch (FileNotFoundException e)
      {
        e.printStackTrace();
      }
      catch (IOException e)
      {
        e.printStackTrace();
      }
    }

    public boolean next() throws JRException
    {
      boolean retVal = true;
      currentRowIndex++;
      currentColIndex = 0;

      if (currentRowIndex >= totalRows)
      {
        retVal = false;
      }

      return retVal;
    }

    public Object getFieldValue(JRField arg0) throws JRException
    {
      String value = null;
      String[] currentRow = (String[]) rows.get(currentRowIndex);
      value = currentRow[currentColIndex];
      currentColIndex++;

      return value;
    }

    public void moveFirst() throws JRException
    {
      currentRowIndex = 0;
      currentColIndex = 0;
    }
  }
}
```

In this example, the constructor initializes an instance of `au.com.bytecode.`
`opencsv.CSVReader`, a class provided by OpenCsv. The constructor passes an
instance of `java.io.Reader` as a parameter.

We then proceed to call the `readAll()` method of `CSVReader`. This method reads the contents of the CSV file and stores it into a `java.util.List` containing String arrays as its elements. Each String array represents a row of values in the CSV file, mapping them as they appear on the file. The `List` will have as many elements as there are rows in the CSV file. The contents of our CSV file, `AircraftData.csv`, are as follows:

```
N263Y,T-11,39 ROSCOE TRNR RACER,R1830 SERIES
N4087X,BA100-163,BRADLEY AEROBAT,R2800 SERIES
N43JE,HAYABUSA 1,NAKAJIMA KI-43 IIIA,R1830 SERIES
N912S,9973CC,PA18-150,R-1820 SER
```

After reading the contents of this CSV file, the `CSVReader.readAll()` method will return a list containing four arrays of Strings:

```
{"N263Y", "T-11", "39 ROSCOE TRNR RACER","R1830 SERIES"}
{"N4087X", "BA100-163", "BRADLEY AEROBAT","R2800 SERIES"}
{"N43JE", "HAYABUSA 1", "NAKAJIMA KI-43 IIIA","R1830 SERIES"}
{"N912S", "9973CC", "PA18-150","R-1820 SER"}
```

As we can see, the layout corresponds to the layout of the CSV file just described.

JasperReports datasources contain 'elements' and 'fields'. When using a database as a datasource, a database row is considered as an element, and the columns as fields. When using Java objects as datasources, each object is an element, and each attribute of the object is a field. For our custom CSV datasource, each row in the CSV file is considered an element, and each column, a field.

The `next()` method defined in `JRDataSource` moves the cursor to the next element in the datasource. It returns a Boolean, indicating if the move was successful or not. In our implementation, we have a `currentRowIndex` variable, indicating the current element in the `List` returned by `CSVReader.readAll()` method. In the `next()` method, we increase the value of `currenRowIndex` by one, and return `false` if its value is larger than the size of the list; otherwise, we return `true`.

The `getFieldValue()` method retrieves the value for the current field in the datasource. It takes an instance of `net.sf.jasperreports.engine.JRField` class as its only argument. The `JRField` interface contains a `getName()` method that is used to retrieve the value of the field from its name. The way in which it is done depends on the type of datasource. For example, `JRBeanCollectionDataSource` uses utility classes from `Jakarta commons-beanutils` to retrieve the bean's `property` value from its name. `JRXmlDataSource` uses a combination of `Xalan`, an XML transformation library, and `Jakarta commons` for its implementation.

For our `getFieldValue()` implementation, since a CSV file does not map names to its fields, we simply ignore the parameter. All we do is obtain the array of strings in the `List` returned by `CSVReader.readAll()` corresponding to `currentRowIndex`. We, then, obtain the field corresponding to `currentColumnIndex` from it.

For our `moveFirst()` implementation, we simply reset the values of `currentRowIndex` and `currentColumnIndex` to 0.

# Using the Custom JRDataSource Implementation

Writing code to take advantage of a custom `JRDataSource` implementation is not much different from writing code that uses standard JasperReports datasources. After all, both custom and standard datasources implement the `JRDataSource` interface. The following example illustrates how to take advantage of our custom `CSVDataSource`:

```
package net.ensode.jasperbook;
import java.io.IOException;
import java.io.InputStream;
import java.io.InputStreamReader;
import java.io.PrintWriter;
import java.io.StringWriter;
import java.util.HashMap;

import javax.servlet.ServletException;
import javax.servlet.ServletOutputStream;
import javax.servlet.http.HttpServlet;
import javax.servlet.http.HttpServletRequest;
import javax.servlet.http.HttpServletResponse;
import net.sf.jasperreports.engine.JasperRunManager;
public class CsvDSReportServlet extends HttpServlet
{

  protected void doGet(HttpServletRequest request, HttpServletResponse
                    response) throws ServletException, IOException
  {
    ServletOutputStream servletOutputStream = response.
                                        getOutputStream();
    InputStream reportStream = getServletConfig().getServletContext()
          .getResourceAsStream("/reports/AircraftReport.jasper");
    try
    {

      CsvDataSource csvDataSource = new CsvDataSource(new
                            InputStreamReader(
        getServletConfig().getServletContext().getResourceAsStream(
          "/reports/AircraftData.csv")));
      JasperRunManager.runReportToPdfStream(reportStream,
```

```
                    servletOutputStream, new HashMap(), csvDataSource);
        response.setContentType("application/pdf");
        servletOutputStream.flush();
        servletOutputStream.close();
      }
      catch (Exception e)
      {
        // display stack trace in the browser
        StringWriter stringWriter = new StringWriter();
        PrintWriter printWriter = new PrintWriter(stringWriter);
        e.printStackTrace(printWriter);
        response.setContentType("text/plain");
        response.getOutputStream().print(stringWriter.toString());
      }
    }
  }
```

Since the constructor for `CSVDataSource` takes an instance of `java.io.Reader` as its only argument, and `javax.servlet.ServletContext.getResourceAsStream()` returns a `java.io.InputStream`, we take advantage of the `java.io.InputStreamReader` class. This class takes an `InputStream` and converts it to a `Reader`. We then pass this `Reader` to `CSVDataSource`, and proceed just as we have in previous examples. This example assumes that the CSV file is saved as `AircraftData.csv`.

# Summary

This chapter has given us a quick run through all the non-database datasources supported by JasperReports, including how to create our own.

We have created reports that use no external datasources by using an empty datasource and have also used instances of a class implementing `java.util.Map` as a datasource by taking advantage of the `net.sf.jasperreports.engine.data.JRMapArrayDataSource` class. We learned to use plain Java objects as datasources by employing the `net.sf.jasperreports.engine.JRBeanArrayDataSource` and `net.sf.jasperreports.engine.JRBeanCollectionDataSource` classes. Besides, we also saw the use of a Swing `TableModel` and an XML document as a datasource by implementing the `net.sf.jasperreports.engine.data.JRTableModelDataSource` and `net.sf.jasperreports.engine.data.JRXmlDataSource` classes respectively.

We have covered not only the datasources supported by JasperReports, but also created custom datasources by creating our own `JRDataSource` implementation. In addition to datasources, we also discussed how to pass data in the form of report parameters.

# 6
# Report Layout and Design

All reports that we have created so far contain simple layouts. In this chapter, we will cover how to create elaborate layouts, including, among other JasperReports features, adding background images or text to a report, logically grouping report data, conditionally printing report data, and creating subreports.

In this chapter, we will cover the following topics:

- How to control report-wide layout properties
- How to use styles to control the look of report elements
- How to add a background text to a report
- How to add multiple columns to a report
- How to divide report data into logical groups
- How to add dynamic data to a report via report expressions and variables
- How to allow report text fields to stretch to display large amounts of data
- How to control the layout of the report elements, including how to control their position, width, and height, among other layout elements
- How to use the `<frame>` element to visually group report elements
- How to hide the repeated values to conditionally print data based on a report expression
- How to create subreports

Since most of the techniques described in this chapter are encapsulated in the JRXML template, for most examples we will not be showing Java code, since it would illustrate nothing we haven't seen before. The code to generate all the reports in this chapter can be found in this book's website at `http://www.packtpub.com/support`.

# Controlling Report-Wide Layout Properties

The `<jasperReport>` root element of the JRXML template contains a number of attributes that allow us to control report layout. The following table summarizes these attributes:

| Attribute | Description | Valid Values | Default Value |
|---|---|---|---|
| pageWidth | Determines the width of the page, in pixels. | Any non-negative integer | 595 |
| pageHeight | Determines the height of the page, in pixels. | Any non negative integer | 842 |
| leftMargin | Determines the left margin of the page, in pixels. | Any non-negative integer | 20 |
| rightMargin | Determines the right margin of the page, in pixels. | Any non-negative integer | 20 |
| topMargin | Determines the top margin of the page, in pixels. | Any non-negative integer | 30 |
| bottomMargin | Determines the top margin of the page, in pixels. | Any non-negative integer | 30 |
| orientation | Determines the orientation of the page. | Portrait, Landscape | Portrait |
| whenNoDataType | Determines how to create report with no data in its datasource. | NoPages, BlankPage, AllSectionsNoDetail | NoPages |
| isTitleNewPage | Determines if the title section of the report will be printed on a separate page. | true, false | false |
| isSummaryNewPage | Determines if the summary section of the report will be printed on a separate page. | true, false | false |

Most of the attributes in the table are self explanatory, and their use should be intuitive. However, the `whenNoDataType` attribute deserves more explanation.

When there is no data in the report's datasource, by default, JasperReports will not generate a report. This happens because the default value of `whenNoDataType` is `NoPages`. Setting `whenNoDataType` to `NoPages` will result in a report containing zero pages. If we would like a report displaying all sections, except the detail section, we can accomplish this by setting `whenNoDataType` to `AllSectionsNoDetail`.

# Setting Text Properties

JasperReports provides several ways to control the properties of the text in the report (bold, italic, font, underline, etc.).

# Styles

One way JasperReports allows us to control text properties, is by using the `<style>` element. This element allows us to control the foreground color, background color, whether the font is bold, italic, or normal, the font size, a border for the font, and many other attributes. Styles can extend other styles, and add to, or override properties of the parent style.

 Styles were introduced in JasperReports 1.1 and are not supported by previous versions of JasperReports.

The following JRXML template illustrates the use of styles:

```xml
<?xml version="1.0" encoding="UTF-8"?>
<!DOCTYPE jasperReport PUBLIC "//JasperReports//DTD Report Design//EN"
  "http://jasperreports.sourceforge.net/dtds/jasperreport.dtd">
<jasperReport name="ReportStylesDemo">
  <style name="parentStyle" isDefault="true" fontName="Times"
         isBold="true" fontSize="13" pdfFontName="Helvetica-Bold"/>
  <style name="childStyle" fontSize="9"/>
  <detail>
    <band height="60">
      <staticText>
        <reportElement x="0" y="0" width="555" height="35"/>
        <text>
          <![CDATA[This text uses the default report style, in this
          report it is called "parentStyle".]]>
        </text>
      </staticText>
    </band>
```

```
<staticText>
  <reportElement x="0" y="35" width="555" height="25"
                 style="childStyle"/>
  <text>
    <![CDATA[This text uses the style called "childStyle", this
      style inherits all the properties of its parents, and
      overrides only the size.]]>
  </text>
</staticText>
      </band>
    </detail>
</jasperReport>
```

There are a few things to be noted about this example. Notice the isDefault="true" attribute of the parentStyle. By default, this attribute makes all report elements use this style without having to explicitly declare it. Since the first <staticText> element does not indicate what style to use, it will use the style named parentStyle, by default. What style report elements use is defined by the style attribute of the <reportElement>, as can be seen in the second <staticText> element in the preceding template.

After compiling, filling, and exporting the JRXML template, we should have a report like the following:

**This text uses the default report style, in this report it is called "parentStyle".**

This text uses the style called "childStyle", this style inherits all the properties of its parents, and overrides only the size.

The <style> element contains numerous attributes. Some of the most commonly used are outlined in the following table. Refer to the JasperReports website at http://jasperreports.sourceforge.net/reference/index2.html#style for the complete list.

| Attribute | Description | Valid Values |
| --- | --- | --- |
| forecolor | Indicates the text color. | Either a hexadecimal RGB value preceded by the # character, or one of the following predefined values:<br><br>black, blue, cyan, darkGray, gray, green, lightGray, magenta, orange, pink, red, yellow, white |

| Attribute | Description | Valid Values |
|---|---|---|
| `backcolor` | Indicates the text background color. | Refer to the valid values of `forecolor` given in the preceding row. |
| `hAlign` | Indicates the horizontal alignment of the element. | `Center`, `Justified`, `Left`, `Right` |
| `vAlign` | Indicates the vertical alignment of the element. | `Bottom`, `Middle`, `Top` |
| `border` | Indicate the element border. | `1Point`, `2Point`, `4Point`, `Dotted`, `None`, `Thin` |
| `borderColor` | Indicates the border color. | Refer to the given valid values of `forecolor`. |
| `padding` | The amount of spacing between the element and its border. | An integer indicating the amount of padding (in pixels) to use. |
| `fontName` | Indicates what font to use for the element. | A String indicating the font to use. |
| `fontSize` | Indicates the size of the font. | An integer indicating the text size to use. |
| `isBold` | Indicates whether the font is bold. | `true`, `false` |
| `isItalic` | Indicates whether the font is italic. | `true`, `false` |
| `IsUnderline` | Indicates whether the font is underlined. | `true`, `false` |
| `isStrikeThrough` | Indicates whether the font is strikethrough style. | `true`, `false` |
| `lineSpacing` | Determines the spacing between lines of text. A value of `1_1_2` indicates a line and a half of space between lines of text. | `1_1_2`, `Double`, `Single` |
| `rotation` | Indicates the element direction by rotating it 90 degrees in the specified direction. | `Left`, `None`, `Right` |
| `isStyledText` | Indicates whether the element text is styled. | `true`, `false` |

All the attributes that are not specific to textual information (padding, border, etc.) can be used not only for textual elements, but also for any kind of element. The `isStyledText` attribute is used to allow segments of the text to be styled individually. This is covered in detail, later in this chapter.

# Setting Text Style for Individual Report Elements

Report styles can be shared among several report elements. By setting attributes in the `<textElement>` sub-element of `<staticText>` and `<textField>`, JasperReports allows us to set some properties for individual report elements. These attributes are outlined in the following table:

| Attribute | Description | Valid Values |
|---|---|---|
| `lineSpacing` | Determines the spacing between lines of text. A value of `1_1_2` indicates a line and a half of space between lines of text. | `1_1_2`, `Double`, `Single` |
| `rotation` | Indicates the text direction by rotating it 90 degrees in the specified direction. | `Left`, `None`, `Right` |
| `textAlignment` | Indicates the horizontal alignment of the text. | `Center`, `Justified`, `Left`, `Right` |
| `verticalAlignment` | Indicates the vertical alignment of the text. | `Bottom`, `Middle`, `Top` |
| `isStyledText` | Indicates whether the element text is styled. | `true`, `false` |

The following snippet of a JRXML template illustrates how to use these attributes:

```
<staticText>
  <reportElement x="0" y="0" width="555" height="30"/>
  <textElement lineSpacing="Double" textAlignment="center"
            verticalAlignment="Middle"/>
  <text>
    <![CDATA[This text is not really important.]]>
  </text>
</staticText>
```

This snippet would generate text using double spacing, horizontally, and vertically centered. The `<textElement>` element is a sub-element of both `<staticText>` and `<textField>`.

> **Use Styles to Create More Maintainable Reports**
>
> It is usually faster to set the text properties using the `<textElement>` element. However, doing it this way prevents us from reusing the styles across several elements. Report styles allow us to do this, and they provide much more control than the attributes in `<textElement>`.

# Setting Styles for Text Segments

The text property modification techniques described so far apply the text properties to a complete text element. Sometimes we want to have certain segments of a text element use a different style. For example, we might want to emphasize a word by making it bold or italic. JasperReports allows us to do this by using styled text.

As we have seen in previous sections, the `<textElement>` and the `<style>` element both contain an `isStyledText` attribute. We need to set this attribute to `true` to use styled text. When this attribute is set to `true`, the text inside a `<textField>` or `<staticText>` element is not interpreted as regular text, but as XML. The text to be styled needs to be nested between `<style>` elements to obtain a different style from the rest of the text. This style element contains similar attributes to before, but is not the same as the `<style>` element discussed previously.

The following table lists all the attributes available to this `<style>` element:

| Attribute | Description | Valid Values |
|---|---|---|
| fontName | Indicates what font to use for the element. | A String indicating the font to use. |
| size | Indicates the size of the font. | An integer indicating the text size to use. |
| isBold | Indicates whether the font is bold. | true, false |
| isItalic | Indicates whether the font is italic. | true, false |
| IsUnderline | Indicates whether the font is underlined. | true, false |
| isStrikeThrough | Indicates whether the font is strikethrough style. | true, false |
| pdfFontName | Indicates the name of the font to use if the report is exported to PDF. | Courier, Courier-Bold, Courier-BoldOblique, Courier-Oblique, Helvetica, Helvetica Bold, Helvetica BoldOblique, Helvetica Oblique, Symbol, Times-Roman, Times-Bold, Times-BoldItalic, Times-Italic, ZapfDingbats |
| pdfEncoding | Indicates the encoding to use if the report is exported to PDF. | A String indicating the encoding to use when the report is exported to PDF. |

| Attribute | Description | Valid Values |
|---|---|---|
| `isPdfEmbedded` | Indicates if the PDF font should be embedded in the document. | `true`, `false` |
| `forecolor` | Indicates the color of the text. | See valid values for `forecolor` in the *Styles* section of this chapter. |
| `backcolor` | Indicates the background color of the text. | See valid values for `backcolor` in the *Styles* section of this chapter. |

We will be using styled text throughout this chapter. To see an example, see the JRXML templates in the *Subreports* section later in this chapter.

 There is one more way to set text properties, and that is by using the `<reportFont>` and `<font>` elements. As of JasperReports 1.1, these elements are deprecated and should not be used. Therefore, we will not discuss them here. Refer to the **quick reference** section of the JasperReports website if you need to use them: `http://jasperreports.sourceforge.net/quick.reference.html`.

# Setting a Report's Background

Reports can have elements that appear in the report background, behind all other report elements. We can add any report element to the background by using the JRXML `<background>` element. The following JRXML template demonstrates how to do this:

```
<?xml version="1.0" encoding="UTF-8"?>
<!DOCTYPE jasperReport PUBLIC "//JasperReports//DTD Report Design//EN"
 "http://jasperreports.sourceforge.net/dtds/jasperreport.dtd">
<jasperReport name="BackgroundDemoReport">
  <style name="centeredText" hAlign="Center" vAlign="Middle"/>
  <style name="boldCentered" style="centeredText" isBold="true"/>
  <style name="backgroundStyle" style="boldCentered"
        fontName="Helvetica" pdfFontName="Helvetica-Bold"
        forecolor="lightGray" fontSize="90"/>
  <background>
    <band height="782">
      <staticText>
        <reportElement x="0" y="0" width="555" height="782"
                       style="backgroundStyle" mode="Transparent"/>
```

```
          <textElement rotation="None"/>
          <text>
            <![CDATA[SAMPLE]]>
          </text>
        </staticText>
      </band>
    </background>
    <title>
      <band height="60">
        <staticText>
          <reportElement x="0" y="0" width="555" height="60"
                         style="boldCentered"/>
          <text>
            <![CDATA[Report Background Demo]]>
          </text>
        </staticText>
      </band>
    </title>
    <detail>
      <band height="600">
        <staticText>
          <reportElement x="0" y="300" width="555" height="60"
                         mode="Transparent" style="centeredText"/>
          <text>
            <![CDATA[This report demonstrates how to set the report
            background.]]>
          </text>
        </staticText>
      </band>
    </detail>
  </jasperReport>
```

The JRXML <background> element, just like all other JRXML elements that create
a report section, contains a single <band> element as its only sub-element. The
<background> element is different from other section elements because it is designed
to span a complete page, with its contents shown behind all other report elements.
It is worth noting that to allow report backgrounds to display correctly, the mode
attribute of other report sections must be set to Transparent.

After compiling this above JRXML template and filling the resulting Jasper template, we should obtain a report like the following:

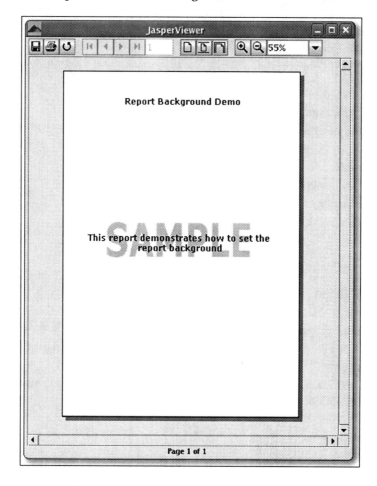

Notice how the background text appears to be behind the text in the `<band>` sub-element of the `<detail>` element.

It is common to set an image as a report background, usually a company logo set as a watermark. In the next chapter, we will cover how to add images to a report. The techniques explained there can be used to add an image as a report background.

# Adding Multiple Columns to a Report

JasperReports allows us to generate reports with multiple columns. Reports we have seen so far look like they have multiple columns. For example, the report we created in the previous chapter, has four separate columns for Model, Tail Number, Serial Number, and Engine. However, all four of these fields are laid out in a single <band>.

When we add multiple columns to a report, we should think of the data inside a <band> as being in a cell, regardless of how the data is laid out inside that band.

The FlightStats database that we used for the examples in Chapter 4 contains the country, state, and city where an aircraft is registered. Let us create a report displaying the tail number of all the aircraft registered in the state of New York, in the United States. Our report will display the data in three columns. The following JRXML template will generate a report with the desired layout:

```xml
<?xml version="1.0" encoding="UTF-8"?>
<!DOCTYPE jasperReport PUBLIC "//JasperReports//DTD Report Design//EN"
  "http://jasperreports.sourceforge.net/dtds/jasperreport.dtd">
<jasperReport name="MultipleColumnDemo" columnCount="3"
                columnWidth="180">
  <queryString>
    <![CDATA[select a.tail_num
            from aircraft a
            where a.country = 'US'
            and a.state = 'NY'
            order by a.tail_num]]>
  </queryString>
  <field name="tail_num" class="java.lang.String"/>
  <columnHeader>
    <band height="20">
      <staticText>
        <reportElement x="0" y="0" height="20" width="84"/>
        <text>Tail Number</text>
      </staticText>
    </band>
  </columnHeader>
  <detail>
    <band height="20">
      <textField>
        <reportElement x="0" y="0" height="20" width="84"/>
        <textFieldExpression>
          <![CDATA[$F{tail_num}]]>
```

```
    </textFieldExpression>
   </textField>
  </band>
 </detail>
</jasperReport>
```

As we can see in the above JRXML template, the number of columns and the column width are specified by the `columnCount` and `columnWidth` attributes of the `<jasperReport>` root element.

 The column width defaults to `555`, which is also the default width of a report page, excluding its margins. If we want to create a report with multiple columns, we must specify a smaller `columnWidth` attribute than the default; otherwise, our JRXML template will fail to compile.

As can be seen in the example above, we can define a column header to be displayed at the top of every column. This can be accomplished by the `<columnHeader>` JRXML element. We can also choose to display a footer at the bottom of every column by adding a `<columnFooter>` element to our JRXML template (not shown in the example). Just like all the other JRXML templates defining report sections, `<columnHeader>` and `<columnFooter>` contain a single `<band>` element as their only child element. The `<band>` element can contain report fields, static text, images, graphs, or anything else we can display on any of the other report sections.

The following servlet will generate a PDF report from the Jasper file generated from the above JRXML template and direct it to the browser:

```
package net.ensode.jasperbook;

import java.io.IOException;
import java.io.InputStream;
import java.io.PrintWriter;
import java.io.StringWriter;
import java.sql.Connection;
import java.sql.DriverManager;
import java.util.HashMap;

import javax.servlet.ServletException;
import javax.servlet.ServletOutputStream;
import javax.servlet.http.HttpServlet;
import javax.servlet.http.HttpServletRequest;
import javax.servlet.http.HttpServletResponse;
import net.sf.jasperreports.engine.JasperRunManager;
```

```java
public class MultipleColumnDemoServlet extends HttpServlet
{

  protected void doGet(HttpServletRequest request, HttpServletResponse
                       response) throws ServletException, IOException
  {
    Connection connection;
    ServletOutputStream servletOutputStream =
                                        response.getOutputStream();
    InputStream reportStream =
         getServletConfig().getServletContext().getResourceAsStream(
                           "/reports/MultipleColumnDemo.jasper");

    try
    {
      Class.forName("com.mysql.jdbc.Driver");

      connection = DriverManager.getConnection("jdbc:mysql://
        localhost:3306/flightstats" + "?user=dbuser&password=secret");

      JasperRunManager.runReportToPdfStream(reportStream,
                   servletOutputStream, new HashMap(), connection);

      connection.close();

      response.setContentType("application/pdf");
      servletOutputStream.flush();
      servletOutputStream.close();
    }
    catch (Exception e)
    {
      // display stack trace in the browser
      StringWriter stringWriter = new StringWriter();
      PrintWriter printWriter = new PrintWriter(stringWriter);
      e.printStackTrace(printWriter);
      response.setContentType("text/plain");
      response.getOutputStream().print(stringWriter.toString());
    }
  }
}
```

There is nothing in this servlet we haven't seen before. The data multiple column logic is encapsulated in the JRXML. After deploying this servlet and directing the browser to its URL, we should see a report like the following:

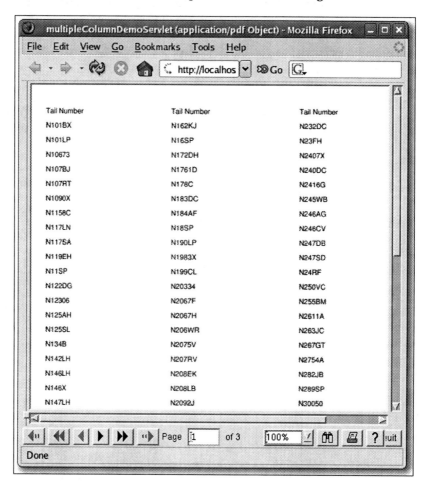

As we can see, the data is displayed in three columns. This way we can create the whole report using about one-third of the pages we would have had to use with one column.

# A Few Things about Report Columns

Before we move on, there are a few more things we should know about report columns. These features are pretty straightforward. Although there are no examples explaining them, yet we should be aware of them.

Report columns, by default, have no space between them (in the preceding report, the columns are wider than the displayed tail number; there is a lot of whitespace inside the columns). We can change this default behavior by using the `columnSpacing` attribute of the root `<jasperReport>` element of the JRXML template.

By default, report columns are filled vertically, that is, the first column is filled to completion first, then the second, then the third, and so on. If we want to fill the columns by row, that is, fill the first row of every column first, then the second, and so on, we can achieve this by setting the `printOrder` attribute of the root `<jasperReport>` element to `Horizontal`.

Column footers, by default, are printed at the bottom of the page. If a report column does not have enough data to fill a page, there will be some blank space between the end of the column and the column footer. If we want the column footer to be printed right after the end of the column, we can do it by setting the `isFloatColumnFooter` attribute of the `<jasperReport>` element to `true`.

# Grouping Report Data

JasperReports allows us to group report data in a logical manner. For example, if we were creating a report about cars, we could group the data by car make and/or model. Similarly, if we were creating a report about sales figures, we could group the report data by geographical area.

The FlightStats database we used for the examples in Chapter 4 contains the country, state, and city where an aircraft is registered. Let us create a report displaying aircraft data registered in any state starting with the letter 'A' in the United States. We will group the report data by state abbreviation. The JRXML template for the report follows:

```
<?xml version="1.0" encoding="UTF-8"?>
<!DOCTYPE jasperReport PUBLIC "//JasperReports//DTD Report Design//EN"
  "http://jasperreports.sourceforge.net/dtds/jasperreport.dtd">
<jasperReport name="DataGroupingDemo">
  <queryString>
    <![CDATA[select a.tail_num, a.aircraft_serial, am.model, a.state
            from aircraft a, aircraft_models am
            where a.aircraft_model_code = am.aircraft_model_code
            and a.country = 'US'
            and state like 'A%'
            order by state, model]]>
  </queryString>
```

```
<field name="tail_num" class="java.lang.String"/>
<field name="aircraft_serial" class="java.lang.String"/>
<field name="model" class="java.lang.String"/>
<field name="state" class="java.lang.String"/>
<group name="StateGroup">
  <groupExpression>
   <![CDATA[$F{state}]]>
  </groupExpression>
  <groupHeader>
    <band height="40">
      <staticText>
        <reportElement x="0" y="10" width="115" height="20"/>
        <textElement>
          <font isBold="true"/>
        </textElement>
        <text>Aircraft Registered In:</text>
      </staticText>
      <textField>
        <reportElement x="116" y="10" width="20" height="20"/>
        <textFieldExpression>$F{state}</textFieldExpression>
      </textField>
    </band>
  </groupHeader>
  <groupFooter>
    <band height="40">
      <staticText>
        <reportElement x="0" y="10" width="140" height="20"/>
        <textElement>
          <font isBold="true"/>
        </textElement>
        <text>End Aircraft Registered In:</text>
      </staticText>
      <textField>
        <reportElement x="141" y="10" width="20" height="20"/>
        <textFieldExpression>$F{state}</textFieldExpression>
      </textField>
    </band>
  </groupFooter>
</group>
<detail>
  <band height="20">
    <staticText>
      <reportElement x="20" y="0" height="20" width="35"/>
      <text>Model:</text>
    </staticText>
    <textField>
```

```
      <reportElement x="56" y="0" height="20" width="164"/>
      <textFieldExpression>
        <![CDATA[$F{model}]]>
      </textFieldExpression>
    </textField>
    <staticText>
      <reportElement x="220" y="0" height="20" width="65"/>
      <text>Tail Number:</text>
    </staticText>
    <textField>
      <reportElement x="286" y="0" height="20" width="84"/>
      <textFieldExpression>
        <![CDATA[$F{tail_num}]]>
      </textFieldExpression>
    </textField>
    <staticText>
      <reportElement x="380" y="0" height="20" width="75"/>
      <text>Serial Number:</text>
    </staticText>
    <textField>
      <reportElement x="456" y="0" height="20" width="94"/>
      <textFieldExpression>
        <![CDATA[$F{aircraft_serial}]]>
      </textFieldExpression>
    </textField>
    </band>
  </detail>
</jasperReport>
```

As can be seen in this example, a group is defined by the <group> element. The <group> element must contain a name attribute defining the group's name. A group must also contain a <groupExpression> sub-element. This sub-element indicates the data that must change to start a new data group. In the example above, every time the state changes, we begin a new data grouping.

A group can optionally contain <groupHeader> and <groupFooter> elements. They are useful to place labels at the beginning and at the end of the grouped data. The group header and footer contain a single <band> element as their only child element. The <band> element is a regular <band> element. We can place any report element we wish in it, just as if it was inside any of the other report sections (title, page header, column header, detail, etc.). In this example, we chose to place some static text and report field identifying the state that the aircrafts in the group are registered to.

The servlet to generate a PDF report is virtually identical to the one we saw in the previous section. The only difference is the location of the Jasper template. After deploying this servlet and directing the browser to its URL, we should see a report like the following:

Here, a screenshot of page 3 of the report is displayed to illustrate the group header and footer.

The `<group>` element contains attributes that allow us to control how grouped data is laid out. The following table summarizes these attributes:

| Attribute | Description |
|---|---|
| isStartNewPage | When set to 'true', each data group will begin on a new page. |
| isStartNewColumn | When set to 'true', each data group will begin on a new column. |
| isReprintHeaderOnEachPage | When set to 'true', the group header will be reprinted on every page. |
| isResetPageNumber | When set to 'true', the report page number will be reset every time a new group starts. |

Each of the attributes described in this table default to `false`.

# Report Expressions

Report expressions are a feature of JasperReports that allows us to display calculated data on a report. Calculated data is data that is not static and not specifically passed as a report parameter or a datasource field.

Report expressions are built from combining report parameters, fields, and static data. By default, report expressions can be built using the Java language. However, JasperReports can support any other language supported by the JVM. The JasperReports project file includes examples of using BeanShell and Groovy to build report expressions.

 Since by far the most commonly used report expressions are Java expressions, we will only cover those. Refer to the examples distributed with the JasperReports project ZIP file, if you need to create expressions in BeanShell or Groovy.

We have already seen simple report expressions in the form of report parameters and fields. We can use any valid Java language expression that returns a String or a numeric value in report expressions. For example, we can concatenate Strings or call any method in a report expression. The following JRXML template demonstrates these concepts:

```xml
<?xml version="1.0" encoding="UTF-8"?>
<!DOCTYPE jasperReport PUBLIC "//JasperReports//DTD Report Design//EN"
  "http://jasperreports.sourceforge.net/dtds/jasperreport.dtd">
<jasperReport name="ReportExpressionsDemo">
  <queryString>
```

```
      <![CDATA[select (select count(*)
                   from aircraft_models am
                   where am.aircraft_type_id = 4) as
                   fixed_wing_single_engine_cnt,
                   (select count(*)
                   from aircraft_models am
                   where am.aircraft_type_id = 5) as
                   fixed_wing_multiple_engine_cnt,
                   (select count(*)
                   from aircraft_models am
                   where am.aircraft_type_id = 6) as
                   rotorcraft_cnt]]>
  </queryString>
  <field name="fixed_wing_single_engine_cnt" class="java.lang.Integer"/>
  <field name="fixed_wing_multiple_engine_cnt" class="java.lang.
          Integer"/>
  <field name="rotorcraft_cnt" class="java.lang.Integer"/>
  <detail>
    <band height="100">
      <textField>
        <reportElement x="20" y="0" height="20" width="500"/>
        <textFieldExpression>
          <![CDATA["Total Fixed Wing Single Engine Aircraft Models: "
                  +$F{fixed_wing_single_engine_cnt}]]>
        </textFieldExpression>
      </textField>
      <textField>
        <reportElement x="20" y="20" height="20" width="500"/>
        <textFieldExpression>
          <![CDATA["Total Fixed Wing Multiple Engine Aircraft Models:"
                  +$F{fixed_wing_multiple_engine_cnt}]]>
        </textFieldExpression>
      </textField>
      <textField>
        <reportElement x="20" y="40" height="20" width="500"/>
        <textFieldExpression>
          <![CDATA["Total Fixed Wing Aircraft Models: " +
                  ($F{fixed_wing_single_engine_cnt}.intValue() +
                   $F{fixed_wing_multiple_engine_cnt}.intValue())]]>
        </textFieldExpression>
      </textField>
      <textField>
```

```
        <reportElement x="20" y="60" height="20" width="500"/>
        <textFieldExpression>
          <![CDATA["Total Rotorcraft Aircraft Models: " +
                   $F{rotorcraft_cnt}]]>
        </textFieldExpression>
      </textField>
      <textField>
        <reportElement x="20" y="80" height="20" width="500"/>
        <textFieldExpression>
          <![CDATA["Total Aircraft Models Reported: " +
                   ($F{fixed_wing_single_engine_cnt}.intValue() +
                    $F{fixed_wing_multiple_engine_cnt}.intValue() +
                    $F{rotorcraft_cnt}.intValue())]]>
        </textFieldExpression>
      </textField>
    </band>
  </detail>
</jasperReport>
```

This JRXML generates a report on the total number of fixed-wing single-engine, fixed-wing multiple-engine, and rotorcraft aircraft in the FlightStats database. It then calculates the total number of fixed-wing aircrafts in the database by adding the first two fields. Lastly, it calculates the total number of aircraft reported by adding all three fields.

The following servlet generates a PDF report from the Jasper file generated by the above JRXML template and directs it to the browser:

```
package net.ensode.jasperbook;

import java.io.IOException;
import java.io.InputStream;
import java.io.PrintWriter;
import java.io.StringWriter;
import java.sql.Connection;
import java.sql.DriverManager;
import java.util.HashMap;

import javax.servlet.ServletException;
import javax.servlet.ServletOutputStream;
import javax.servlet.http.HttpServlet;
import javax.servlet.http.HttpServletRequest;
import javax.servlet.http.HttpServletResponse;

import net.sf.jasperreports.engine.JasperRunManager;
```

```java
public class ReportExpressionsDemoServlet extends HttpServlet
{

  protected void doGet(HttpServletRequest request, HttpServletResponse
                    response) throws ServletException, IOException
  {
    Connection connection;
    ServletOutputStream servletOutputStream =
                                        response.getOutputStream();
    InputStream reportStream = getServletConfig().getServletContext().
        getResourceAsStream("/reports/ReportExpressionsDemo.jasper");

    try
    {
      Class.forName("com.mysql.jdbc.Driver");

      connection = DriverManager.getConnection("jdbc:mysql://
            localhost:3306/flightstats?user=dbuser&password=secret");

      JasperRunManager.runReportToPdfStream(reportStream,
                    servletOutputStream, new HashMap(), connection);

      connection.close();

      response.setContentType("application/pdf");
      servletOutputStream.flush();
      servletOutputStream.close();
    }
    catch (Exception e)
    {
      // display stack trace in the browser
      StringWriter stringWriter = new StringWriter();
      PrintWriter printWriter = new PrintWriter(stringWriter);
      e.printStackTrace(printWriter);
      response.setContentType("text/plain");
      response.getOutputStream().print(stringWriter.toString());
    }
  }
}
```

There is nothing in this code that we haven't seen before, since the logic to add report expressions is encapsulated in the JRXML template.

After deploying this servlet and directing the browser to its URL, we should see a report like the following:

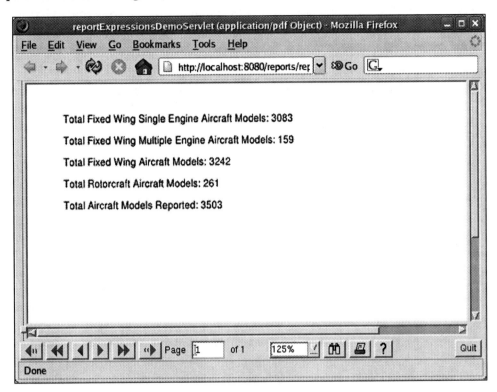

# Report Variables

When we wrote the report in the previous section, we had to type the following expression twice:

```
$F{fixed_wing_single_engine_cnt}.intValue() +
$F{fixed_wing_multiple_engine_cnt}.intValue())
```

This expression was typed once to calculate the number of fixed-wing aircraft reported, and again to calculate the total number of aircraft reported. This duplication is not a good thing, since if we need to change the expression for any reason we would have to do it twice. JasperReports allows us to assign report expressions to a variable, eliminating the need to type the expression multiple times. The following JRXML template is a modified version of the one we wrote in the previous section. This version takes advantage of report variables to eliminate the duplicate expression.

```xml
<?xml version="1.0" encoding="UTF-8"?>
<!DOCTYPE jasperReport PUBLIC "//JasperReports//DTD Report Design//EN"
    "http://jasperreports.sourceforge.net/dtds/jasperreport.dtd">
<jasperReport name="ReportVariablesDemo">
  <queryString>
    <![CDATA[select (select count(*)
                from aircraft_models am
                where am.aircraft_type_id = 4) as
                fixed_wing_single_engine_cnt,
            (select count(*)
             from aircraft_models am
             where am.aircraft_type_id = 5) as
             fixed_wing_multiple_engine_cnt,
            (select count(*)
             from aircraft_models am
             where am.aircraft_type_id = 6) as rotorcraft_
             cnt]]>
  </queryString>
  <field name="fixed_wing_single_engine_cnt" class="java.lang.Integer"/>
  <field name="fixed_wing_multiple_engine_cnt" class="java.lang.
            Integer"/>
  <field name="rotorcraft_cnt" class="java.lang.Integer"/>
  <variable name="fixed_wing_engine_cnt" class="java.lang.Integer">
    <variableExpression>
      <![CDATA[new Integer($F{fixed_wing_single_engine_cnt}.intValue() +
                    $F{fixed_wing_multiple_engine_cnt}.intValue())]]>
    </variableExpression>
  </variable>
  <detail>
    <band height="100">
      <textField>
        <reportElement x="20" y="0" height="20" width="500"/>
```

```
            <textFieldExpression>
              <![CDATA["Total Fixed Wing Single Engine Aircraft Models: " +
                       $F{fixed_wing_single_engine_cnt}]]>
            </textFieldExpression>
          </textField>
          <textField>
            <reportElement x="20" y="20" height="20" width="500"/>
            <textFieldExpression>
              <![CDATA["Total Fixed Wing Multiple Engine Aircraft Models: " +
                       $F{fixed_wing_multiple_engine_cnt}]]>
            </textFieldExpression>
          </textField>
          <textField>
            <reportElement x="20" y="40" height="20" width="500"/>
            <textFieldExpression>
              <![CDATA["Total Fixed Wing Aircraft Models: " +
                       $V{fixed_wing_engine_cnt}]]>
            </textFieldExpression>
          </textField>
          <textField>
            <reportElement x="20" y="60" height="20" width="500"/>
            <textFieldExpression>
              <![CDATA["Total Rotorcraft Aircraft Models: " +
                       $F{rotorcraft_cnt}]]>
            </textFieldExpression>
          </textField>
          <textField>
            <reportElement x="20" y="80" height="20" width="500"/>
            <textFieldExpression>
              <![CDATA["Total Aircraft Models Reported: " +
                       ($V{fixed_wing_engine_cnt}.intValue() +
                        $F{rotorcraft_cnt}.intValue())]]>
            </textFieldExpression>
          </textField>
        </band>
      </detail>
    </jasperReport>
```

As can be seen in the example, report expressions can be assigned to a variable by using the <variable> element in a JRXML file. We give the variable a name, by using the name attribute of the <variable> field. The actual expression we want to assign to a variable must be enclosed inside a <variableExpression>

element. Variable values can be accessed in other report expressions by using the `$V{variable_name}` notation, where `variable_name` is the name we gave to the variable by using the `name` attribute in the `<variable>` element.

Output for the preceding example is identical to the output of the example given in the previous section on *Report Expressions*.

The JRXML `<variable>` element contains a number of attributes. These attributes are summarized in the following table:

| Attribute | Description | Valid Values | Default Value |
|---|---|---|---|
| name | Sets the variable name. | Any valid XML attribute value. | N/A |
| class | Sets the variable class. | Any Java class available in the CLASSPATH. | java.lang. String |
| calculation | Determines what calculation to perform on the variable when filling the report. | Average: The variable value is the average of every non-null value of the variable expression. Valid for numeric variables only. | Nothing |
| | | Count: The variable value is the count of non-null instances of the variable expression. | |
| | | First: The variable value is the value of the first instance of the variable expression. Subsequent values are ignored. | |
| | | Highest: The variable value is the highest value for the variable expression. | |
| | | Lowest: The variable value is the lowest value in the report for the variable expression. | |
| | | Nothing: No calculations are performed on the variable. | |
| | | StandardDeviation: The variable value is the standard deviation of all non-null values matching the report expression. Valid for numeric variables only. | |
| | | Sum: The variable value is the sum of all non-null values matching the report expression. | |

| Attribute | Description | Valid Values | Default Value |
|---|---|---|---|
| | | System: The variable value is a custom calculation.<br><br>Variance: The variable value is the variance of all non-null values matching the report expression. | |
| incrementer FactoryClass | Determines the class used to calculate the value of the variable when filling the current record on the report. | Any class implementing net.sf.jasperreports. engine.fill.<br><br>JRIncrementerFactory | N/A |
| incrementType | Determines when to recalculate the value of the variable. | Column: The variable value is recalculated at the end of each column.<br><br>Group: The variable value is recalculated when the group specified by incrementGroup changes.<br><br>None: The variable value is recalculated with every record.<br><br>Page: The variable value is recalculated at the end of every page.<br><br>Report: The variable value is recalculated once, at the end of the report. | None |
| incrementGroup | Determines the name of the group at which the variable value is recalculated, when incrementType is Group. | The name of any group declared in the JRXML report template. | N/A |

| Attribute | Description | Valid Values | Default Value |
|---|---|---|---|
| resetType | Determines when the value of a variable is reset. | Column: The variable value is reset at the beginning of each column. | Report |
| | | Group: The variable value is reset when the group specified by incrementGroup changes. | |
| | | None: The variable value is never reset. | |
| | | Page: The variable value is recalculated at the beginning of every page. | |
| | | Report: The variable value is recalculated once, at the beginning of the report. | |
| resetGroup | Determines the name of the group at which the variable value is reset, when resetType is Group. | The name of any group declared in the JRXML report template. | N/A |

As can be inferred from the table, JasperReports variables can be used not only to simplify report expressions, but also to perform calculations, and to display the result of those calculations on the report.

Let us modify the report we developed in the previous section so that it displays the total number of aircraft in each state. To accomplish this, we need to create a report variable and set its calculation attribute to Count. The following JRXML template illustrates this concept:

```
<?xml version="1.0" encoding="UTF-8"?>
<!DOCTYPE jasperReport PUBLIC "//JasperReports//DTD Report Design//EN"
  "http://jasperreports.sourceforge.net/dtds/jasperreport.dtd">
<jasperReport name="VariableCalculationDemo">
  <queryString>
    <![CDATA[select a.tail_num, a.aircraft_serial, am.model, a.state
        from aircraft a, aircraft_models am
        where a.aircraft_model_code = am.aircraft_model_code
        and a.country = 'US' and state like 'A%'
```

```
                    order by state, model]]>
</queryString>
<field name="tail_num" class="java.lang.String"/>
<field name="aircraft_serial" class="java.lang.String"/>
<field name="model" class="java.lang.String"/>
<field name="state" class="java.lang.String"/>
<variable name="aircraft_count" class="java.lang.Integer"
          calculation="Count" resetType="Group"
          resetGroup="StateGroup">
  <variableExpression>
    <![CDATA[$F{aircraft_serial}]]>
  </variableExpression>
  <initialValueExpression>
    <![CDATA[new java.lang.Integer(0)]]>
  </initialValueExpression>
</variable>
<group name="StateGroup">
  <groupExpression>
    <![CDATA[$F{state}]]>
  </groupExpression>
  <groupHeader>
    <band height="40">
      <staticText>
        <reportElement x="0" y="10" width="115" height="20"/>
        <textElement>
          <font isBold="true"/>
        </textElement>
        <text>Aircraft Registered In:</text>
      </staticText>
      <textField>
        <reportElement x="116" y="10" width="20" height="20"/>
        <textFieldExpression>$F{state}</textFieldExpression>
      </textField>
    </band>
  </groupHeader>
  <groupFooter>
    <band height="40">
      <textField>
        <reportElement x="0" y="10" width="325" height="20"/>
        <textFieldExpression>
          <![CDATA["Total Number Of Aircraft Registered In " +
                  $F{state} + ": " +
                  $V{aircraft_count}]]>
```

```
                  </textFieldExpression>
                </textField>
              </band>
            </groupFooter>
          </group>
          <detail>
            <band height="20">
              <staticText>
                <reportElement x="20" y="0" height="20" width="35"/>
                <text>Model:</text>
              </staticText>
              <textField>
                <reportElement x="56" y="0" height="20" width="164"/>
                <textFieldExpression>
                  <![CDATA[$F{model}]]>
                </textFieldExpression>
              </textField>
              <staticText>
                <reportElement x="220" y="0" height="20" width="65"/>
                <text>Tail Number:</text>
              </staticText>
              <textField>
                <reportElement x="286" y="0" height="20" width="84"/>
                <textFieldExpression>
                  <![CDATA[$F{tail_num}]]>
                </textFieldExpression>
              </textField>
              <staticText>
                <reportElement x="380" y="0" height="20" width="75"/>
                <text>Serial Number:</text>
              </staticText>
              <textField>
                <reportElement x="456" y="0" height="20" width="94"/>
                <textFieldExpression>
                  <![CDATA[$F{aircraft_serial}]]>
                </textFieldExpression>
              </textField>
            </band>
          </detail>
        </jasperReport>
```

In this report template, setting the `calculation` attribute of the `<variable>` field to `Count` allowed us to obtain the number of aircrafts in each state. By setting the report expression to `$F{aircraft_serial}`, each time a serial number is displayed in the report, the variable value is increased by one. Setting the `resetType` attribute to `Group` allows us to reset the variable value to its initial value, which in turn is set by the `<initialValueExpression>` field.

We are familiar with the code for the servlet that fills and exports the Jasper file generated by this JRXML template. Therefore, it is not shown. After directing the browser to its URL, we should see a report like the following:

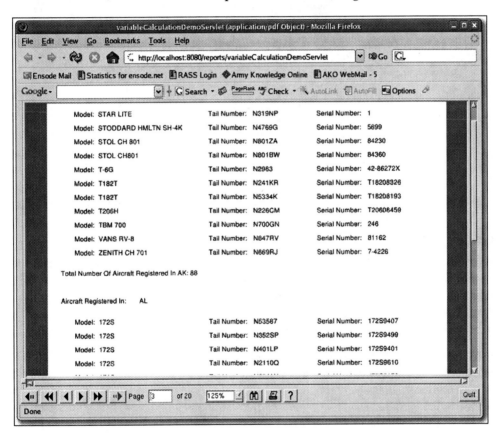

The concepts we saw here can be applied for the other calculation values and reset types.

# Built-In Report Variables

JasperReports has a number of built-in report variables that we can use in our reports without having to declare them. They are listed and described in the following table:

| Built-In Variable | Description |
|---|---|
| PAGE_COUNT | Contains the total number of pages in the report. |
| PAGE_NUMBER | Contains the current page number. |
| COLUMN_COUNT | Contains the total number of columns in the report. |
| COLUMN_NUMBER | Contains the current column number. |
| REPORT_COUNT | Contains the total number of records in the report. |
| NameOfGroup_COUNT | Contains the total number of records in the group named "NameOfGroup". The exact report variable name will match the group name in the report. For example, for a group named "MyGroup" the variable name will be MyGroup_COUNT. |

# Stretching Text Fields to Accommodate Data

By default, `<textField>` elements have a fixed size. If the data they need to display does not fit into their defined size, it is simply not displayed in the report. This is rarely the behavior we would want. Luckily, JasperReports allows us to alter this default behavior. This is accomplished by setting the `isStretchWithOverflow` attribute of the `<textField>` element to `true`.

The following JRXML template demonstrates how to allow text fields to stretch so that they can accommodate large amounts of data:

```xml
<?xml version="1.0" encoding="UTF-8"?>
<!DOCTYPE jasperReport PUBLIC "//JasperReports//DTD Report Design//EN"
  "http://jasperreports.sourceforge.net/dtds/jasperreport.dtd">
<jasperReport name="TextFieldStretchDemo">
  <field name="lots_of_data" class="java.lang.String"/>
  <detail>
    <band height="30">
      <textField isStretchWithOverflow="true">
        <reportElement x="0" y="0" width="100" height="24"/>
```

```xml
      <textFieldExpression class="java.lang.String">
        <![CDATA[$F{lots_of_data}]]>
      </textFieldExpression>
    </textField>
  </band>
</detail>
</jasperReport>
```

The following servlet fills the Jasper template generated from this JRXML and directs the generated report to the browser window in PDF format:

```java
package net.ensode.jasperbook;

import java.io.IOException;
import java.io.InputStream;
import java.io.PrintWriter;
import java.io.StringWriter;
import java.util.ArrayList;
import java.util.Collection;
import java.util.HashMap;

import javax.servlet.ServletException;
import javax.servlet.ServletOutputStream;
import javax.servlet.http.HttpServlet;
import javax.servlet.http.HttpServletRequest;
import javax.servlet.http.HttpServletResponse;

import net.sf.jasperreports.engine.JRDataSource;
import net.sf.jasperreports.engine.JasperRunManager;
import net.sf.jasperreports.engine.data.JRMapCollectionDataSource;

public class TextFieldStretchDemoServlet extends HttpServlet
{
  private JRDataSource createReportDataSource()
  {
    JRMapCollectionDataSource dataSource;
    Collection reportRows = initializeMapCollection();

    dataSource = new JRMapCollectionDataSource(reportRows);

    return dataSource;
  }

  private Collection initializeMapCollection()
  {
    ArrayList reportRows = new ArrayList();
    HashMap datasourceMap = new HashMap();
```

```
        datasourceMap
            .put(
                "lots_of_data",
                "This element contains so much data, "
            + "there is no way it will ever fit in the text field
                without it stretching.");

    reportRows.add(datasourceMap);

    return reportRows;
}

protected void doGet(HttpServletRequest request, HttpServletResponse
                    response) throws ServletException, IOException
{
    ServletOutputStream servletOutputStream =
                                        response.getOutputStream();
    InputStream reportStream = getServletConfig().getServletContext().
        getResourceAsStream("/reports/TextFieldStretchDemo.jasper");

    try
    {

        JRDataSource dataSource = createReportDataSource();

        JasperRunManager.runReportToPdfStream(reportStream,
                        servletOutputStream, new HashMap(), dataSource);

        response.setContentType("application/pdf");
        servletOutputStream.flush();
        servletOutputStream.close();
    }
    catch (Exception e)
    {
        // display stack trace in the browser
        StringWriter stringWriter = new StringWriter();
        PrintWriter printWriter = new PrintWriter(stringWriter);
        e.printStackTrace(printWriter);
        response.setContentType("text/plain");
        response.getOutputStream().print(stringWriter.toString());
    }
  }
}
```

We should see a report like the following after directing the browser to this servlet's URL:

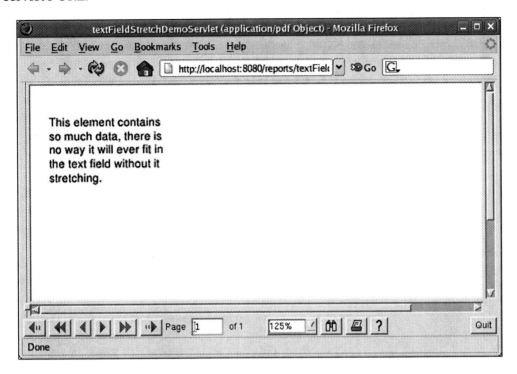

When a `<textField>` element stretches to accommodate its data, its parent `<band>` element stretches accordingly. When a `<band>` element stretches due to one of its child `<textField>` element's stretching, JasperReports allows us to control how other child elements of the `<band>` will be positioned when the band stretches. This will be discussed in detail in the next section.

# Laying Out Report Elements

As we saw in Chapter 3, a report can contain a report title, a page header, a page footer, a column header, a column footer, a detail section, a report summary, and a last page footer. These sections are defined by the `<title>`, `<pageHeader>`, `<pageFooter>`, `<columnHeader>`, `<columnFooter>`, `<detail>`, `<summary>`, and `<lastPageFooter>` JRXML elements, respectively.

Each of these elements contains a single `<band>` element as its only sub-element. The `<band>` element can contain zero or more `<line>`, `<rectangle>`, `<ellipse>`, `<image>`, `<staticText>`, `<textField>`, `<subReport>`, or `<elementGroup>` sub-elements. Except for `<elementGroup>`, each of these elements must contain a single `<reportElement>` as its first element. `<reportElement>` determines how data is laid out for that particular element. In this section, we will see how the different attributes of `<reportElement>` affect the way data in its parent element is laid out.

The following table summarizes all the attributes of `<reportElement>`:

| Attribute | Description | Valid Values |
| --- | --- | --- |
| x | Specifies the x coordinate of the element within the band. | An integer value indicating the x coordinate of the element in pixels. This attribute is required. |
| y | Specifies the y coordinate of the element within the band. | An integer value indicating the y coordinate of the element in pixels. This attribute is required. |
| width | Specifies the width of the element. | An integer value indicating the element width in pixels. This attribute is required. |
| height | Specifies the height of the element. | An integer value indicating the element height in pixels. This attribute is required. |
| key | Uniquely identifies the element within the band; does not affect layout. | A unique string used to identify the containing element. |
| stretchType | Specifies how the element stretches when the containing band stretches. | NoStretch (default): The element will not stretch. |
| | | RelativeToTallestObject: The element will stretch to accommodate the tallest object in its group. |
| | | RelativeToBand: The element will stretch to fit the band's height. |
| positionType | Specifies the element's position when the band stretches. | Float: The element will move depending on the size of the surrounding elements. |
| | | FixRelativeToTop (default): The element will maintain a fixed position relative to the band's top. |
| | | FixRelativeToBottom: The element will maintain a fixed position relative to the band's bottom. |

| Attribute | Description | Valid Values |
|---|---|---|
| isPrintRepeated Values | Specifies if repeated values are printed. | true (default): Repeated values will be printed.<br><br>false: Repeated values will not be printed. |
| mode | Specifies the background mode of the element. | Opaque, Transparent |
| isRemoveLineWhen Blank | Specifies if the element should be removed when it is blank and there are no other elements in the same horizontal space. | true, false |
| isPrintInFirst WholeBand | Specifies if the element must be printed in a whole band, that is, a band that is not divided between report pages or columns. | true, false |
| isPrintWhenDetail OverFlows | Specifies if the element will be printed when the band overflows to a new page or column. | true, false |
| printWhenGroup Changes | Specifies that the element will be printed when the specified group changes. | A string corresponding to the group that must change for the element to be printed. |
| forecolor | Specifies the foreground color of the element. | Either a hexadecimal RGB value preceded by the # character, or one of the following predefined values:<br><br>black, blue, cyan, darkGray, gray, green, lightGray, magenta, orange, pink, red, yellow, white. |
| backcolor | Specifies the background color of the element. | Refer to the valid values of forecolor in the preceding row. |

Most of the <reportElement> attributes described in the table are self explanatory. We will discuss some of them in the next few sections.

# Setting the Size and Position of a Report Element

The x and y attributes of `<reportElement>` specify the x and y coordinates (in pixels) of the element within the band. An initial common mistake is to assume that the x and y coordinates, which are defined here, are absolute for the page. Again, the x and y coordinates, defined by the x and y attributes, are relative to the `<band>` where the element is contained. Coordinates (0, 0) are at the top left of the band. The x and y attributes of `<reportElement>` are required.

The `width` and `height` elements of `<reportElement>`, unsurprisingly, define the width and height (in pixels) of the element, respectively. The `width` and `height` attributes of `<reportElement>` are required. We have already seen several examples demonstrating the use of the x, y, `width`, and `height` elements of `<reportElement>`. Here is the JRXML template for the report we created in Chapter 3:

```xml
<?xml version="1.0"?>
<!DOCTYPE jasperReport
  PUBLIC "-//JasperReports//DTD Report Design//EN"
  "http://jasperreports.sourceforge.net/dtds/jasperreport.dtd">
<jasperReport name="FirstReport">
  <detail>
    <band height="20">
      <staticText>
        <reportElement x="20" y="0" width="200" height="20"/>
        <text><![CDATA[If you don't see this, it didn't work]]></text>
      </staticText>
    </band>
  </detail>
</jasperReport>
```

In this example, the static text will appear 20 pixels from the left margin, aligned with the top of the band. Refer to Chapter 3 to see a rendered report based on this template.

The `positionType` attribute defines the element's position when the band is stretched. As can be seen in the table overleaf, there are three legal values for this attribute, namely, `Float`, `FixRelativeToTop`, and `FixRelativeToBottom`. Let us modify the example we showed in the *Allowing Text Fields to Stretch to Accommodate their Data* section by adding some static text right under the existing text field. We will see the effect the different `positionType` values have on its positioning.

```xml
<?xml version="1.0" encoding="UTF-8"?>
<!DOCTYPE jasperReport PUBLIC "//JasperReports//DTD Report Design//EN"
  "http://jasperreports.sourceforge.net/dtds/jasperreport.dtd">
<jasperReport name="TextFieldStretchDemo" >
  <field name="lots_of_data" class="java.lang.String"/>
  <detail>
    <band height="55">
      <textField isStretchWithOverflow="true">
        <reportElement x="0" y="0" width="100" height="24"/>
        <box border="Thin"/>
        <textFieldExpression class="java.lang.String">
          <![CDATA[$F{lots_of_data}]]>
        </textFieldExpression>
      </textField>
      <staticText>
        <reportElement width="500" y="25" x="0" height="30"
                       positionType="FixRelativeToTop"/>
        <box border="Thin"/>
        <text>
          <![CDATA[This staticText element has a default positionType
          of "FixRelativeToTop"]]>
        </text>
      </staticText>
    </band>
  </detail>
</jasperReport>
```

The `<textField>` element in the JRXML template has a y position of 0, and a height of 24. We positioned the new `<staticText>` element to have a y position of 25, just below the `<textField>`.

> For clarity, we explicitly set the `positionType` attribute of `<reportElement>` to FixRelativeToTop. It was not really necessary to do it, since `FixRelativeToTop` is the default value.

Notice the `<box>` element we added to the `<textField>` and `<staticText>` elements. This `<box>` field allows us to display a border around the elements, making it very clear where the element starts and ends. We chose to do this to be able to easily see the position of the elements within the report.

Again, the code to fill and export the report is similar to what we have seen before. Therefore, we chose not to display it. The generated report should look like this:

The `FixRelativeToTop` value of the `positionType` attribute of `<reportElement>` forces the element to stay in the same position regardless of whether any other element stretches. Hence, we ended up with the two elements overlapping each other, which is probably not what we want.

It would be nice if the `<staticText>` element would be pushed down, if the `<textField>` element stretches. We can accomplish this by setting `positionType` to `Float`.

```xml
<?xml version="1.0" encoding="UTF-8"?>
<!DOCTYPE jasperReport PUBLIC "//JasperReports//DTD Report Design//EN"
  "http://jasperreports.sourceforge.net/dtds/jasperreport.dtd">
<jasperReport name="FloatDemo" >
  <field name="lots_of_data" class="java.lang.String"/>
  <detail>
    <band height="55">
      <textField isStretchWithOverflow="true">
        <reportElement x="0" y="0" width="100" height="24"/>
        <box border="Thin"/>
        <textFieldExpression class="java.lang.String">
          <![CDATA[$F{lots_of_data}]]>
        </textFieldExpression>
      </textField>
      <staticText>
        <reportElement width="500" y="25" x="0" height="30"
                       positionType="Float"/>
        <box border="Thin"/>
        <text>
          <![CDATA[This staticText element has a positionType of
                  "Float"]]>
        </text>
      </staticText>
    </band>
  </detail>
</jasperReport>
```

After compiling, filling, and exporting the preceding JRXML template, we should get a report that looks like the following:

```
This element contains
so much data, there is
no way it will ever fit in
the text field without it
stretching.



This staticText element has a positionType of "Float"
```

As we can see, setting the `positionType` attribute of `<reportElement>` to `Float` made JasperReports ignore the y position of the `<staticText>` element, which was pushed down by the stretched `<textField>` element.

The third possible value for `positionType` is `FixRelativeToBottom`. This value is similar to `FixRelativeToTop`, with the only difference being that the element keeps its position relative to the bottom of the band, as opposed to its top.

It is not only possible to control the position of elements inside a band, when one of its elements stretches, but also possible to control their size. This is accomplished by the `stretchType` attribute of `<reportElement>`. The following example demonstrates how we can set a report element to stretch to match the tallest element in its group:

```
<?xml version="1.0" encoding="UTF-8"?>
<!DOCTYPE jasperReport PUBLIC "//JasperReports//DTD Report Design//EN"
  "http://jasperreports.sourceforge.net/dtds/jasperreport.dtd">
<jasperReport name="RelativeToTallestObjectDemo">
  <field name="lots_of_data" class="java.lang.String"/>
  <detail>
    <band height="50">
      <elementGroup>
        <textField isStretchWithOverflow="true">
          <reportElement x="0" y="0" width="100" height="24"/>
          <box border="Thin"/>
          <textFieldExpression class="java.lang.String">
            <![CDATA[$F{lots_of_data}]]>
          </textFieldExpression>
        </textField>
        <textField isStretchWithOverflow="true">
          <reportElement x="101" y="0" width="150" height="24"/>
          <box border="Thin"/>
          <textFieldExpression class="java.lang.String">
```

```
          <![CDATA[$F{lots_of_data}]]>
        </textFieldExpression>
      </textField>
      <staticText>
        <reportElement width="300" y="0" x="252" height="24"
                       stretchType="RelativeToTallestObject"/>
        <box border="Thin"/>
        <text>
          <![CDATA[staticText element stretchType is
            "RelativeToTallestObject"]]>
        </text>
      </staticText>
    </elementGroup>
    <staticText>
      <reportElement width="250" y="25" x="0" height="24"
                     positionType="Float"/>
      <box border="Thin"/>
      <text>
        <![CDATA[This text is here to stretch the band a bit
          more.]]>
      </text>
    </staticText>
  </band>
 </detail>
</jasperReport>
```

After compiling the above JRXML template, and filling the resulting Jasper template, we should see a report like the following:

Once again we decided to display borders around every element, to make it clear where an element's boundaries are. As we can see in the screenshot, the static text is stretched to match the height of the tallest object. This is because we set the value of the stretchType property of <reportElement> to be RelativeToTallestObject.

Notice the <elementGroup> element in the above JRXML template. The purpose of this element is to group elements together so that we can better control the behavior of report elements when one of them stretches. The RelativeToTallestObject stretch type will stretch the appropriate element to match the height of the tallest object in the element's group. All elements between `<elementGroup>` and `</elementGroup>` are in the same group. The `<elementGroup>` element can have other nested `<elementGroup>` elements. If no `<elementGroup>` element is defined inside a `<band>`, then all elements inside the band are considered to be in the same group.

# Using the <frame> Element

JasperReports 1.1 introduced a new report element, the `<frame>` element. The `<frame>` element allows us to group elements together and give them a common look. For example, we can set the background color of the frame and it will be inherited across all elements contained within the frame. Frames also provide a straightforward way of placing a border around multiple report elements. The following JRXML template is a new version of the example in the previous section. It has been modified to illustrate the use of frames.

```xml
<?xml version="1.0" encoding="UTF-8"?>
<!DOCTYPE jasperReport PUBLIC "//JasperReports//DTD Report Design//EN"
 "http://jasperreports.sourceforge.net/dtds/jasperreport.dtd">
<jasperReport name="FrameDemo">
<field name="lots_of_data" class="java.lang.String"/>
<detail>
  <band height="60">
    <frame>
      <reportElement x="0" y="0" width="555" height="60"
                     mode="Opaque" backcolor="lightGray"/>
      <box border="Dotted" padding="1"/>
      <textField isStretchWithOverflow="true">
        <reportElement x="0" y="0" width="100" height="24"/>
        <box border="Thin"/>
        <textFieldExpression class="java.lang.String">
          <![CDATA[$F{lots_of_data}]]>
        </textFieldExpression>
      </textField>
      <textField isStretchWithOverflow="true">
        <reportElement x="101" y="0" width="150" height="24"/>
        <box border="Thin"/>
        <textFieldExpression class="java.lang.String">
          <![CDATA[$F{lots_of_data}]]>
        </textFieldExpression>
      </textField>
      <staticText>
        <reportElement width="290" y="0" x="252" height="24"
                       stretchType="RelativeToTallestObject"/>
        <box border="Thin"/>
```

```
        <text>
          <![CDATA[staticText element stretchType is
            "RelativeToTallestObject"]]>
        </text>
      </staticText>
      <staticText>
      <reportElement width="250" y="25" x="0" height="24"
                     positionType="Float"/>
      <box border="Thin"/>
      <text>
        <![CDATA[This text is here to stretch the band a bit more.]]>
      </text>
      </staticText>
    </frame>
  </band>
 </detail>
</jasperReport>
```

In this JRXML template, we replaced the `<elementGroup>` element in the previous example with a `<frame>` element and slightly modified some of the element's sizes. We added a `<reportElement>` sub-element to the `<frame>` element to set the frame to have a light gray background. We then added a `<box>` element to set the frame's element. Since `<reportElement>` and `<box>` apply for the whole frame, they are applied to all the elements inside the frame. After compiling and filling the above JRXML template, it should generate a report like the following:

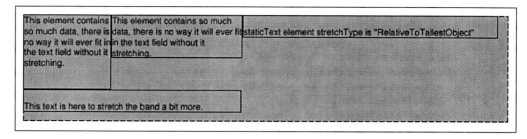

The code to generate the report is similar to what we have seen before. Therefore, we are not showing it.

# Hiding Repeated Values

Sometimes report elements can have the same value over and over. For example, the report we created in the *Grouping Report Data* section is sorted by model number. For aircraft with the same model, we see the model number repeated over and over again. Perhaps, the report would be easier to read if we printed the model number only when it is different from the previous one. This will improve report readability, since the person reading the report would not have to look at the model number unless it is different from the previous one. In the following example, we will modify the JRXML template discussed in that section to accomplish this:

```
<?xml version="1.0" encoding="UTF-8"?>
<!DOCTYPE jasperReport PUBLIC "//JasperReports//DTD Report Design//EN"
  "http://jasperreports.sourceforge.net/dtds/jasperreport.dtd">
<jasperReport name="IsPrintRepeatedValuesDemo">
  <queryString>
      <![CDATA[select a.tail_num, a.aircraft_serial, am.model, a.state
              from aircraft a, aircraft_models am
              where a.aircraft_model_code = am.aircraft_model_code
              and a.country = 'US' and state like 'A%'
              order by state, model]]>
  </queryString>
  <field name="tail_num" class="java.lang.String"/>
  <field name="aircraft_serial" class="java.lang.String"/>
  <field name="model" class="java.lang.String"/>
  <field name="state" class="java.lang.String"/>
  <group name="StateGroup">
    <groupExpression>
      <![CDATA[$F{state}]]>
    </groupExpression>
    <groupHeader>
      <band height="40">
        <staticText>
          <reportElement x="0" y="10" width="115" height="20"/>
          <textElement>
            <font isBold="true"/>
          </textElement>
          <text>Aircraft Registered In:</text>
        </staticText>
        <textField>
          <reportElement x="116" y="10" width="20" height="20"/>
          <textFieldExpression>$F{state}</textFieldExpression>
        </textField>
      </band>
    </groupHeader>
    <groupFooter>
```

```
      <band height="40">
        <staticText>
          <reportElement x="0" y="10" width="140" height="20"/>
          <textElement>
            <font isBold="true"/>
          </textElement>
          <text>End Aircraft Registered In:</text>
        </staticText>
        <textField>
          <reportElement x="141" y="10" width="20" height="20"/>
          <textFieldExpression>$F{state}</textFieldExpression>
        </textField>
      </band>
    </groupFooter>
  </group>
  <detail>
    <band height="20">
      <textField>
        <reportElement x="56" y="0" height="20" width="164"
                       isPrintRepeatedValues="false"/>
        <textFieldExpression>
          <![CDATA["Model: " + $F{model}]]>
        </textFieldExpression>
      </textField>
      <staticText>
        <reportElement x="220" y="0" height="20" width="65"/>
        <text>Tail Number:</text>
      </staticText>
      <textField>
        <reportElement x="286" y="0" height="20" width="84"/>
        <textFieldExpression>
          <![CDATA[$F{tail_num}]]>
        </textFieldExpression>
      </textField>
      <staticText>
        <reportElement x="380" y="0" height="20" width="75"/>
        <text>Serial Number:</text>
      </staticText>
      <textField>
        <reportElement x="456" y="0" height="20" width="94"/>
        <textFieldExpression>
```

```
        <![CDATA[$F{aircraft_serial}]]>
      </textFieldExpression>
    </textField>
  </band>
 </detail>
</jasperReport>
```

The two main differences between this JRXML template and the one discussed in the *Grouping Report Data* section is that we consolidated the `<staticText>` rendering the string `Model` and the `<textField>` rendering the `Model` field into a single `<textField>` element. The other, and more significant change, is that we set the `isPrintRepeatedValues` element in the corresponding `<reportElement>` element to `false`. After compiling the JRXML template, filling the resulting Jasper template, and exporting the resulting report, we should see a report like the following:

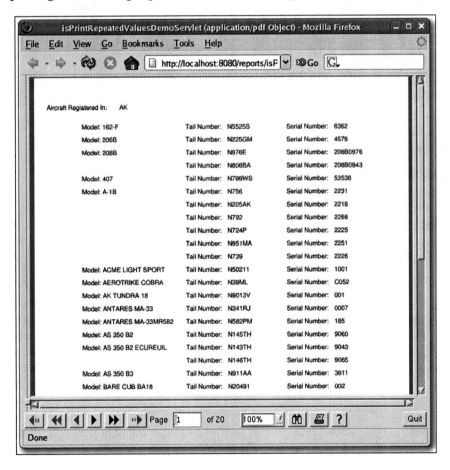

As we can see from the screenshot, the aircraft model is only displayed when the model number changes. This layout makes it a lot easier to see which aircraft are of the same model.

 When setting isPrintRepeatedValues="false" in a
<reportElement> element inside an <image> element,
the image will not be displayed repeatedly, unless its
isUsingCache attribute is set to true and its corresponding
image expression is the same for each row. Adding images to a
report is discussed in detail in the next chapter.

# Subreports

One nice feature of JasperReports is that it allows incorporating a report within another report, that is, one report can be a subreport of another. Subreports allow us to keep report designs simple, since we can create many simple reports and encapsulate them into a master report.

Let us create a more detailed version of the report discussed in the previous section. This new version divides the report on the number of aircraft in the city they are registered to. We will create one report that displays the aircraft registered in each city for a particular state, and use that report as a subreport for a master report that divides the aircraft by state. The JRXML template for the subreport is as follows:

```
<?xml version="1.0" encoding="UTF-8"?>
<!DOCTYPE jasperReport PUBLIC "//JasperReports//DTD Report Design//EN"
  "http://jasperreports.sourceforge.net/dtds/jasperreport.dtd">
<jasperReport name="AircraftCityReport">
  <parameter name="state" class="java.lang.String"/>
  <parameter name="city" class="java.lang.String"/>
  <queryString>
    <![CDATA[select a.tail_num, a.aircraft_serial, am.model, a.state
        from aircraft a, aircraft_models am
        where a.aircraft_model_code = am.aircraft_model_code
        and a.country = 'US' and a.state = $P{state}
        and a.city = $P{city}
        order by model]]>
  </queryString>
  <field name="tail_num" class="java.lang.String"/>
  <field name="aircraft_serial" class="java.lang.String"/>
  <field name="model" class="java.lang.String"/>
```

```
<title>
   <band height="30">
     <textField>
       <reportElement x="0" y="0" width="300" height="24"/>
       <textElement isStyledText="true"/>
       <textFieldExpression>
         <![CDATA["<style isBold=\"true\"
                   pdfFontName=\"Helvetica-Bold\">Aircraft
                   Registered in " +  $P{city} + ", " +
                   $P{state} + "</style>"]]>
       </textFieldExpression>
     </textField>
   </band>
</title>
<pageHeader>
   <band height="30">
     <staticText>
       <reportElement width="100" x="0" y="0" height="30"/>
       <textElement isStyledText="true" verticalAlignment="Middle"/>
       <text>
         <![CDATA[<style isBold="true" pdfFontName=
                 "Helvetica-Bold">Model</style>]]>
       </text>
     </staticText>
     <staticText>
       <reportElement width="100" x="110" y="0" height="30"/>
       <textElement isStyledText="true" verticalAlignment="Middle"/>
       <text>
         <![CDATA[<style isBold="true" pdfFontName="Helvetica-Bold">
                 Tail Number</style>]]>
       </text>
     </staticText>
     <staticText>
       <reportElement width="105" x="220" y="0" height="30"/>
       <textElement isStyledText="true" verticalAlignment="Middle"/>
       <text>
         <![CDATA[<style isBold="true" pdfFontName="Helvetica-Bold">
                 Serial Number</style>]]>
       </text>
     </staticText>
```

```
        </band>
    </pageHeader>
    <detail>
      <band height="24">
        <textField>
          <reportElement x="0" y="0" width="100" height="24"/>
            <textElement verticalAlignment="Middle"/>
            <textFieldExpression>
              <![CDATA[$F{model}]]>
            </textFieldExpression>
        </textField>
        <textField>
          <reportElement x="110" y="0" width="100" height="24"/>
            <textElement verticalAlignment="Middle"/>
            <textFieldExpression>
              <![CDATA[$F{tail_num}]]>
            </textFieldExpression>
        </textField>
        <textField>
          <reportElement x="220" y="0" width="100" height="24"/>
            <textElement verticalAlignment="Middle"/>
            <textFieldExpression>
              <![CDATA[$F{aircraft_serial}]]>
            </textFieldExpression>
        </textField>
      </band>
    </detail>
</jasperReport>
```

As we can see, we did not have to do anything special to make this report a subreport. This is because any report can be used as a subreport. Let us see what the parent report's JRXML looks like.

```
<?xml version="1.0" encoding="UTF-8"?>
<!DOCTYPE jasperReport PUBLIC "//JasperReports//DTD Report Design//EN"
  "http://jasperreports.sourceforge.net/dtds/jasperreport.dtd">
<jasperReport name="AircraftStateReport">
  <parameter name="state" class="java.lang.String"/>
  <queryString>
    <![CDATA[select city
```

```
            from aircraft
            where state = $P{state}]]>
    </queryString>
    <field name="city" class="java.lang.String"/>
    <title>
      <band height="30">
        <textField>
          <reportElement x="0" y="0" width="300" height="24"/>
          <textElement isStyledText="true"/>
          <textFieldExpression>
            <![CDATA["<style isBold=\"true\"
                    pdfFontName=\"Helvetica-Bold\">Aircraft
                    Registered in " +  $P{state} + "</style>"]]>
          </textFieldExpression>
        </textField>
      </band>
    </title>
    <detail>
      <band height="30">
        <subreport>
          <reportElement x="0" y="0" height="30" width="500"
                         isPrintWhenDetailOverflows="true"/>
          <subreportParameter name="state">
            <subreportParameterExpression>
              <![CDATA[$P{state}]]>
            </subreportParameterExpression>
          </subreportParameter>
          <subreportParameter name="city">
            <subreportParameterExpression>
              <![CDATA[$F{city}]]>
            </subreportParameterExpression>
          </subreportParameter>
          <connectionExpression>
            <![CDATA[$P{REPORT_CONNECTION}]]>
          </connectionExpression>
          <subreportExpression class="java.lang.String">
            <![CDATA["http://localhost:8080/reports
            /reports/AircraftCityReport.jasper"]]>
          </subreportExpression>
        </subreport>
      </band>
    </detail>
</jasperReport>
```

As can be seen in the preceding JRXML, we place a subreport into a master report by using the `<subreport>` element. The `<subreportParameter>` element is used to pass parameters to the subreport. The `<connectionExpression>` is used to pass a `java.sql.Connection` to the subreport. However, it only needs to be used if the subreport template needs a database connection (as opposed to a datasource) to be filled. Recall from Chapter 5 that the built-in report parameter `REPORT_CONNECTION` resolves a reference to the instance of `java.util.Connection` passed to the report. If the parent report uses a datasource instead of a Connection, and the subreport needs a Connection, the easiest way to pass the Connection to the subreport is to pass it as a parameter to the parent report. The parameter can then pass it to the subreport by using the corresponding parameter name in `<connectionExpression>`. The `<subreportExpression>` indicates where to find the compiled report template for the subreport.

When the `class` attribute of `<subreportExpression>` is a String, JasperReports attempts to resolve a URL for the String contents. If that fails, it assumes that the String contents represent the template's location in the file system and tries to load the report template from disk. If that fails too, it assumes the String represents a CLASSPATH location and attempts to load the report template from the CLASSPATH. If all of these fail, JasperReports will throw an exception since it will not be able to find the template for the subreport.

Other valid values for the `class` attribute of a report expression include `net.sf.jasperreports.engine.JasperReport`, `java.io.File`, `java.io.InputStream`, and `java.net.URL`. The most common way to obtain these is to have the Java code filling the report pass them as a parameter and resolve them inside the `<subreportExpression>` tags using the `$P{paramName}` syntax we have seen before.

After compiling, filling, and exporting this JRXML template, the following report will be generated:

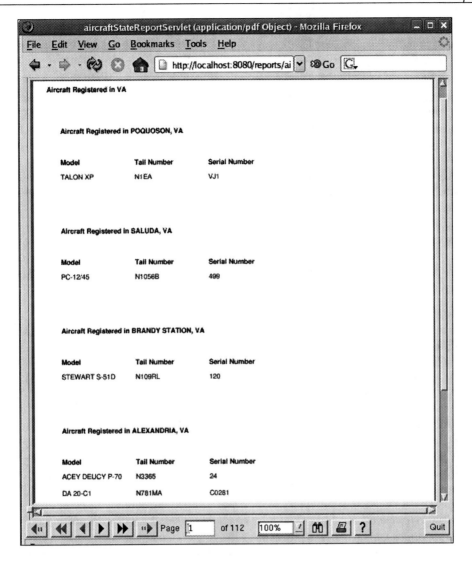

Each record in the report is a subreport. Each time we pass a different city as a parameter, a report for the appropriate city is generated.

The `<subreport>` JRXML element can contain a number of sub-elements that were not used in this example. These sub-elements include:

- `<dataSourceExpression>`: This is used to pass a datasource to the subreport. This datasource is usually obtained from a parameter in the master report or by using the built-in `REPORT_DATA_SOURCE` parameter to pass the parent report's datasource to the subreport.

- `<parametersMapExpression>`: This is used to pass a map containing report parameters to the subreport. The map is usually obtained from a parameter in the master report, or by using the built-in REPORTS_PARAMETERS_MAP parameter to pass the parent report's parameters to the subreport.

- `<returnValue>`: This is used to assign the value of one of the subreport's variables to one of the master report's variables. The subreportVariable attribute is used to indicate the subreport variable to use, and the toVariable attribute is used to indicate the master report variable to use.

One last note about subreports is that subreports can have other subreports, which in turn can have more subreports. There is no limit to the subreport nesting level.

# Summary

In this chapter, we discussed several of JasperReports features that allow us to control the layout of a report.

By setting the appropriate attributes of the `<jasperReport>` JRXML element, we can control report-wide layout properties like margins, page width, page orientation, and others. Text properties like size and font can be set by using report styles or by setting the appropriate attributes of the `<text>` JRXML element. We can use styled text to modify the style of individual words, phrases, or sentences by setting the isStyledText attribute of the `<textElement>` JRXML element.

We learned to add multiple columns to a report by setting the columnCount attribute of the `<jasperReport>` JRXML element as well as to divide report data into logical groups by using the `<group>` JRXML element. The chapter also dealt with displaying dynamic data in a report by using report expressions, using report variables to encapsulate report expressions, and performing automated report calculations.

The chapter discussed how to allow text fields to stretch to accommodate large amounts of data by setting the isStretchWithOverflow attribute of the `<textField>` JRXML element to `true`. We went about setting the appropriate attributes of the `<reportElement>` JRXML element, to control the layout of individual report elements, including their size, width, height, and how they react to having another element stretch beyond its declared size. We also learned to set properties that affect a group of elements by grouping them in a frame via the `<frame>` JRXML element as well as to set the isPrintRepeatedValues attributes of the `<reportElement>` JRXML element to `false` to avoid printing repeated values between datasource records. Lastly, we created subreports by taking advantage of the `<subReport>` JRXML element.

# 7
# Adding Charts and Graphics to Reports

All the reports we have seen so far contain only textual data. JasperReports has the capability to create reports with graphical data in them, including simple geometric shapes, images, and charts. Adding graphical representation of the data makes it easier to visualize. Moreover, adding images and other graphical elements allows us to create more appealing reports. In this chapter, we will cover how to take advantage of JasperReports' graphical features.

The following topics will be covered in this chapter:

- Adding simple geometrical shapes to a report
- Adding images to a report
- Adding different types of 2-D and 3-D charts to a report

## Adding Geometrical Shapes to a Report

JasperReports supports adding lines, rectangles, and ellipses to a report. This capability allows us to display simple graphics in a report. The following sections will discuss each one of these elements in detail.

## Adding Lines to a Report

Lines can be added to a report by using the JRXML `<line>` element. Lines are drawn as a diagonal from one corner of the area, defined by the `<reportElement>` sub-element, to the other. The JRXML `<line>` element has a single attribute called `direction`. This attribute has two valid values, namely, `BottomUp`, which indicates that the line will go from the bottom corner to the top corner, and `TopDown`, which indicates that the line will go from the top corner to the bottom corner. The default value for the `direction` attribute is `TopDown`.

The following example demonstrates the use of the `<line>` element:

```xml
<?xml version="1.0" encoding="UTF-8"?>
<!DOCTYPE jasperReport PUBLIC "//JasperReports//DTD Report Design//EN"
 "http://jasperreports.sourceforge.net/dtds/jasperreport.dtd">
<jasperReport name="LineDemoReport">
  <detail>
    <band height="100">
      <line>
        <reportElement x="0" y="0" width="555" height="25"/>
      </line>
      <line direction="BottomUp">
        <reportElement x="0" y="26" width="555" height="25"/>
      </line>
      <line>
        <reportElement x="0" y="50" width="0" height="25"/>
      </line>
      <line>
        <reportElement x="0" y="75" width="555" height="0"/>
      </line>
    </band>
  </detail>
</jasperReport>
```

After compiling the JRXML template and filling the resulting binary Jasper template, we should get a report that looks like the following:

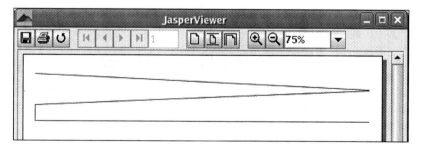

As can be seen in the example, the default value for `direction` is `TopDown`. Moreover, since there is no way to directly create a vertical or horizontal line, one way that we can achieve this is by setting either the width (for vertical lines) or height (for horizontal lines) of the `<reportElement>` sub-element of `<line>`, to be 0. Notice how the lines go from one corner of the area defined by `<reportElement>` to the other. Altering the value of the `direction` attribute allows us to define which way the line will slope.

# Adding Rectangles to a Report

Adding a rectangle to a report can be achieved by using the JRXML `<rectangle>` element. A rectangle simply outlines the area defined by its `<reportElement>` sub-element. We can create rectangles with round corners by setting the `radius` property of the `<rectangle>` element. The following JRXML template illustrates how to create rectangles in a report:

```xml
<?xml version="1.0" encoding="UTF-8"?>
<!DOCTYPE jasperReport PUBLIC "-//JasperReports//DTD Report Design//
  EN" "http://jasperreports.sourceforge.net/dtds/jasperreport.dtd">
<jasperReport name="RectangleDemoReport">
  <detail>
    <band height="100">
      <rectangle>
        <reportElement x="0" y="0" width="555" height="30"/>
      </rectangle>
      <rectangle radius="5">
        <reportElement x="0" y="70" width="555" height="30"
                       forecolor="lightGray"/>
        <graphicElement pen="4Point"/>
      </rectangle>
    </band>
  </detail>
</jasperReport>
```

After compiling the above JRXML template, and filling the resulting binary Jasper template, we should see a report like the following:

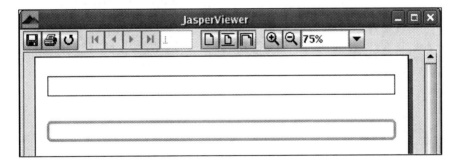

Notice how the line outlining the second rectangle is thicker than the first one. This is because we used the `<graphicElement>` sub-element of the `<rectangle>` element. Just as every text element can contain a `<textElement>` sub-element, every graphic element can contain a `<graphicElement>` sub-element.

The `<graphicElement>` sub-element has only two attributes. The first one is called pen, and is used to control the thickness of the line outlining the graphic element. Valid values for the pen attribute include 1Point, 2Point, 4Point, Dotted, None, and Thin. Each of these gives a different thickness to the line outlining the element. The other attribute of `<graphicElement>` is called fill. It controls the pattern to be used for painting the inside area of the element. Currently, JasperReports supports only one value for this element, Solid, which fills the inside of the element with solid color.

# Adding Ellipses to a Report

Ellipses are added to a report by using the JRXML `<ellipse>` element. The `<ellipse>` element contains no attributes. Its shape is determined by its `<reportElement>` width and height.

The following JRXML template illustrates how to add ellipses to a report:

```
<?xml version="1.0" encoding="UTF-8"?>
<!DOCTYPE jasperReport PUBLIC "-//JasperReports//DTD Report Design//EN"
  "http://jasperreports.sourceforge.net/dtds/jasperreport.dtd">
<jasperReport name="EllipseDemoReport">
  <detail>
    <band height="100">
      <ellipse>
        <reportElement x="280" y="0" height="20" width="20"/>
      </ellipse>
      <ellipse>
        <reportElement x="280" y="20" height="50" width="20"/>
      </ellipse>
      <ellipse>
        <reportElement x="275" y="60" height="40" width="10"/>
      </ellipse>
      <ellipse>
        <reportElement x="295" y="60" height="40" width="10"/>
      </ellipse>
      <ellipse>
        <reportElement x="297" y="25" height="10" width="30"/>
      </ellipse>
      <ellipse>
        <reportElement x="253" y="25" height="10" width="30"/>
      </ellipse>
    </band>
  </detail>
</jasperReport>
```

After compiling the above JRXML template and filling the resultant binary Jasper template, we should see a report like the following:

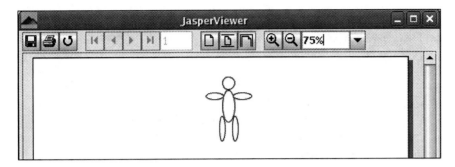

As we can see from the example, we can create a circle by using the same values for the `width` and `height` attributes of the `<reportElement>` element inside the `<ellipse>` element.

# Adding Images to a Report

Images can be added to a report by using the JRXML `<image>` element. Report images can be loaded from memory, from disk, or from a URL. The location from where to obtain the image is determined by the `<imageExpression>` sub-element of the `<image>` element.

The following example illustrates how to add an image to a report:

```
<?xml version="1.0" encoding="UTF-8"?>
<!DOCTYPE jasperReport PUBLIC "-//JasperReports//DTD Report Design//EN"
  "http://jasperreports.sourceforge.net/dtds/jasperreport.dtd">
<jasperReport name="ImageDemoReport">
  <background>
    <band height="391">
      <image>
        <reportElement x="65" y="0" width="391" height="391"/>
        <imageExpression class="java.lang.String">
          <![CDATA["reports/company_logo.gif"]]>
        </imageExpression>
      </image>
    </band>
  </background>
</jasperReport>
```

After compiling this JRXML template and filling the resulting binary Jasper template, we should have a report that looks like the following:

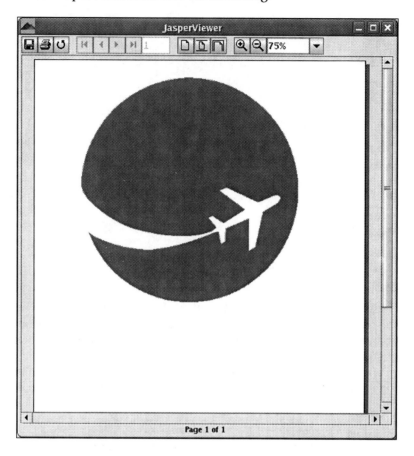

In this example, we set the band's width and height to match the image size. Sometimes the image is not available at the time of report design. Therefore, we might not know the exact image dimensions. We can control how the image will look, if its dimensions do not match the area defined by the `<reportElement>` attribute of the `<image>` element. This can be accomplished by using the `scaleImage` attribute of the `<image>` element. Valid values for the `scaleImage` attribute include:

- `Clip`: This includes only the portion of the image that fits into the area defined by `<reportElement>`.

- `FillFrame`: The image will stretch or squash vertically and/or horizontally to fit in the area defined by `<reportElement>`.

- RetainShape: The image will resize itself to fit in the area defined by
  <reportElement>. If the image width changes to fit in this area, the height will
  be proportionally changed so that the image retains it shape, and vice versa.

# Attributes of the <image> Element

The <image> element contains other attributes that allow us to control how the
image will be displayed in the report. The following sections summarize most of
these attributes.

## evaluationTime

This attribute determines when the associated <imageExpression> will be
evaluated. The valid values for this attribute are listed below:

- Band: The expression is evaluated when the containing band has rendered all
  other components.
- Column: The expression is evaluated when the end of the current column
  is reached.
- Group: The expression is evaluated when the group, indicated by the
  evaluationGroup attribute, changes.
- Now: The expression is evaluated when filling the containing band. This is the
  default value.
- Page: The expression is evaluated when the end of the current page
  is reached.
- Report: The expression is evaluated when the end of the report is reached.

## evaluationGroup

When evaluationTime is Group, this attribute determines the group name to be
used to evaluate the associated <imageExpresson>. The value for this attribute must
match the name of the group we would like to use as the evaluationGroup.

## hAlign

The hAlign attribute indicates the horizontal alignment of the image. The valid
values for this attribute are listed below:

- Center: The image will be centered.
- Left: The image will be left-aligned. This is the default value.
- Right: The image will be right-aligned.

# vAlign

The `vAlign` attribute indicates the vertical alignment of the image. The valid values for this attribute are listed below:

- `Bottom`: The image will be placed at the bottom of the area defined by its `<reportElement>`.
- `Middle`: The image will be vertically centered between the top and bottom boundaries defined by its `<reportElement>`.
- `Top`: The image will be placed at the top of the area defined by its `<reportElement>`. This is the default value.

# isLazy

This attribute determines whether the image is loaded when the report is filled, or when the report is viewed or exported. The valid values for this attribute are listed below:

- `true`: The image will be loaded when the report is viewed or exported.
- `false`: The image will be loaded when the report is filled. This is the default value for this attribute.

# isUsingCache

This attribute indicates whether images loaded from the same `<imageExpression>` will be cached. The valid values for this attribute are listed below:

- `true`: The image will be cached. This is the default value.
- `false`: The image will not be cached.

# onErrorType

This determines the report's behavior when there is a problem loading the image. The valid values for this attribute are listed below:

- `Blank`: This value will display blank space instead of the image.
- `Error`: This value will throw an exception and the report will not be filled or viewed. It is the default value for this attribute.
- `Icon`: This value displays an icon indicating a missing image.

The `<image>` element contains other attributes to support hyperlinks and bookmarks. These attributes are discussed in detail in Chapter 8.

# Adding Charts to a Report

JasperReports supports several kinds of charts including pie charts, bar charts, XY bar charts, stacked bar charts, line charts, XY line charts, area charts, XY area charts, scatter-plot charts, bubble charts, time-series charts, high-low charts, and candlestick charts. We will discuss each one of these in detail, but before we do so, let us discuss some common properties across all charts.

There is a JRXML element used to create each type of chart. All of these elements will be discussed in subsequent sections. Each of these elements must contain a `<chart>` element as one of its sub-elements. The `<chart>` element must contain a `<reportElement>` to define the chart's dimensions and position as one of its sub-elements. It may also contain a `<box>` element to draw a border around the chart, a `<chartTitle>` sub-element to define and format the chart's title, and a `<chartSubtitle>` sub-element to define and format the chart's subtitle.

# Attributes of the <chart> Element

The JRXML `<chart>` element contains a number of attributes that allow us to control the way a chart looks and behaves. The most commonly used attributes are listed in the following sections.

## customizerClass

This is the name of a class (optional) that can be used to customize the chart. The value for this element must be a String containing the name of a customizer class.

## evaluationGroup

When `evaluationTime` is `Group`, this attribute determines the name of the group to be used to evaluate the chart's expressions. The value for this attribute must match the name of the group we would like to use as the chart's evaluation group.

## evaluationTime

This attribute determines when the chart's expression will be evaluated. The valid values for this attribute are listed below:

- `Band`: The chart expression is evaluated when the containing band has finished rendering all other elements.
- `Column`: The chart expression is evaluated when rendering all other elements in the current column is finished.

- `Group`: The chart expression is evaluated when the group specified by `evaluationGroup` changes.

- `Now`: The chart expression is evaluated when its containing band is filled. This is the default value for this attribute.

- `Page`: The chart expression is evaluated when rendering all other elements in the same page is finished.

- `Report`: The chart expression is evaluated when rendering all other elements in the report is finished.

## isShowLegend

This attribute is used to determine if a chart legend will be displayed on the report. The valid values for this attribute are listed below:

- `true`: A legend will be displayed on the report. This is the default value.

- `false`: A legend will not be displayed on the report.

# Chart Customization

JasperReports uses `JFreeChart` as the underlying charting library. `JFreeChart` contains features not directly supported by JasperReports. By supplying a customizer class via the `customizerClass` attribute, we can take advantage of `JFreeChart` features.

All customizer classes must implement `net.sf.jasperreports.engine.JRChartCustomizer`. This interface contains a single method. The method signature is:

```
customize(org.jfree.chart.JFreeChart chart, JRChart jasperChart)
```

`org.jfree.chart.JFreeChart` is `JFreeChart`'s representation of a `chart`; `JRChart` is JasperReports representation of a `jasperChart`. Since the `customize()` method is automatically called by JasperReports when filling a report, we don't need to worry about instantiating and initializing instances of these classes.

Chart customization is more of a `JFreeChart` feature rather than a JasperReports feature. Therefore, an example has not been shown.

More information about `JFreeChart` can be found at `http://www.jfree.org/jfreechart/`.

The JRXML `<chart>` element contains some attributes used to support bookmarks and hyperlinks. These attributes are discussed in detail in Chapter 8.

# Chart Datasets

Another common property across all chart types is a <dataset>. Each chart type contains different sub-elements to define a chart's expressions that define the data used to generate the chart, yet all of these sub-elements contain a <dataset> element that defines when the chart's expressions are evaluated and reset.

## Attributes of the <dataset> Element

The following sections describe all of the attributes for the JRXML <dataset> element.

### incrementType

This attribute determines when to recalculate the value of the chart expression. The valid values for this attribute are listed below:

- Column: The chart expression is recalculated at the end of each column.
- Group: The chart expression is recalculated when the group specified by incrementGroup changes.
- None: The chart expression is recalculated with every record. This is the default value.
- Page: The chart expression is recalculated at the end of every page.
- Report: The chart expression is recalculated once, at the end of the report.

### incrementGroup

When the incrementType is Group, this attribute determines the name of the group at which the chart expression is recalculated. The value for this attribute must match the name of a group declared in the JRXML report template.

### resetType

This attribute determines when the value of the chart expression is to be reset. The valid values for this attribute are listed below:

- Column: The chart expression is reset at the beginning of each column.
- Group: The chart expression is reset when the group specified by incrementGroup changes.
- None: The chart expression is never reset.
- Page: The chart expression is reset at the beginning of every page.
- Report: The chart expression is reset once, at the beginning of the report. This is the default value.

## resetGroup

When `resetType` is `Group`, this attribute determines the name of the group at which the chart expression value is reset. The value for this attribute must match the name of any group declared in the JRXML report template.

# Plotting Charts

Another common JRXML element through all chart types is the `<plot>` element. The JRXML `<plot>` element allows us to define several of the chart's characteristics like orientation and background color.

# Attributes of the <plot> Element

All attributes for the JRXML `<plot>` element are described in the following sections.

## backcolor

This attribute defines the chart's background color. Any six digit hexadecimal value is a valid value for this attribute. The hexadecimal value must be preceded by a `#`. It represents the RGB value of the chart's background color.

## backgroundAlpha

This attribute defines the transparency of the chart's background color. The valid values for this attribute include any decimal number between `0` and `1`, inclusive. The higher the number, the less transparent the background will be. The default value is `1`.

## foregroundAlpha

This attribute defines the transparency of the chart's foreground colors. The valid values for this attribute include any decimal number between `0` and `1`, inclusive. The higher the number, the less transparent the background will be. The default value is `1`.

## orientation

This attribute defines the chart's orientation (vertical or horizontal). The valid values for this attribute are listed below:

- `Horizontal`
- `Vertical`

Default value is `Vertical`. Now that we have seen the attributes that are common to all types of charts, let us look at all the different types of charts that JasperReports supports.

# Pie Charts

JasperReports allows us to create pie charts both in two and three dimensions. The procedure to create 2-D and 3-D pie charts is almost identical. Therefore, we will discuss them together.

Suppose, we are asked to create a report indicating the most popular aircraft models registered in a particular city, in the order they appear in the FlightStats database (refer to Chapter 4). This kind of information can be nicely summarized in a pie chart. The following screenshot shows a report displaying this information for the city of Washington, DC.

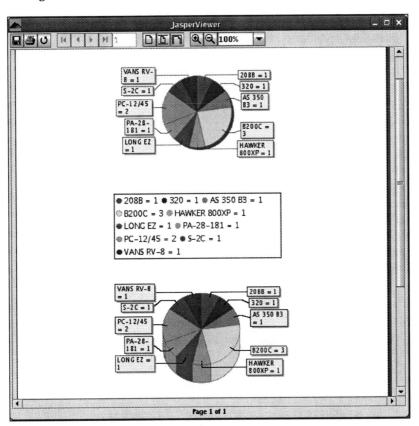

The JRXML to create the report looks like this:

```
<?xml version="1.0" encoding="UTF-8"?>
<!DOCTYPE jasperReport PUBLIC "//JasperReports//DTD Report Design//EN"
  "http://jasperreports.sourceforge.net/dtds/jasperreport.dtd">
<jasperReport name="PieChartDemoReport">
```

```xml
<queryString>
  <![CDATA[select am.model
          from aircraft a, aircraft_models am
          where city='WASHINGTON'
          and state='DC'
          and a.aircraft_model_code = am.aircraft_model_code
          order by model]]>
</queryString>
<field name="model" class="java.lang.String"/>
<variable name="totalAircraft" class="java.lang.Integer"
             calculation="Count" resetType="Group"
             resetGroup="modelGroup">
  <variableExpression>
    <![CDATA[$F{model}]]>
  </variableExpression>
  <initialValueExpression>
    <![CDATA[new java.lang.Integer(0)]]>
  </initialValueExpression>
</variable>
<group name="modelGroup">
  <groupExpression>
    <![CDATA[$F{model}]]>
  </groupExpression>
</group>
<summary>
  <band height="750">
    <!-- Start 2D Pie Chart -->
    <pieChart>
      <chart evaluationTime="Report">
        <reportElement x="135" y="0" width="270" height="350"/>
      </chart>
      <pieDataset>
        <dataset incrementType="None"/>
        <keyExpression>
          <![CDATA[$F{model}]]>
        </keyExpression>
        <valueExpression>
          <![CDATA[$V{totalAircraft}]]>
        </valueExpression>
      </pieDataset>
      <piePlot>
        <plot/>
      </piePlot>
    </pieChart>
    <!-- End 2D Pie Chart -->
```

```
  <!-- Start 3D Pie Chart -->
<pie3DChart>
  <chart evaluationTime="Report" isShowLegend="false">
    <reportElement x="125" y="375" width="300" height="200"/>
  </chart>
  <pieDataset>
    <dataset incrementType="None"/>
    <keyExpression>
      <![CDATA[$F{model}]]>
    </keyExpression>
    <valueExpression>
      <![CDATA[$V{totalAircraft}]]>
    </valueExpression>
  </pieDataset>
  <pie3DPlot>
    <plot/>
  </pie3DPlot>
</pie3DChart>
  <!-- End 3D Pie Chart -->
</band>
</summary>
</jasperReport>
```

As we can see from this example, the JRXML element to create a two-dimensional pie chart is `<pieChart>`, and the JRXML element to create a three-dimensional pie chart is called `<pie3DChart>`. Just like all JRXML chart elements, these elements contain a `<chart>` sub-element. They also contain a `<pieDataset>` sub-element, which in turn contains the `<dataset>` element for the chart, a `<keyExpression>` sub-element, and a `<valueExpression>` sub-element. The `<keyExpression>` sub-element contains a report expression indicating what to use as a key in the chart. The `<valueExpression>` sub-element contains an expression used to calculate the value for the key. The values we see to the left of the equal sign in the chart label correspond to the `<keyExpression>` (aircraft model, in this case). The values we see to the right of the equal sign in the chart label correspond to the `<valueExpression>` (number of aircraft of a particular model, in this case).

In this example, the aircraft model is used as the key. It is represented by the report field called `model`. The value to be used in the chart is the total number of aircrafts of that model, represented by the `totalAircraft` report variable.

`<pieChart>` must contain a `<piePlot>` sub-element containing the chart's `<plot>` element. `<pie3Dchart>` must contain an analogous `<pie3DPlot>` element. Although `<piePlot>` has no attributes, `<pie3DPlot>` has a single optional attribute called `depthFactor`. This attribute indicates the depth (how 'tall' or 'short' the pie chart is) of the 3-D pie chart. Its default value is `0.2`.

# Bar Charts

Just like pie charts, bar charts can be used to illustrate quantitative differences between chart elements. They can be used to display the same data a pie chart displays, but in a different way. One advantage that bar charts have over pie charts is that the same data for more than one category can be displayed.

For example, suppose we are asked to produce a report comparing the number of aircraft registered in Washington, DC with the number of aircraft registered in New York City. Also, the report must illustrate the most popular aircraft models in each city. If we wanted to display this data graphically via a pie chart, we would have to create a pie chart for each city. With a bar chart, we can display the whole picture using a single chart, as can be seen in the following screenshot:

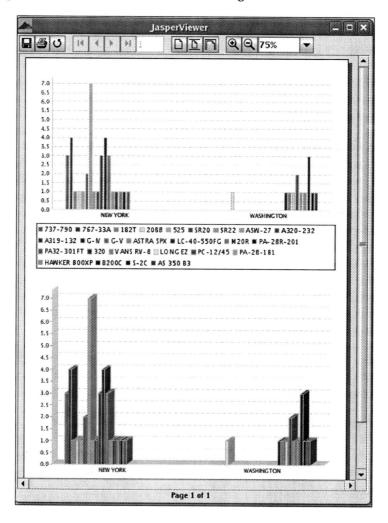

The JRXML template used to generate this report is as follows:

```xml
<?xml version="1.0" encoding="UTF-8"?>
<!DOCTYPE jasperReport PUBLIC "//JasperReports//DTD Report Design//EN"
 "http://jasperreports.sourceforge.net/dtds/jasperreport.dtd">
<jasperReport name="BarChartDemoReport">
  <queryString>
    <![CDATA[(select a.city, am.model
            from aircraft a, aircraft_models am
            where city='NEW YORK'
            and state='NY'
            and a.aircraft_model_code = am.aircraft_model_code
            order by model)
            UNION ALL (select a.city, am.model
                    from aircraft a, aircraft_models am
                    where city='WASHINGTON'
                    and state='DC'
                    and a.aircraft_model_code =
                    am.aircraft_model_code
                    order by model)]]>
  </queryString>
  <field name="city" class="java.lang.String"/>
  <field name="model" class="java.lang.String"/>
  <variable name="totalAircraft" class="java.lang.Integer"
    calculation="Count" resetType="Group" resetGroup="modelGroup">
    <variableExpression>
      <![CDATA[$F{model}]]>
    </variableExpression>
    <initialValueExpression>
      <![CDATA[new java.lang.Integer(0)]]>
    </initialValueExpression>
  </variable>
  <group name="modelGroup">
    <groupExpression>
      <![CDATA[$F{model}]]>
    </groupExpression>
  </group>
  <summary>
    <band height="750">
```

```xml
<!-- Start 2D Bar Chart -->
<barChart>
  <chart evaluationTime="Report">
    <reportElement x="0" y="0" width="555" height="350"/>
  </chart>
  <categoryDataset>
    <dataset incrementType="None"/>
    <categorySeries>
      <seriesExpression>
        <![CDATA[$F{model}]]>
      </seriesExpression>
      <categoryExpression>
        <![CDATA[$F{city}]]>
      </categoryExpression>
      <valueExpression>
        <![CDATA[$V{totalAircraft}]]>
      </valueExpression>
    </categorySeries>
  </categoryDataset>
  <barPlot isShowTickMarks="false">
    <plot/>
  </barPlot>
</barChart>
<!-- End 2D Bar Chart -->
<!-- Start 3D Bar Chart -->
<bar3DChart>
  <chart evaluationTime="Report" isShowLegend="false">
    <reportElement x="0" y="375" width="555" height="350"/>
  </chart>
  <categoryDataset>
    <dataset incrementType="None"/>
    <categorySeries>
      <seriesExpression>
        <![CDATA[$F{model}]]>
      </seriesExpression>
      <categoryExpression>
        <![CDATA[$F{city}]]>
      </categoryExpression>
      <valueExpression>
        <![CDATA[$V{totalAircraft}]]>
      </valueExpression>
```

```
        </categorySeries>
      </categoryDataset>
      <bar3DPlot>
        <plot />
      </bar3DPlot>
    </bar3DChart>
    <!-- End 3D Bar Chart -->
  </band>
 </summary>
</jasperReport>
```

As we can see from the given example, the process used to create bar charts is very similar to creating pie charts. This example creates two bar charts, a two-dimensional one and a three-dimensional one. Let us discuss the two-dimensional one first.

The JRXML element used to create a two-dimensional bar chart is `<barchart>`. Just like all charts in JasperReports, it must contain a `<chart>` sub-element, which contains a `<reportElement>` sub-element defining the chart's dimensions and position.

The `<dataset>` element in a bar chart must be enclosed between `<categoryDataSet>` and `</categoryDataset>` JRXML elements. `<categoryDataSet>` must contain a `<categorySeries>` element. This element defines what data element the bars will represent (aircraft models, in this example). `<categoryDataSet>` must also contain a `<categoryExpression>` element, which defines how the data will be separated into categories for comparison. In the previous example, data is separated by city. The `<valueExpression>` element defines what expression to use to determine the value of each bar in the chart.

If we want to create 3-D bar charts, the JRXML element to use is `<bar3Dchart>`, which works almost exactly the same way as `<barChart>`. The only difference is that the `<plot/>` element must be a sub-element of `<bar3DPlot>`. `<bar3DPlot>` contains three attributes, `isShowLabels`, which determines if labels will be shown in the chart, `xOffset`, and `yOffset`, whose valid values are numeric values indicating the number of pixels to use for the 3-D effect on the x and y axis, respectively.

# XY Line Charts

XY line charts allow us to view the relationship between two numerical values. For our next example, let us suppose we need to generate a report for a flight school to illustrate how much the operating cost will be for flying a particular model of their aircraft. Let us assume the flight school has an inventory of 43 of these aircraft, and that the operating cost per day of each aircraft is $45. The JRXML template to generate a report with a chart illustrating the operating cost would look like this:

```xml
<?xml version="1.0" encoding="UTF-8"?>
<!DOCTYPE jasperReport PUBLIC "//JasperReports//DTD Report Design//EN"
 "http://jasperreports.sourceforge.net/dtds/jasperreport.dtd">
<jasperReport name="XYLineChartReportDemo">
  <queryString>
    <![CDATA[select tail_num
            from aircraft
            where aircraft_model_code = 0033001]]>
  </queryString>
  <field name="tail_num" class="java.lang.String"/>
  <variable name="grandTotalAircraft" class="java.lang.Integer"
          calculation="Count" resetType="Report">
    <variableExpression>
      <![CDATA[$F{tail_num}]]>
    </variableExpression>
    <initialValueExpression>
      <![CDATA[new java.lang.Integer(0)]]>
    </initialValueExpression>
  </variable>
  <summary>
    <band height="750">
      <!-- Start XY Line Chart -->
      <xyLineChart>
        <chart evaluationTime="Report">
          <reportElement x="0" y="0" width="555" height="350"/>
        </chart>
        <xyDataset>
          <dataset incrementType="None"/>
          <xySeries>
            <seriesExpression>
              <![CDATA["CH 2000"]]>
            </seriesExpression>
            <xValueExpression>
              <![CDATA[$V{grandTotalAircraft}]]>
            </xValueExpression>
            <yValueExpression>
              <![CDATA[new Long( $V{grandTotalAircraft}.longValue() *
                      45L)]]>
            </yValueExpression>
```

```
          </xySeries>
        </xyDataset>
        <linePlot>
          <plot/>
        </linePlot>
      </xyLineChart>
      <!-- End XY Line Chart -->
    </band>
  </summary>
</jasperReport>
```

The generated report would look like this:

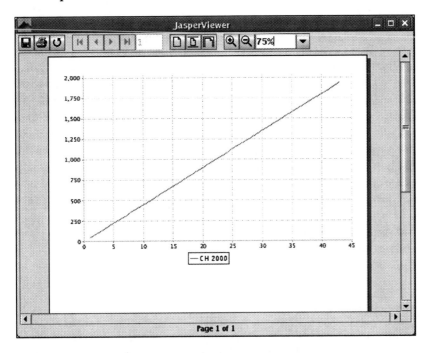

As we can see in the example for XY line chart, the `<dataset>` element must be inside an `<xyDataset>` element. This element has no attributes. In addition to the `<dataset>` element, `<xyDataset>` may contain one or more `<xySeries>` element.

`<xySeries>` may contain a `<seriesExpression>` element, which is used to generate the label at the bottom of the chart in this example. It may also contain an `<xValueExpression>` element and a `<yValueExpression>` element. The last two elements contain report expressions for the X and Y values in the chart, respectively.

# Other Types of Charts

As we have seen in previous examples, all JRXML elements used to display a chart follow a pattern. First, we have the element that determines what chart to plot (`<pieChart>`, `<barChart>`, etc.). Inside that element we have a `<chart>` element, followed by an element enclosing the `<dataset>` element (`<pieDataset>`, `<categoryDataset>`, etc.), followed by another element enclosing the `<plot>` element (`<piePlot>`, `<barPlot>`, etc.). Since all charts follow the same pattern, it would be redundant to show examples for all chart types supported by JasperReports. In the following table, we will discuss the elements used to create all other supported chart types, without explicitly showing examples. The JasperReports project files include examples for all chart types. They can be found in the `demo/samples/charts` directory.

| Chart Type | Chart Element | Dataset Element | Plot Element |
|---|---|---|---|
| XY Bar Chart | `<xyBarChart>` | `<xyDataset>` | `<barPlot>` |
| Stacked Bar Chart | `<stackedBarChart>` | `<categoryDataset>` | `<barPlot>` |
| Line Chart | `<lineChart>` | `<categoryDataset>` | `<linePlot>` |
| Area Chart | `<areaChart>` | `<categoryDataset>` | `<areaPlot>` |
| XY Area Chart | `<xyAreaChart>` | `<xyDataset>` | `<areaPlot>` |
| Scatter Plot Chart | `<scatterChart>` | `<xyDataset>` | `<scatterPlot>` |
| Bubble Chart | `<bubbleChart>` | `<xyzDataset>` | `<bubblePlot>` |
| Time Series Chart | `<timeSeriesChart>` | `<timeSeriesDataset>` | `<timeSeriesPlot>` |
| High Low Chart | `<highLowChart>` | `<highLowDataset>` | `<highLowPlot>` |
| Candlestick Chart | `<candlestickChart>` | `<highLowDataset>` | `<candlestickPlot>` |

You can find details of the attributes for each of these at `http://jasperreports.sourceforge.net/reference/index.html`.

# Summary

In this chapter, we learned to further customize our reports by adding graphical elements. We added geometric figures like rectangles, ellipses, and lines to our reports by using the `<line>`, `<rectangle>`, and `<ellipse>` JRXML elements. Images, such as company logos, can be added to our reports by making use of the `<image>` JRXML element. JasperReports supports several types of charts and these can be easily added to our reports by using the appropriate JRXML element such as `<pieChart>`, `<barChart>`, `<xyLineChart>`, etc.

# 8
# Other JasperReports Features

JasperReports has several features that allow us to create elaborate reports. Some of the features we will cover in this chapter include:

- How to display report text in different languages by using report localization/internationalization
- How to execute snippets of Java code by using scriptlets
- How to create cross-tabulation (crosstab) reports
- How to use subdatasets to run a query with the results of a different query
- How to add anchors, hyperlinks, and bookmarks to reports to ease navigation between report sections
- How to handle large reports using the report virtualization feature of JasperReports

## Report Localization

JasperReports takes advantage of the Java language's internationalization features to generate reports in different languages. The following JRXML template will generate a report displaying a line of text that will be different depending on the locale used:

```
<?xml version="1.0" encoding="UTF-8"?>
<!DOCTYPE jasperReport PUBLIC "//JasperReports//DTD Report Design//EN"
 "http://jasperreports.sourceforge.net/dtds/jasperreport.dtd">
<jasperReport name="LocalizationDemoReport"
  resourceBundle="localizationdemo">
  <summary>
    <band height="60">
```

```
<textField>
  <reportElement x="0" y="0" width="200" height="30" />
  <textFieldExpression>
   <![CDATA[$R{localization.text1}]]>
  </textFieldExpression>
</textField>
          </band>
        </summary>
      </jasperReport>
```

The `resourceBundle` attribute of the `<jasperReport>` element tells JasperReports where to get the localized strings to use for the report. In order for this attribute to work correctly, a property file with a root name matching the value of the attribute must exist anywhere in the CLASSPATH when filling the report. In this example, a property file with the name `localizationdemo.properties` must exist in the CLASSPATH when using the default locale. To use a different locale, the name of the file must be `localizationdemo_[locale].properties`. For example, to use a Spanish locale, the name would be `localizationdemo_es.properties`.

The following property file can be used with the preceding template to generate the report using the default locale:

```
localization.text1=This is English text.
```

This, of course, assumes that the default locale uses the English language. In order for JasperReports to pick it up as the resource bundle for the default locale, the file must be saved as `localizationdemo.properties`.

To generate a report from the preceding template in Spanish, `localization_es.properties` must look like this:

```
localization.text1=Este texto es en Español.
```

Notice how in both the property files the key (text before the equal sign) is the same. This must be the case for each locale property file that we wish to use, since this key is what JasperReports uses to obtain the localized text to display in the report. As can be seen in the previous example, the syntax to obtain the value for `resourceBundle` properties is `$R{key}`.

To let JasperReports know what locale we wish to use, we need to assign a value to a built-in parameter. This parameter's name is defined as a constant called `REPORT_LOCALE`, and this constant is defined in the `net.sf.jasperreports.engine.JRParameter` class. The constant's value must be an instance of `java.util.Locale`. The following example demonstrates this procedure.

```
package net.ensode.jasperbook;
import java.util.HashMap;
import java.util.Locale;

import net.sf.jasperreports.engine.JREmptyDataSource;
import net.sf.jasperreports.engine.JRException;
import net.sf.jasperreports.engine.JRParameter;
import net.sf.jasperreports.engine.JasperFillManager;
public class LocalizationDemoReportFill
{
  public static void main(String[] args)
  {
    try
    {
      HashMap parameterMap = new HashMap();
      if (args.length > 0)
      {
        parameterMap.put(JRParameter.REPORT_LOCALE, new
        Locale(args[0]));
      }

      System.out.println("Filling report...");
      JasperFillManager.fillReportToFile(
          "reports/LocalizationDemoReport.jasper",
          parameterMap, new JREmptyDataSource());
      System.out.println("Done!");
    }
    catch (JRException e)
    {
      e.printStackTrace();
    }
  }
}
```

This example assumes we have already created a Jasper template from the JRXML template. If no command-line parameters are sent to the preceding code, it will use the default locale; otherwise, it will use the first command-line parameter as the locale. If we pass the String es as the first command-line parameter, the report will be generated in Spanish. The generated report will look like this:

# Scriptlets

JasperReports allows us to execute snippets of Java code at certain points during the report filling process. We can accomplish this by writing scriptlets. All scriptlets must extend either `net.sf.jasperreports.engine.JRAbstractScriptlet` or `net.sf.jasperreports.engine.JRDefaultScriptlet`. Following is a brief explanation on these classes:

- `JRAbstractScriptlet` contains a number of abstract methods that must be overridden in every implementation. These methods are called automatically by JasperReports at the appropriate moment.

- `JRDefaultScriptlet` is a convenience class containing default empty implementations of every method in `JRAbstractScriptlet`. It can be used whenever we wish to override only a few of the methods in `JRAbstractScriptlet`.

The following table summarizes these methods:

| Method | Description |
|---|---|
| `public void beforeReportInit()` | Called before report initialization. |
| `public void afterReportInit()` | Called after report initialization. |
| `public void beforePageInit()` | Called before each page is initialized. |
| `public void afterPageInit()` | Called after each page is initialized. |
| `public void beforeColumnInit()` | Called before each column is initialized. |
| `public void afterColumnInit()` | Called after each column is initialized. |
| `public void beforeGroupInit(String groupName)` | Called before the group specified in the parameter is initialized. |
| `public void afterGroupInit(String groupName)` | Called after the group specified in the parameter is initialized. |
| `public void beforeDetailEval()` | Called before each record in the detail section of the report is evaluated. |
| `public void afterDetailEval()` | Called after each record in the detail section of the report is evaluated. |

Scriptlets allow us to add complex functionality to our reports, not easily achievable by report expressions or variables. We indicate that we want to use a scriptlet by setting the `scriptletClass` attribute of the `<jasperReport>` element in the JRXML template to the fully qualified name of the scriptlet (including the entire package name).

Suppose we had a report that was taking a long time to fill. The following scriptlet could help us find out what specific part of the report was taking a long time to fill, and then we would know what to optimize.

```
package net.ensode.jasperbook;
import net.sf.jasperreports.engine.JRAbstractScriptlet;
import net.sf.jasperreports.engine.JRScriptletException;
public class PerformanceScriptlet extends JRAbstractScriptlet
{
  private long reportInitStartTime;
  private long reportInitEndTime;
  private long pageInitStartTime;
  private long pageInitEndTime;
  private long columnInitStartTime;
  private long columnInitEndTime;
  private long groupInitStartTime;
  private long groupInitEndTime;
  private long detailEvalStartTime;
  private long detailEvalEndTime;

  public void beforeReportInit() throws JRScriptletException
  {
    reportInitStartTime = System.currentTimeMillis();

  }

  public void afterReportInit() throws JRScriptletException
  {
    reportInitEndTime = System.currentTimeMillis();
    System.out.println("Report initialization took "
        + (reportInitEndTime - reportInitStartTime)
        + " milliseconds.");
  }

  public void beforePageInit() throws JRScriptletException
  {
    pageInitStartTime = System.currentTimeMillis();
```

```
  }

  public void afterPageInit() throws JRScriptletException
  {
    pageInitEndTime = System.currentTimeMillis();
    Integer pageNum = (Integer) getVariableValue("PAGE_NUMBER");
    System.out.println("Page " + pageNum + " initialization took "
          + (pageInitEndTime - pageInitStartTime) + " milliseconds.");
  }

  public void beforeColumnInit() throws JRScriptletException
  {
    columnInitStartTime = System.currentTimeMillis();

  }

  public void afterColumnInit() throws JRScriptletException
  {
    columnInitEndTime = System.currentTimeMillis();
    Integer columnNum = (Integer) getVariableValue("COLUMN_NUMBER");
    System.out.println("Column " + columnNum + " initialization took "
      + (columnInitEndTime - columnInitStartTime) + " milliseconds.");

  }

  public void beforeGroupInit(String groupName) throws
                                            JRScriptletException
  {
    groupInitStartTime = System.currentTimeMillis();
  }

  public void afterGroupInit(String groupName) throws
                                            JRScriptletException
  {
    groupInitEndTime = System.currentTimeMillis();
    System.out.println("Group " + groupName + " initialization took "
        + (groupInitEndTime - groupInitStartTime) + " milliseconds.");
  }

  public void beforeDetailEval() throws JRScriptletException
  {
    detailEvalStartTime = System.currentTimeMillis();
  }
```

```
public void afterDetailEval() throws JRScriptletException
{
  detailEvalEndTime = System.currentTimeMillis();
  System.out.println("Detail evaluation took "
    + (detailEvalEndTime - detailEvalStartTime) + " milliseconds.");
}
}
```

Each of the methods in the scriptlet would be run at the appropriate time, giving us an idea of the area(s) that is/are suffering from performance problems. As we mentioned previously, all that is needed to use a scriptlet in a report is to provide its fully qualified name to the `scriptlet` attribute of the root `<jasperreport>` element in the JRXML template. The following example illustrates this concept:

```
<?xml version="1.0" encoding="UTF-8"?>
<!DOCTYPE jasperReport PUBLIC "//JasperReports//DTD Report Design//EN"
 "http://jasperreports.sourceforge.net/dtds/jasperreport.dtd">
<jasperReport name="ScriptletDemoReport"
 resourceBundle="localizationdemo"
 scriptletClass="net.ensode.jasperbook.PerformanceScriptlet">
  <summary>
    <band height="60">
      <textField>
        <reportElement x="0" y="0" width="200" height="30"/>
        <textFieldExpression>
          <![CDATA[$R{localization.text1}]]>
        </textFieldExpression>
      </textField>
    </band>
  </summary>
</jasperReport>
```

This JRXML template is a slightly modified version of the template we saw in the previous section. The only difference is that we assigned a value to the scriptlet attribute of `<jasperReport>`. When filling the Jasper template generated by the preceding JRXML template, we should see some console output similar to the following:

```
Column 1 initialization took 0 milliseconds.
Page 1 initialization took 0 milliseconds.
Report initialization took 0 milliseconds.
Detail evaluation took 31 milliseconds.
```

As can be seen in the previous Java source code, scriptlets have access to report variables. Their value can be obtained by calling the getVariableValue() method. In this example, we access built-in variables only; however, there is nothing preventing scriptlets from accessing normal variables. Similarly, scriptlets can access report fields and parameters, both built-in and custom, by calling the getFieldValue() and getParameterValue() methods, respectively. Just like the getVariableValue() method, both of these methods take a single String parameter indicating the name of the field or parameter to obtain. Scriptlets can only access, but not modify, report fields and parameters. However, scriptlets can modify report variable values. This can be accomplished by calling the setVariableValue() method. This method is defined in JRAbstractScriptlet class, which is always the parent class of any scriptlet. The following example illustrates how to modify a report variable from a scriptlet:

```
package net.ensode.jasperbook;
import net.sf.jasperreports.engine.JRDefaultScriptlet;
import net.sf.jasperreports.engine.JRScriptletException;
public class ReportVariableModificationScriptlet extends
JRDefaultScriptlet
{
  public void afterReportInit() throws JRScriptletException
  {
    setVariableValue("someVar", new String(
                 "This value was modified by the scriptlet."));
  }
}
```

The preceding class will modify a variable named someVar to have the value This value was modified by the scriptlet.

> Notice how the preceding scriptlet extends JRDefaultScriptlet instead of JRAbstractScriptlet. JRDefaultScriptlet is a convenience class included with JasperReports. It includes empty implementations of all abstract methods in JRAbstractScriptlet, allowing us to override only those methods that concern our particular use case.

The following JRXML template uses the preceding scriptlet to modify the value of its someVar variable:

```
<?xml version="1.0" encoding="UTF-8"?>
<!DOCTYPE jasperReport PUBLIC "-//JasperReports//DTD Report Design//
EN" "http://jasperreports.sourceforge.net/dtds/jasperreport.dtd">
<jasperReport name="ScriptletVariableModificationReport"
```

```
scriptletClass="net.ensode.jasperbook.
ReportVariableModificationScriptlet">
   <variable name="someVar" class="java.lang.String">
     <initialValueExpression>
       <![CDATA["This is the initial variable value."]]>
     </initialValueExpression>
   </variable>
   <title>
     <band height="30">
       <textField>
         <reportElement width="555" height="30" x="0" y="0"/>
         <textFieldExpression>
           <![CDATA[$V{someVar}]]>
         </textFieldExpression>
       </textField>
     </band>
   </title>
</jasperReport>
```

Compiling and filling this JRXML template results in the following report:

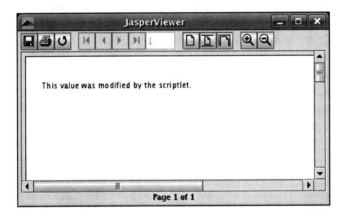

Notice how the report displays the variable value set in the scriptlet.

Before moving on, it is worth mentioning that we can add any additional methods we need to our scriptlets. Reports can call these methods by using the built-in parameter REPORT_SCRIPTLET. For example, if our scriptlet has a method called foo(), a report could access it by using the syntax $P{REPORT_SCRIPTLET}.foo().

# Crosstabs

Crosstab (cross-tabulation) reports are reports containing tables that tabulate data across rows and columns. This feature was introduced in JasperReports 1.1. The following example illustrates the use of crosstab in a report. The JRXML template will generate a report displaying a table containing the number of aircraft in each city in the state of New York. The last column of the table will display the total number of aircraft for all models in the table in each city. The last row will display the total number of aircraft of each model in the table. To avoid having an unmanageable number of columns in the table, we will limit the report to aircraft models that start with the letter C.

```
<?xml version="1.0" encoding="UTF-8"?>
<!DOCTYPE jasperReport PUBLIC "-//JasperReports//DTD Report Design//
 EN" "http://jasperreports.sourceforge.net/dtds/jasperreport.dtd">
<jasperReport name="CrossTabDemoReport" leftMargin="5"
              rightMargin="5">
  <queryString>
    <![CDATA[select
                a.city, am.model, a.tail_num
                from aircraft a, aircraft_models am
                where a.state='NY' and am.model like 'C%'
                and a.aircraft_model_code = am.aircraft_model_code
                order by city, model]]>
  </queryString>
  <field name="tail_num" class="java.lang.String"/>
  <field name="model" class="java.lang.String"/>
  <field name="city" class="java.lang.String"/>
  <summary>
    <band height="60">
      <crosstab>
        <reportElement width="782" y="0" x="0" height="60"/>
        <rowGroup name="cityGroup" width="100" totalPosition="End">
          <bucket>
            <bucketExpression class="java.lang.String">
              <![CDATA[$F{city}]]>
            </bucketExpression>
          </bucket>
          <crosstabRowHeader>
            <cellContents>
              <box border="Thin" borderColor="black"/>
              <textField>
                <reportElement width="100" y="0" x="0" height="20"/>
```

```
            <textElement textAlignment="Right"
                         verticalAlignment="Middle"/>
            <textFieldExpression>
              <![CDATA[$V{cityGroup}]]>
            </textFieldExpression>
          </textField>
        </cellContents>
      </crosstabRowHeader>
      <crosstabTotalRowHeader>
        <cellContents>
          <box borderColor="black" border="Thin"/>
          <staticText>
            <reportElement x="0" y="0" width="60" height="20" />
            <textElement verticalAlignment="Middle"/>
            <text>TOTAL</text>
          </staticText>
        </cellContents>
      </crosstabTotalRowHeader>
    </rowGroup>
    <columnGroup name="modelGroup" height="20"
                 totalPosition="End">
      <bucket>
        <bucketExpression class="java.lang.String">
          $F{model}
        </bucketExpression>
      </bucket>
      <crosstabColumnHeader>
        <cellContents>
          <box border="Thin" borderColor="black"/>
          <textField isStretchWithOverflow="true">
            <reportElement width="60" y="0" x="0" height="20"/>
            <textElement verticalAlignment="Bottom"/>
            <textFieldExpression>
              <![CDATA[$V{modelGroup}]]>
            </textFieldExpression>
          </textField>
        </cellContents>
      </crosstabColumnHeader>
      <crosstabTotalColumnHeader>
        <cellContents>
          <box border="Thin" borderColor="black"/>
          <staticText>
            <reportElement width="60" y="0" x="0" height="20"/>
            <textElement verticalAlignment="Bottom"/>
            <text>TOTAL</text>
          </staticText>
        </cellContents>
```

```
                    </crosstabTotalColumnHeader>
                </columnGroup>
                <measure name="tailNumCount" class="java.lang.Integer"
                        calculation="Count">
                    <measureExpression>$F{tail_num}</measureExpression>
                </measure>
                <crosstabCell height="20" width="60">
                    <cellContents backcolor="#FFFFFF">
                        <box borderColor="black" border="Thin"/>
                        <textField>
                            <reportElement x="5" y="0" width="55" height="20"/>
                            <textElement textAlignment="Left"
                                        verticalAlignment="Bottom"/>
                            <textFieldExpression
                                class="java.lang.Integer">
                                $V{tailNumCount}
                            </textFieldExpression>
                        </textField>
                    </cellContents>
                </crosstabCell>
            </crosstab>
        </band>
    </summary>
</jasperReport>
```

Compiling and filling the above JRXML template results in the following report:

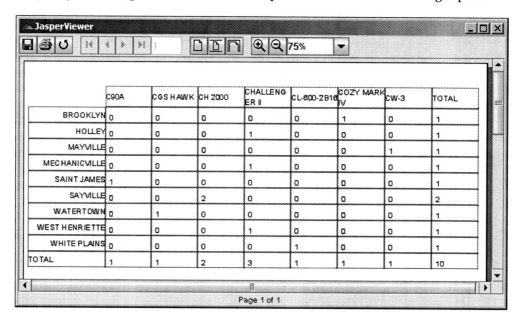

| | C90A | CGS HAWK | CH 2000 | CHALLENGER II | CL-600-2B16 | COZY MARK IV | CW-3 | TOTAL |
|---|---|---|---|---|---|---|---|---|
| BROOKLYN | 0 | 0 | 0 | 0 | 0 | 1 | 0 | 1 |
| HOLLEY | 0 | 0 | 0 | 1 | 0 | 0 | 0 | 1 |
| MAYVILLE | 0 | 0 | 0 | 0 | 0 | 0 | 1 | 1 |
| MECHANICVILLE | 0 | 0 | 0 | 1 | 0 | 0 | 0 | 1 |
| SAINT JAMES | 1 | 0 | 0 | 0 | 0 | 0 | 0 | 1 |
| SAYVILLE | 0 | 0 | 2 | 0 | 0 | 0 | 0 | 2 |
| WATERTOWN | 0 | 1 | 0 | 0 | 0 | 0 | 0 | 1 |
| WEST HENRIETTE | 0 | 0 | 0 | 1 | 0 | 0 | 0 | 1 |
| WHITE PLAINS | 0 | 0 | 0 | 0 | 1 | 0 | 0 | 1 |
| TOTAL | 1 | 1 | 2 | 3 | 1 | 1 | 1 | 10 |

To keep the example as simple as possible, we refrained from adding any style to the text in the crosstab. There is nothing preventing us from altering the text to have different fonts, alignments, etc. as discussed in Chapter 6.

In this example, the crosstab is defined by the <crosstab> element. The <rowGroup> element defines a group to split the data into rows. In the example, each row will display data for a different city. The <bucket> and <bucketExpression> elements define what report expression to use as a group delimiter for <rowGroup>. In the example, here, we used the city field as a delimiter, in order to split the rows by city. The <crosstabRowHeader> element defines the expression to be used as a row header. It contains a single sub-element, namely <cellContents>, which acts like an inner band inside crosstab.

Notice that the variable name for the text field inside <crosstabRowHeader> is not declared in the JRXML template. This is because the name assigned to <rowGroup> (via its name attribute) creates an implicit variable. The <crosstabTotalRowHeader> element defines the contents of the header cell for the entire row. It takes a single <cellContents> element as its only sub-element.

The <columnGroup> element as well as its sub-elements (as illustrated in the preceding example) is analogous to the <rowGroup> element, except that it influences columns instead of rows.

The <measure> element defines the calculation to be performed across rows and columns; possible values for its calculation attribute include Average, Count, First, Highest, Lowest, Nothing, StandardDeviation, Sum, and Variance. These values work just like the analogous values for the calculation attribute for report variables. Refer to the *Report Variables* section in Chapter 6 for an explanation.

The <crosstabCell> element defines how data in non-header cells will be laid out. This element also contains a single <cellContents> element as its only sub-element. If we would like to format cells displaying 'totals' differently from other cells, we can accomplish this by adding additional <crossTabCell> elements and setting their rowTotalGroup and/or columnTotalGroup attributes to match the names defined in <rowGroup> and <columnGroup>.

The <crosstab> element contains a number of sub-elements not shown in the example. The following sections describe all sub-elements of <crosstab>. Most of the elements shown in the following sections contain additional sub-elements. Refer to the **JasperReports Quick Reference Guide** at http://jasperreports. sourceforge.net/reference/index.html for more details.

# <columnGroup>

This element defines a group used to split the data into columns. Attributes for this element include:

- `height`: This defines the height of the column group header.
- `name`: This defines the name of the column group.
- `headerPosition`: This defines the position of the header contents (`Right`, `Left`, `Center`, `Stretch`).
- `totalPosition`: This defines the position of the entire column (`Start`, `End`, `None`).

# <crosstabCell>

This element defines how data in non-header cells will be laid out. Attributes for this element include:

- `columnTotalGroup`: This indicates the group to use to calculate the column total.
- `height`: This defines the height of the cell.
- `rowTotalGroup`: This indicates the group to use to calculate the row total.
- `width`: This defines the width of the cell.

# <crosstabDataset>

This element defines the dataset to use to populate the crosstab (see next section for a detailed explanation). Attributes for this element include:

- `isDataPreSorted`: This indicates whether the data in the dataset is pre-sorted.

# <crosstabParameter>

This element is used to access report variables and parameters from within the crosstab. Attributes for this element include:

- `name`: This defines the parameter name.
- `class`: This indicates the parameter class.

# <measure>

This element defines the calculation to be performed across rows and columns. Attributes for this element include:

- `name`: This defines the measure name.
- `class`: This indicates the measure class.
- `calculation`: This indicates the calculation to be performed between crosstab cell values.

# <parametersMapExpression>

This element is used to pass a report variable or parameter containing an instance of `java.util.Map`, as a set of parameters for the crosstab. This element contains no attributes.

# <reportElement>

This element defines the position, width, and height of the crosstab within its enclosing `<band>`. Attributes for this element include all standard `<reportElement>` attributes.

# <rowGroup>

This element defines a group used to split the data into rows. Attributes for this element include:

- `name`: This defines the name of the row group.
- `width`: This defines the width of the row group.
- `headerPosition`: This defines the position of the header contents (`Top`, `Middle`, `Bottom`, `Stretch`).
- `totalPosition`: This defines the position of the entire column (`Start`, `End`, `None`).

# <whenNoDataCell>

This element defines what to display on an empty crosstab cell. This element contains no attributes.

# Subdatasets

Sometimes we would like to display related charts or crosstabs for similar data grouped differently. For example, in the previous section we generated a crosstab displaying the total number of aircraft of a particular set of models in the state of New York. We can display the same set of data for different states by using subdatasets. The following example illustrates how to do this.

```
<?xml version="1.0" encoding="UTF-8"?>
<!DOCTYPE jasperReport PUBLIC "-//JasperReports//DTD Report Design//
EN" "http://jasperreports.sourceforge.net/dtds/jasperreport.dtd">
<jasperReport name="DatasetDemoReport" leftMargin="5" rightMargin="5">
  <subDataset name="Aircraft_Models">
    <parameter name="StateParam" class="java.lang.String"/>
    <queryString>
      <![CDATA[select
              a.city, am.model, a.tail_num
              from aircraft a, aircraft_models am
              where a.state=$P{StateParam} and am.model like 'C%'
              and a.aircraft_model_code = am.aircraft_model_code
              order by city, model]]>
    </queryString>
    <field name="tail_num" class="java.lang.String"/>
    <field name="model" class="java.lang.String"/>
    <field name="city" class="java.lang.String"/>
  </subDataset>
  <queryString>
    <![CDATA[select distinct state from aircraft where state in (
                              'MD', 'NY', 'VA') order by state]]>
  </queryString>
  <field name="state" class="java.lang.String"/>
  <detail>
    <band height="100">
      <textField>
        <reportElement x="0" y="10" width="500" height="20"/>
        <textFieldExpression><![CDATA[
              "Aircraft registered in" + $F{state}]]>
            </textFieldExpression>
      </textField>
      <crosstab>
        <reportElement width="782" y="30" x="0" height="60"/>
        <crosstabDataset>
          <dataset>
            <datasetRun subDataset="Aircraft_Models">
              <datasetParameter name="StateParam">
                <datasetParameterExpression>
                  <![CDATA[$F{state}]]>
                </datasetParameterExpression>
              </datasetParameter>
            </datasetRun>
          </dataset>
        </crosstabDataset>
        <rowGroup name="cityGroup" width="100" totalPosition="End">
```

```
<bucket>
  <bucketExpression class="java.lang.String">
    <![CDATA[$F{city}]]>
  </bucketExpression>
</bucket>
<crosstabRowHeader>
  <cellContents>
    <box border="Thin" borderColor="black"/>
    <textField>
      <reportElement width="100" y="0" x="0" height="20"/>
      <textElement textAlignment="Right"
                   verticalAlignment="Middle"/>
      <textFieldExpression>
        <![CDATA[$V{cityGroup}]]>
      </textFieldExpression>
    </textField>
  </cellContents>
</crosstabRowHeader>
<crosstabTotalRowHeader>
  <cellContents>
    <box borderColor="black" border="Thin" />
    <staticText>
      <reportElement x="0" y="0" width="60" height="20"/>
      <textElement verticalAlignment="Middle"/>
      <text>TOTAL</text>
    </staticText>
  </cellContents>
</crosstabTotalRowHeader>
</rowGroup>
<columnGroup name="modelGroup" height="20"
             totalPosition="End">
  <bucket>
    <bucketExpression class="java.lang.String">
      $F{model}
    </bucketExpression>
  </bucket>
  <crosstabColumnHeader>
```

```xml
          <cellContents>
            <box border="Thin" borderColor="black"/>
            <textField isStretchWithOverflow="true">
              <reportElement width="60" y="0" x="0" height="20"/>
              <textElement verticalAlignment="Bottom"/>
              <textFieldExpression>
                <![CDATA[$V{modelGroup}]]>
              </textFieldExpression>
            </textField>
          </cellContents>
        </crosstabColumnHeader>
        <crosstabTotalColumnHeader>
          <cellContents>
            <box border="Thin" borderColor="black"/>
            <staticText>
              <reportElement width="60" y="0" x="0" height="20"/>
              <textElement verticalAlignment="Bottom"/>
              <text>TOTAL</text>
            </staticText>
          </cellContents>
        </crosstabTotalColumnHeader>
      </columnGroup>
      <measure name="tailNumCount" class="java.lang.Integer"
             calculation="Count">
        <measureExpression>$F{tail_num}</measureExpression>
      </measure>
      <crosstabCell height="20" width="60">
        <cellContents backcolor="#FFFFFF">
          <box borderColor="black" border="Thin"/>
          <textField>
            <reportElement x="5" y="0" width="55" height="20"/>
            <textElement textAlignment="Left"
                        verticalAlignment="Bottom"/>
            <textFieldExpression class="java.lang.Integer">
              $V{tailNumCount}
            </textFieldExpression>
          </textField>
        </cellContents>
```

```
        </crosstabCell>
      </crosstab>
    </band>
  </detail>
</jasperReport>
```

After compiling this template and filling the resulting Jasper file, we should get a report that looks like the following:

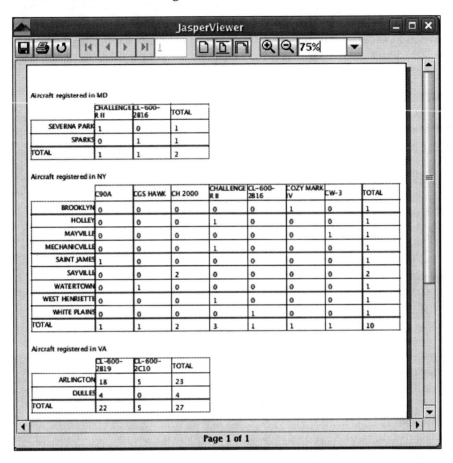

As we can see, the report template generates a different crosstab for each record in the `<detail>` section of the report. To accomplish this, we need to create a query inside the `<subdataSet>` element. The query must have one or more parameters, also defined inside `<subdataSet>`. This parameter needs to be populated with a report expression. In this example, we use the `city` field for this purpose.

To populate the dataset parameters with the desired report expression, we need to use the `<crosstabDataset>` element inside the `<crosstab>`. This element must contain a single `<dataset>` element, which in turn contains a `<datasetRun>` element. This element contains a `name` attribute indicating which subdataset to use to populate the crosstab; it also contains a `<datasetParameterExpression>` sub-element indicating what report element to use to populate the dataset parameter.

Subdatasets can also be used in a similar manner to create related charts in each report record. To accomplish this, the `<dataset>` element must be placed inside the appropriate dataset element for the chart (`<categoryDataset>`, `<pieDataset>`, etc). The following example demonstrates this feature for a bar chart. The report generated by the JRXML template will display a bar chart illustrating the number of aircraft registered in the states of Maryland, New York, and Virginia.

```xml
<?xml version="1.0" encoding="UTF-8"?>
<!DOCTYPE jasperReport PUBLIC "-//JasperReports//DTD Report Design//
  EN" "http://jasperreports.sourceforge.net/dtds/jasperreport.dtd">
<jasperReport name="ChartDatasetDemoReport" leftMargin="5"
                rightMargin="5">
  <subDataset name="Aircraft_Registrations">
    <parameter name="StateParam" class="java.lang.String"/>
    <queryString>
      <![CDATA[select
                a.city, count(*) as aircraft_count
                from aircraft a
                where a.state=$P{StateParam}
                and a.city like 'A%'
                group by city]]>
    </queryString>
    <field name="aircraft_count" class="java.lang.Integer"/>
    <field name="city" class="java.lang.String"/>
  </subDataset>
  <queryString>
    <![CDATA[select distinct state from aircraft where state in ('MD',
            'NY', 'VA') order by state]]>
  </queryString>
  <field name="state" class="java.lang.String"/>
  <detail>
    <band height="200">
      <textField>
        <reportElement x="0" y="10" width="500" height="20"/>
        <textFieldExpression>
```

```
                <![CDATA["Aircraft registered in " + $F{state}]]>
            </textFieldExpression>
        </textField>
        <barChart>
          <chart>
            <reportElement width="500" y="30" x="0" height="170"/>
          </chart>
          <categoryDataset>
            <dataset>
              <datasetRun subDataset="Aircraft_Registrations">
                <datasetParameter name="StateParam">
                  <datasetParameterExpression>
                    <![CDATA[$F{state}]]>
                  </datasetParameterExpression>
                </datasetParameter>
              </datasetRun>
            </dataset>
            <categorySeries>
              <seriesExpression>"City"</seriesExpression>
              <categoryExpression>
                <![CDATA[$F{city}]]>
              </categoryExpression>
              <valueExpression>
                <![CDATA[$F{aircraft_count}]]>
              </valueExpression>
            </categorySeries>
          </categoryDataset>
          <barPlot isShowTickMarks="true"
                   isShowTickLabels="true">
            <plot orientation="Horizontal"/>
          </barPlot>
        </barChart>
      </band>
    </detail>
</jasperReport>
```

Notice how the `<dataset>` element inside `<categoryDataset>` contains a
`<datasetRun>` element, with its subdataset attribute set to the subdataset declared
at the beginning of the report. After compiling the preceding JRXML template and
filling the resulting Jasper template, we should get a report like the following:

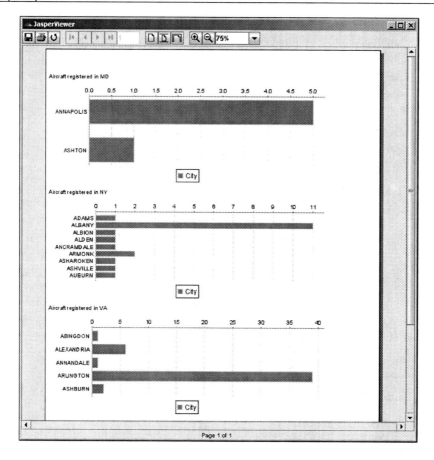

Each chart corresponds to a different state in the main report query, and data in each chart corresponds to cities for the corresponding state.

# Adding Hyperlinks and Anchors to Reports

JasperReports allows us to add hyperlinks and anchors to our reports. The only report elements that can be hyperlinks or anchors are `<textField>`, `<chart>`, and `<image>`. Hyperlinks allow us to quickly navigate between report sections, a feature that is very useful when producing long reports. The following example illustrates how to add hyperlinks to our reports.

```
<?xml version="1.0" encoding="UTF-8"?>
<!DOCTYPE jasperReport PUBLIC "//JasperReports//DTD Report Design//EN"
  "http://jasperreports.sourceforge.net/dtds/jasperreport.dtd">
<jasperReport name="HyperLinkDemoReport">
  <title>
```

```
    <band height="60">
      <staticText>
        <reportElement x="0" y="0" width="555" height="30"/>
        <text>
          <![CDATA[In a rush?]]>
        </text>
      </staticText>
      <textField hyperlinkType="LocalAnchor">
        <reportElement x="0" y="30" width="555" height="30"/>
        <textFieldExpression>
          <![CDATA["Go to summary section."]]>
        </textFieldExpression>
        <hyperlinkAnchorExpression>
          <![CDATA["summary_section"]]>
        </hyperlinkAnchorExpression>
      </textField>
    </band>
  </title>
  <detail>
    <band height="60">
      <textField isStretchWithOverflow="true">
        <reportElement x="0" y="0" width="555" height="30"/>
        <textFieldExpression>
          <![CDATA["This is the main report area, if this area " +
                   "had a lot of text and the person reading " +
                   "the report did not have time to read it all, " +
                   "we can direct them to the summary section " +
                   "by using a hyperlink. Let's add some more " +
                   "text to make this area look more realistic. " +
                   "Boy,if I was reading this report I would be " +
                   "bored by now. Perhaps reading only the " +
                   "summary would be a good idea? Why don't we do " +
                   "just that?"]]>
        </textFieldExpression>
      </textField>
    </band>
  </detail>
  <summary>
    <band height="60">
      <textField isStretchWithOverflow="true">
```

```
            <reportElement x="0" y="0" width="555" height="30"/>
            <textFieldExpression>
              <![CDATA["This is the summary section. It contains less text
                      so that the person reading the report can get the
                      gist of the report data."]]>
            </textFieldExpression>
            <anchorNameExpression>
              <![CDATA["summary_section"]]>
            </anchorNameExpression>
          </textField>
        </band>
      </summary>
    </jasperReport>
```

As we can see from the example, we can turn a `<textField>` into a hyperlink by using the `hyperlinkType` attribute. In this example, we set `hyperLinkType` to be `LocalAnchor`, which means that the hyperlink target is another area of the report specified by an anchor expression. The `<hyperlinkAnchorExpression>` element indicates what the target for the hyperlink will be. To create the target for the anchor, we need to use the `<anchorNameExpression>` JRXML element. Notice, in the example, how the contents of the `<anchorNameExpression>` match the contents of `<hyperLinkAnchorExpression>`. This is how we link hyperlinks with the corresponding anchor.

In addition to pointing to specific anchors in the reports, hyperlinks can point to external resources or specific pages in the report. When a hyperlink points to an external resource, the enclosing element (`<textField>`, `<image>`, or `<chart>`) must contain a `<hyperlinkReferenceExpression>` element containing a report expression indicating the name of the external resource (usually a URL).

The following table summarizes the different types of hyperlinks supported by JasperReports:

| Hyperlink Type | Description | Elements Defining Hyperlink Target |
| --- | --- | --- |
| LocalAnchor | Hyperlink points to an anchor in the report, defined by the `<anchorNameExpression>` element. | `<hyperlinkAnchorExpression>` |
| LocalPage | Hyperlink points to a page in the current report. | `<hyperlinkPageExpression>` |
| None | Used to indicate that the element containing the `hyperlinkType` attribute is not an anchor (this is the default). | N/A |

| Hyperlink Type | Description | Elements Defining Hyperlink Target |
|---|---|---|
| Reference | Hyperlink points to an external resource. | `<hyperlinkReferenceExpression>` |
| RemoteAnchor | Hyperlink points to an anchor in an external resource. | `<hyperlinkAnchorExpression>` `<hyperlinkReferenceExpression>` |
| RemotePage | Hyperlink points to a page in an external resource. | `<hyperlinkPageExpression>` `<hyperlinkReferenceExpression>` |

The `<textField>`, `<chart>`, or `<image>` containing the `hyperlinkType` attribute must contain the corresponding element defining the hyperlink target as shown in the table. The only one out of these elements we haven't discussed is the `<hyperlinkPageExpression>` element. This element must contain a report expression resolving into a numeric value corresponding to the page number where the hyperlink will take us.

# Bookmarks

PDF documents can have a tree-like 'table of contents' that allows easy navigation between the document sections. This 'table of contents' is labeled **Bookmarks** in most PDF viewers. JasperReports can generate bookmarks in reports exported to PDF by setting the `bookmarkLevel` attribute of any `<image>`, `<chart>`, or `<textField>` containing an `<anchorExpression>` sub-element. The following JRXML template illustrates the use of the `bookmarkLevel` attribute to create bookmarks. It is a slightly modified version of the second subdataset example from the previous section.

```
<?xml version="1.0" encoding="UTF-8"?>
<!DOCTYPE jasperReport PUBLIC "-//JasperReports//DTD Report Design//
 EN" "http://jasperreports.sourceforge.net/dtds/jasperreport.dtd">
<jasperReport name="BookmarkDemoReport" leftMargin="5"
              rightMargin="5">
  <subDataset name="Aircraft_Registrations">
    <parameter name="StateParam" class="java.lang.String" />
    <queryString>
      <![CDATA[select
               a.city, count(*) as aircraft_count
               from aircraft a
               where a.state=$P{StateParam}
               and a.city like 'A%'
               group by city]]>
    </queryString>
```

```
    <field name="aircraft_count" class="java.lang.Integer"/>
    <field name="city" class="java.lang.String"/>
</subDataset>
<queryString>
    <![CDATA[select distinct state from aircraft where state in ('MD',
    'NY', 'VA') order by state]]>
</queryString>
<field name="state" class="java.lang.String"/>
<detail>
  <band height="200">
    <textField bookmarkLevel="1">
      <reportElement x="0" y="10" width="500" height="20"/>
      <textFieldExpression>
        <![CDATA["Aircraft registered in " + $F{state}]]>
      </textFieldExpression>
      <anchorNameExpression>
        <![CDATA["Aircraft registered in " + $F{state}]]>
      </anchorNameExpression>
    </textField>
    <barChart>
      <chart bookmarkLevel="2">
      <reportElement width="500" y="30" x="0" height="170"/>
        <anchorNameExpression>
          <![CDATA["Chart"]]>
        </anchorNameExpression>
      </chart>
      <categoryDataset>
        <dataset>
          <datasetRun
            subDataset="Aircraft_Registrations">
            <datasetParameter name="StateParam">
              <datasetParameterExpression>
                <![CDATA[$F{state}]]>
              </datasetParameterExpression>
            </datasetParameter>
          </datasetRun>
        </dataset>
        <categorySeries>
          <seriesExpression>"City"</seriesExpression>
          <categoryExpression>
```

```
        <![CDATA[$F{city}]]>
      </categoryExpression>
      <valueExpression>
        <![CDATA[$F{aircraft_count}]]>
      </valueExpression>
    </categorySeries>
  </categoryDataset>
  <barPlot isShowTickMarks="true"
           isShowTickLabels="true">
    <plot orientation="Horizontal"/>
  </barPlot>
  </barChart>
  </band>
  </detail>
</jasperReport>
```

The value for the `bookmarkLevel` attribute must be a positive integer indicating the relative position of the item in the bookmark tree structure. A value of 1 indicates a root node in the tree. After compiling, filling, and exporting this JRXML template we should get a PDF containing bookmarks, with the chart titles as root nodes and the charts themselves as child nodes.

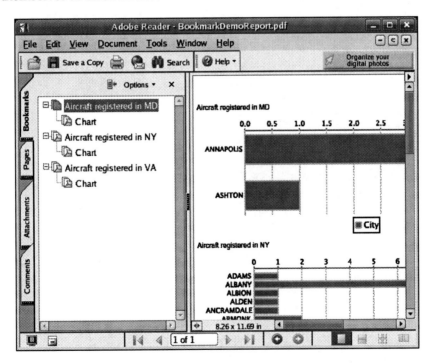

Clicking on the nodes will direct the main window to the appropriate anchor.

# Handling Very Large Reports

Sometimes, when filling a report, the report datasource may have a lot of data. In some cases, the generated report can become very large, larger than the memory allocated for the JVM, causing an OutOfMemoryException.

It is possible to set up JasperReports so that it stores segments of a report on disk in order to free up some memory. This can be accomplished by using the REPORT_ VIRTUALIZER built-in report parameter. The value for this parameter must be an instance of a class implementing net.sf.jasperreports.engine.JRVirtualizer. JasperReports comes with an implementation of this interface, namely net. sf.jasperreports.engine.fill.JRFileVirtualizer. This implementation is sufficient to handle the vast majority of large reports. If for some reason this implementation is not sufficient for our needs, we can always create our own implementation of net.sf.jasperreports.engine.JRVirtualizer. The following example illustrates typical usage of JRVirtualizer.

```
package net.ensode.jasperbook;
import java.sql.Connection;
import java.sql.DriverManager;
import java.sql.SQLException;
import java.util.HashMap;

import net.sf.jasperreports.engine.JRException;
import net.sf.jasperreports.engine.JRParameter;
import net.sf.jasperreports.engine.JasperFillManager;
import net.sf.jasperreports.engine.fill.JRFileVirtualizer;
public class DbConnectionReportFill
{
  Connection connection;
  public void generateReport(String reportName)
  {
    String reportDirectory = "reports";
    JRFileVirtualizer fileVirtualizer =
                              new JRFileVirtualizer(3, "cacheDir");
    HashMap parameterMap = new HashMap(); parameterMap.
              put(JRParameter.REPORT_VIRTUALIZER, fileVirtualizer);
    try
    {
      Class.forName("com.mysql.jdbc.Driver");
```

```
          connection = DriverManager.getConnection("jdbc:mysql:
            //localhost:3306/flightstats?" + "user=user&password=secret");
          System.out.println("Filling report...");
          JasperFillManager.fillReportToFile(reportDirectory + "/" +
                        reportName + ".jasper", parameterMap,connection);
          System.out.println("Done!");
          connection.close();
        }
        catch (JRException e)
        {
          e.printStackTrace();
        }
        catch (ClassNotFoundException e)
        {
          e.printStackTrace();
        }
        catch (SQLException e)
        {
          e.printStackTrace();
        }
      }

      public static void main(String[] args)
      {
        new DbConnectionReportFill().generateReport(args[0]);
      }
    }
```

JRFileVirtualizer has two constructors. The one we chose to use in the example takes two parameters. The first parameter is the maximum number of report pages that will be stored in primary memory (RAM) before sections of the report are stored in virtual memory (disk), and the second parameter is the directory that will be used to store the segments of the report that will be stored on disk. The other constructor takes a single parameter, an int indicating the maximum number of report pages that will be stored in primary memory. When using this constructor, the cached portions of the report will be stored in the running application's working directory. We need to do nothing special in the JRXML template to be able to cache them to disk.

The process described in this section makes filling a report a much slower process than usual. Therefore, report virtualization should be used only when there is a good possibility that the report will cause the JVM to run out of memory.

# Summary

In this chapter, we discussed several features that allow us to create elaborate reports. We learned to render localized reports by using the `resourceBundle` attribute of the `<jasperReport>` JRXML element. We used scriptlets to add complex functionality to reports, including variable value modification and performance measurement. We saw how to add cross-tabulation tables (crosstabs) to our reports by taking advantage of the `<crosstab>` JRXML element as well as to display related charts or crosstabs for each record in a report by using subdatasets. To ease the task of report navigation, we learned how to add hyperlinks, anchors, and bookmarks to our reports. There are times when we need to generate reports larger than the available memory. We can safely generate such reports by taking advantage of report virtualization.

# 9
# Exporting to Other Formats

Reports can be exported to several formats. Since reports in native JasperReports format can only be viewed by using the JasperReports API (or by using the JasperViewer utility included with JasperReports), exporting reports is a very common requirement since exported reports can be viewed with readily available software like PDF viewers, word processors, and web browsers. In this chapter, we will cover how to export our reports to all formats supported by JasperReports, which include:

- Exporting reports to PDF
- Exporting reports to RTF
- Exporting reports to Excel
- Exporting reports to HTML
- Exporting reports to XML
- Exporting reports to CSV
- Exporting reports to Plain Text
- Directing HTML reports to a browser

## Exporting Overview

Exporting reports is done via a series of classes that implement the `net.sf.jasperreports.engine.JRExporter` interface. This interface contains, among others, the following two methods:

- `public void setParameter(JRExporterParameter parameter, java.lang.Object value)`
- `public void exportReport()`

The setParameter() method is used to set parameters used to export the report. In most cases, two parameters need to be set: the jasperPrint object containing the native report and the name of the output file or output stream used to output the exported report. We would set the output file any time we are sure we want to save the exported report to disk. We would set the output stream parameter for sending the exported report through the network or when we are not sure if we want to save the exported report to disk or stream it through the network. Since an output stream can be easily saved to disk or streamed through the network, the decision can be made at run time.

As can be seen in the given method signature, setParameter() takes an instance of net.sf.jasperreports.engine.JRExporterParameter as its first argument. JRExporterParameter contains a number of static constants that are typically used as the first argument to setParameter(). To accommodate the most common cases, the JRExporterParameter constants that are of interest are:

- JRExporterParameter.JASPER_PRINT, used to set the JasperPrint object to export

- JRExporterParameter.OUTPUT_FILE_NAME, used to set the output file name

- JRExporterParameter.OUTPUT_STREAM, used to set the output stream

> There are several other constants defined in JRExporterParameter. Consult the JavaDoc documentation for JRExporterParameter at http://jasperreports. sourceforge.net/api/net/sf/jasperreports/ engine/JRExporterParameter.html for details.

As we will see in the following sections, exporting to different formats follows the same pattern in all cases. Once we are familiar with the procedure to export to one format, learning to export to other formats will be trivial.

Exporting reports functionality is done entirely in Java code. The JRXML template does not need to be modified at all. For most of the examples in this chapter, we will be using the *subdatasets* example from the previous chapter.

Before moving on, it is worth mentioning that for most formats, exported reports keep their formatting (fonts, colors, etc.). The only two formats that lose their formatting are CSV and Plain Text, since both of these are plain text files containing no formatting information.

# Exporting to PDF

We have already seen examples of exporting reports to PDF in previous chapters. However, all examples we have seen so far stream a PDF report straight to the browser window. In this example, we will export a report to PDF and save it to the file system.

```java
package net.ensode.jasperbook;

import java.io.File;

import net.sf.jasperreports.engine.JRException;
import net.sf.jasperreports.engine.JRExporterParameter;
import net.sf.jasperreports.engine.JasperPrint;
import net.sf.jasperreports.engine.export.JRPdfExporter;
import net.sf.jasperreports.engine.util.JRLoader;

public class PdfExportDemo
{
  public static final String REPORT_DIRECTORY = "reports";

  public void pdfExport(String reportName)
  {
    File file = new File(REPORT_DIRECTORY + "/" + reportName +
                                                ".jrprint");

    try
    {
      JasperPrint jasperPrint = (JasperPrint)
      JRLoader.loadObject(file);
      JRPdfExporter pdfExporter = new JRPdfExporter();

      pdfExporter.setParameter(JRExporterParameter.
                            JASPER_PRINT, jasperPrint);
      pdfExporter.setParameter(JRExporterParameter.OUTPUT_FILE_NAME,
                    REPORT_DIRECTORY + "/" + reportName + ".pdf");
      System.out.println("Exporting report...");
      pdfExporter.exportReport();
      System.out.println("Done!");
    }
    catch (JRException e)
    {
      e.printStackTrace();
    }
  }
```

```
public static void main(String[] args)
{
  new PdfExportDemo().pdfExport(args[0]);
}

}
```

As we can see in the example, the JRExporter implementation used to export to PDF is net.sf.jasperreports.engine.export.JRPdfExporter. We need to pass it the compiled report in native JasperReports format by setting the JRExporterParameter.JASPER_PRINT parameter to the appropriate instance of net.sf.jasperreports.engine.JasperPrint.

Since in this case we are saving the report to disk, we set the output file name to the report name. The only difference is we substitute the file extension to .pdf.

The code above will generate a PDF that looks like the following screenshot:

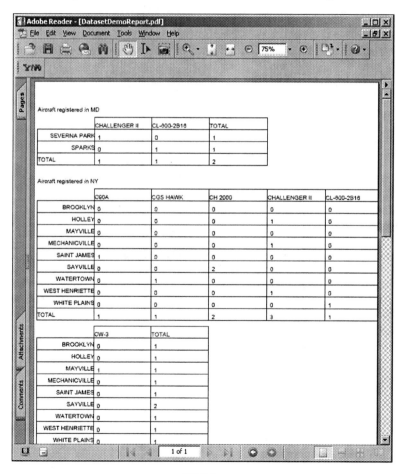

# Exporting to RTF

**Rich Text Format (RTF)** is a document file format that is supported by most word processors. Exporting to RTF allows our documents to be read by Microsoft Word and several other word processors.

 Unfortunately, RTF documents generated by JasperReports are not always readable by OpenOffice.org or StarOffice writer, since these office suites are not fully compliant with the RTF specification.

In the following example, we will export a report to RTF format.

```java
package net.ensode.jasperbook;

import java.io.File;

import net.sf.jasperreports.engine.JRException;
import net.sf.jasperreports.engine.JRExporterParameter;
import net.sf.jasperreports.engine.JasperPrint;
import net.sf.jasperreports.engine.export.JRRtfExporter;
import net.sf.jasperreports.engine.util.JRLoader;

public class RtfExportDemo
{
  public static final String REPORT_DIRECTORY = "reports";

  public void rtfExport(String reportName)
  {
    File file = new File(REPORT_DIRECTORY + "/" + reportName +
                                            ".jrprint");

    try
    {
      JasperPrint jasperPrint = (JasperPrint)
                          JRLoader.loadObject(file);
      JRRtfExporter rtfExporter = new JRRtfExporter();

      rtfExporter.setParameter(JRExporterParameter.
                          JASPER_PRINT, jasperPrint);
      rtfExporter.setParameter(JRExporterParameter.OUTPUT_FILE_NAME,
                    REPORT_DIRECTORY + "/" + reportName + ".rtf");
      System.out.println("Exporting report...");
```

```
        rtfExporter.exportReport();
        System.out.println("Done!");
    }
    catch (JRException e)
    {
        e.printStackTrace();
    }
}

public static void main(String[] args)
{
    new RtfExportDemo().rtfExport(args[0]);
}

}
```

As we can see in the example, net.sf.jasperreports.engine.export.
JRRtfExporter is the JRExporter implementation we need to use to export to RTF.
Like the previous example, we tell the exporter what report to export by supplying
an instance of net.sf.jasperreports.engine.JasperPrint as the value for the
JRExporterParameter.JASPER_PRINT parameter, and we set the output file to the
report name by setting the JRExporterParameter.OUTPUT_FILE_NAME with the
appropriate value.

The code will generate an RTF document as shown in the following screenshot:

Aircraft registered in MD

| | CHALLENGER II | CL-600-2B16 | TOTAL |
|---|---|---|---|
| SEVERNA PARK | 1 | 0 | 1 |
| SPARKS | 0 | 1 | 1 |
| TOTAL | 1 | 1 | 2 |

Aircraft registered in NY

| | C90A | CGS HAWK | CH 2000 | CHALLENGER II | CL-600-2B16 |
|---|---|---|---|---|---|
| BROOKLYN | 0 | 0 | 0 | 0 | 0 |
| HOLLEY | 0 | 0 | 0 | 1 | 0 |
| MAYVILLE | 0 | 0 | 0 | 0 | 0 |
| MECHANICVILLE | 0 | 0 | 0 | 1 | 0 |
| SAINT JAMES | 1 | 0 | 0 | 0 | 0 |
| SAYVILLE | 0 | 0 | 2 | 0 | 0 |
| WATERTOWN | 0 | 1 | 0 | 0 | 0 |
| WEST HENRIETTE | 0 | 0 | 0 | 1 | 0 |
| WHITE PLAINS | 0 | 0 | 0 | 0 | 1 |
| TOTAL | 1 | 1 | 2 | 3 | 1 |

| | CW-3 | TOTAL |
|---|---|---|
| BROOKLYN | 0 | 1 |
| HOLLEY | 0 | 1 |
| MAYVILLE | 1 | 1 |
| MECHANICVILLE | 0 | 1 |
| SAINT JAMES | 0 | 1 |
| SAYVILLE | 0 | 2 |
| WATERTOWN | 0 | 1 |
| WEST HENRIETTE | 0 | 1 |
| WHITE PLAINS | 0 | 1 |

# Exporting to Excel

It is not uncommon to request reports in Microsoft Excel format since Excel allows easy manipulation of report data to perform calculations. JasperReports provides built-in capability to export reports to Excel. The following example demonstrates this functionality:

```
package net.ensode.jasperbook;

import java.io.File;

import net.sf.jasperreports.engine.JRException;
import net.sf.jasperreports.engine.JRExporterParameter;
```

```
import net.sf.jasperreports.engine.JasperPrint;
import net.sf.jasperreports.engine.export.JRXlsExporter;
import net.sf.jasperreports.engine.export.JExcelApiExporter;
import net.sf.jasperreports.engine.util.JRLoader;

public class XlsExportDemo
{
  public static final String REPORT_DIRECTORY = "reports";

  public void xlsExport(String reportName)
  {
    File file = new File(REPORT_DIRECTORY + "/" + reportName +
                                      ".jrprint");

    try
    {
      JasperPrint jasperPrint = (JasperPrint)
                            JRLoader.loadObject(file);
      JExcelApiExporter xlsExporter = new JExcelApiExporter();

      xlsExporter.setParameter(JRExporterParameter.
                          JASPER_PRINT, jasperPrint);
      xlsExporter.setParameter(JRExporterParameter.OUTPUT_FILE_NAME,
                      REPORT_DIRECTORY + "/" + reportName + ".xls");
      System.out.println("Exporting report...");
      xlsExporter.exportReport();
      System.out.println("Done!");
    }
    catch (JRException e)
    {
      e.printStackTrace();
    }
  }

  public static void main(String[] args)
  {
    new XlsExportDemo().xlsExport(args[0]);
  }

}
```

This example follows the same pattern as the previous examples in this chapter. The
JRExporter implementation needed to export to Excel is net.sf.jasperreports.
engine.export.JExcelApiExporter. Again, we set the report to export and the
output file name by setting the appropriate parameters on JExcelApiExporter.

The code will generate an Excel spreadsheet that looks like the following screenshot:

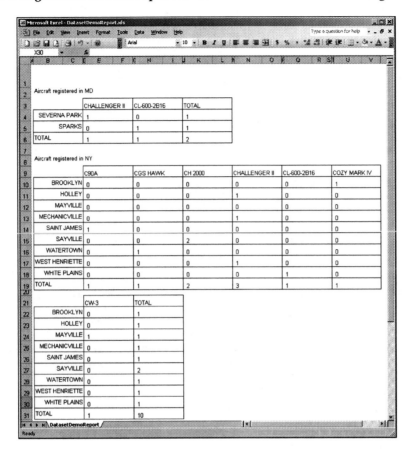

 JasperReports includes two Excel exporters, `JExcelApiExporter` and `JRXlsExporter`. It is preferable to use `JExcelApiExporter` since `JRXlsExporter` does not support exporting images. `JExcelApiExporter` is the newer Excel exporter. `JRXlsExporter` is still included for backward compatibility.

# Exporting to HTML

Exporting to HTML is another common requirement. The following example demonstrates how to do it:

```
package net.ensode.jasperbook;

import java.io.File;
```

```java
import net.sf.jasperreports.engine.JRException;
import net.sf.jasperreports.engine.JRExporterParameter;
import net.sf.jasperreports.engine.JasperPrint;
import net.sf.jasperreports.engine.export.JRHtmlExporter;
import net.sf.jasperreports.engine.util.JRLoader;

public class HtmlExportDemo
{
  public static final String REPORT_DIRECTORY = "reports";

  public void htmlExport(String reportName)
  {
    File file = new File(REPORT_DIRECTORY + "/" + reportName +
                                           ".jrprint");

    try
    {
      JasperPrint jasperPrint = (JasperPrint)
                          JRLoader.loadObject(file);
      JRHtmlExporter htmlExporter = new JRHtmlExporter();

      htmlExporter.setParameter(JRExporterParameter.
                        JASPER_PRINT, jasperPrint);
      htmlExporter.setParameter(JRExporterParameter.OUTPUT_FILE_NAME,
                    REPORT_DIRECTORY + "/" + reportName + ".html");
      System.out.println("Exporting report...");
      htmlExporter.exportReport();
      System.out.println("Done!");
    }
    catch (JRException e)
    {
      e.printStackTrace();
    }
  }

  public static void main(String[] args)
  {
    new HtmlExportDemo().htmlExport(args[0]);
  }

}
```

In this example, we generate an HTML file and save it to disk. The JRExporter implementation for HTML export is net.sf.jasperreports.engine.export. JRHtmlExporter. Just as in previous examples, we set the report to export and the file name by setting the appropriate parameters.

>  A common requirement when exporting to HTML is to have the exported report directed to a browser window. This technique will be covered in the last section in this chapter.

The code in the example will generate an HTML report that looks like the following screenshot:

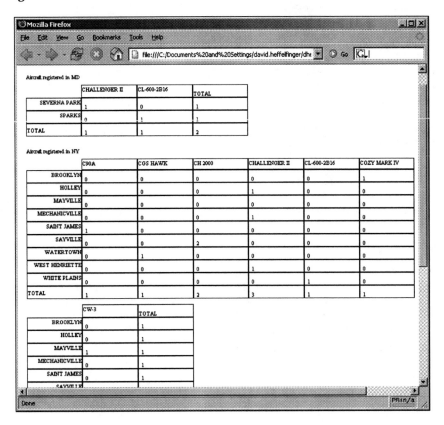

Reports exported to HTML result in a single HTML file, regardless of how many pages the original report has.

# Exporting to XML

Reports can be exported to XML as well. JasperReports uses a DTD file to generate XML reports. XML reports can be exported back to compiled reports by using the `net.sf.jasperreports.engine.xml.JRPrintXmlLoader` class. The following example demonstrates how to export a report to XML.

```
package net.ensode.jasperbook;

import java.io.File;

import net.sf.jasperreports.engine.JRException;
import net.sf.jasperreports.engine.JRExporterParameter;
import net.sf.jasperreports.engine.JasperPrint;
import net.sf.jasperreports.engine.export.JRXmlExporter;
import net.sf.jasperreports.engine.util.JRLoader;

public class XmlExportDemo
{
  public static final String REPORT_DIRECTORY = "reports";

  public void xmlExport(String reportName)
  {
    File file = new File(REPORT_DIRECTORY + "/" + reportName +
                                        ".jrprint");

    try
    {
      JasperPrint jasperPrint = (JasperPrint) JRLoader.
                                            loadObject(file);
      JRXmlExporter xmlExporter = new JRXmlExporter();

      xmlExporter.setParameter(JRExporterParameter.
                        JASPER_PRINT, jasperPrint);
      xmlExporter.setParameter(JRExporterParameter.OUTPUT_FILE_NAME,
                  REPORT_DIRECTORY + "/" + reportName + ".jrpxml");
      System.out.println("Exporting report...");
      xmlExporter.exportReport();
      System.out.println("Done!");
    }
    catch (JRException e)
    {
      e.printStackTrace();
    }
  }

  public static void main(String[] args)
  {
    new XmlExportDemo().xmlExport(args[0]);
  }

}
```

As we can see in the example, the `JRExporter` implementation used to export to XML is `net.sf.jasperreports.engine.export.JRXmlExporter`. The same procedure used in previous examples is used to set the report to export and the resulting file name.

> Notice the file name used for the exported report contains the extension `.jrpxml`. Even though exported reports are standard XML files, it is customary to use this extension instead of `.xml`.

The following is a partial listing of the generated XML file:

```xml
<?xml version="1.0" encoding="UTF-8"?>
<!DOCTYPE jasperPrint PUBLIC "-//JasperReports//DTD Report Design//EN"
 "http://jasperreports.sourceforge.net/dtds/jasperprint.dtd">
<jasperPrint name="DatasetDemoReport" pageWidth="595"
            pageHeight="842">
  <page>
    <text textHeight="13.578125" lineSpacingFactor="1.3578125"
          leadingOffset="-3.1972656">
      <reportElement x="5" y="40" width="500" height="20"/>
      <textContent><![CDATA[Aircraft registered in MD]]></textContent>
    </text>
    <rectangle radius="0">
      <reportElement mode="Opaque" x="5" y="60" width="782"
                     height="80" forecolor="#000000"/>
      <graphicElement pen="None" fill="Solid"/>
    </rectangle>
    <frame>
      <reportElement x="105" y="80" width="100" height="20"
                     backcolor="#FFFFFF"/>
      <box border="Thin" borderColor="#000000"/>
      <text textAlignment="Left" verticalAlignment="Bottom"
            textHeight="13.578125" lineSpacingFactor="1.3578125"
            leadingOffset="-3.1972656">
        <reportElement x="5" y="0" width="55" height="20"/>
        <textContent><![CDATA[1]]></textContent>
      </text>
    </frame>
  </page>
</jasperPrint>
```

The **Document Type Definition (DTD)** for the generated XML when exporting to this format can be found at http://jasperreports.sourceforge.net/dtds/jasperprint.dtd.

Reports exported to XML can be viewed with the JasperViewer utility included with JasperReports. To view a report exported to XML, the -XML argument needs to be passed to JasperViewer. For example, to view the above XML report, the following command needs to be typed in the command line (assuming all required libraries are already in the CLASSPATH):

```
net.sf.jasperreports.view.JasperViewer -Freports/DatasetDemoReport.
jrpxml -XML
```

Exporting reports to XML has some advantages over using the compiled report directly. For example, exported reports are human readable and editable, and they can easily be stored in a database without resorting to **BLOBS (Binary Large Objects)**.

# Exporting to CSV

**CSV (Comma Separated Values)** files contain a number of values separated by commas. There are several pieces of software that can parse CSV files. JasperReports includes built-in functionality to export reports to CSV files. The following example illustrates the process:

```
package net.ensode.jasperbook;

import java.io.File;

import net.sf.jasperreports.engine.JRException;
import net.sf.jasperreports.engine.JRExporterParameter;
import net.sf.jasperreports.engine.JasperPrint;
import net.sf.jasperreports.engine.export.JRCsvExporter;
import net.sf.jasperreports.engine.util.JRLoader;

public class CsvExportDemo
{
  public static final String REPORT_DIRECTORY = "reports";

  public void csvExport(String reportName)
  {
    File file = new File(REPORT_DIRECTORY + "/" + reportName +
                                           ".jrprint");

    try
```

```
       {
          JasperPrint jasperPrint = (JasperPrint)
                                JRLoader.loadObject(file);
          JRCsvExporter csvExporter = new JRCsvExporter();

          csvExporter.setParameter(JRExporterParameter.
                          JASPER_PRINT, jasperPrint);
          csvExporter.setParameter(JRExporterParameter.OUTPUT_FILE_NAME,
                          REPORT_DIRECTORY + "/" + reportName + ".csv");
          System.out.println("Exporting report...");
          csvExporter.exportReport();
          System.out.println("Done!");
       }
       catch (JRException e)
       {
          e.printStackTrace();
       }
     }

     public static void main(String[] args)
     {
       new CsvExportDemo().csvExport(args[0]);
     }

}
```

Again, this example follows the same pattern we have seen in previous examples. The JRExporter implementation used to export to CSV is net.sf.jasperreports. engine.export.JRCsvExporter. The report to export and the file name of the exported report are set by assigning the appropriate values to the JRExporterParameter.JASPER_PRINT and JRExporterParameter.OUTPUT_FILE_NAME parameters.

The above code will generate a CSV file that looks like the following:

```
Aircraft registered in MD,,,,,,,,,,,,,
CHALLENGER II,,CL-600-2B16,,TOTAL,,,,,,,
SEVERNA PARK,,1,,0,,1,,,,,,
SPARKS,,0,,1,,1,,,,,,
TOTAL,,1,,1,,2,,,,,,
Aircraft registered in NY,,,,,,,,,,,,,
C90A,,CGS HAWK,,CH 2000,,CHALLENGER II,,CL-600-2B16,,COZY MARK IV,
BROOKLYN,,0,,0,,0,,0,,0,,1
HOLLEY,,0,,0,,0,,1,,0,,0
```

```
MAYVILLE,,0,,0,,0,,0,,0,,0
MECHANICVILLE,,0,,0,,0,,1,,0,,0
SAINT JAMES,,1,,0,,0,,0,,0,,0
SAYVILLE,,0,,0,,2,,0,,0,,0
WATERTOWN,,0,,1,,0,,0,,0,,0
WEST HENRIETTE,,0,,0,,0,,1,,0,,0
WHITE PLAINS,,0,,0,,0,,0,,1,,0
TOTAL,,1,,1,,2,,3,,1,,1,,
CW-3,,TOTAL,,,,,,,,,
BROOKLYN,,0,,1,,,,,,,,,
HOLLEY,,0,,1,,,,,,,,,
MAYVILLE,,1,,1,,,,,,,,,
MECHANICVILLE,,0,,1,,,,,,,,,
SAINT JAMES,,0,,1,,,,,,,,,
SAYVILLE,,0,,2,,,,,,,,,
WATERTOWN,,0,,1,,,,,,,,,
WEST HENRIETTE,,0,,1,,,,,,,,,
WHITE PLAINS,,0,,1,,,,,,,,,
TOTAL,,1,,10,,,,,,,,,
Aircraft registered in VA,,,,,,,,,,,,,,
CL-600-2B19,,CL-600-2C10,,TOTAL,,,,,,,
ARLINGTON,,18,,5,,23,,,,,,
DULLES,,4,,0,,4,,,,,,
TOTAL,,22,,5,,27,,,,,,
```

Here is how the CSV file is rendered by OpenOffice.org's spreadsheet component, Calc:

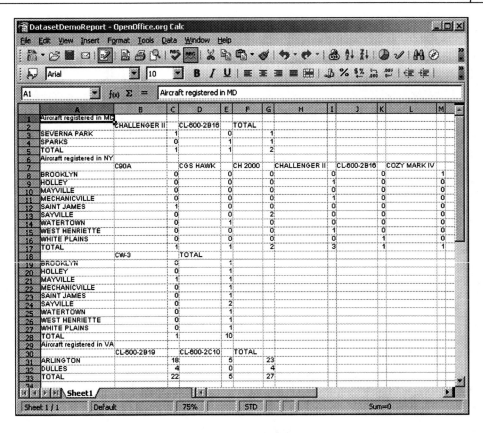

# Exporting to Plain Text

Reports can be exported to plain text. For this section, we will export a more textual report than the one we used for previous sections. The JRXML template for the report we will export is as follows:

```
<?xml version="1.0" encoding="UTF-8"?>
<!DOCTYPE jasperReport PUBLIC "-//JasperReports//DTD Report Design//
 EN" "http://jasperreports.sourceforge.net/dtds/jasperreport.dtd">
<jasperReport name="PlainTextExportDemoReport">
  <title>
    <band height="30">
      <staticText>
        <reportElement x="0" y="0" width="555" height="30"/>
        <text>
          <![CDATA[Text Heavy Report]]>
        </text>
```

```
      </staticText>
    </band>
  </title>
  <detail>
    <band height="100">
      <staticText>
        <reportElement x="0" y="0" width="555" height="100"/>
        <text>
          <![CDATA[
Exporting to plain text makes more sense when the report is completely
                                            (or mostly) text.
Since tables and graphical elements don't translate to plain text
                                            very well.
We created this report template to demonstrate exporting to plain text.
Exciting, isn't it?]]>
        </text>
      </staticText>
    </band>
  </detail>
</jasperReport>
```

The following Java code fragment will export the JasperReports' native report
generated by the above JRXML template into plain text:

```
package net.ensode.jasperbook;

import java.io.File;

import net.sf.jasperreports.engine.JRException;
import net.sf.jasperreports.engine.JRExporterParameter;
import net.sf.jasperreports.engine.JasperPrint;
import net.sf.jasperreports.engine.export.JRTextExporter;
import net.sf.jasperreports.engine.export.JRTextExporterParameter;
import net.sf.jasperreports.engine.util.JRLoader;

public class PlainTextExportDemo
{
  public static final String REPORT_DIRECTORY = "reports";

  public void plainTextExport(String reportName)
  {
    File file = new File(REPORT_DIRECTORY + "/" + reportName +
                                        ".jrprint");
```

```
   try
   {
      JasperPrint jasperPrint = (JasperPrint) JRLoader.loadObject(file);
      JRTextExporter textExporter = new JRTextExporter();

      textExporter.setParameter(JRExporterParameter.JASPER_PRINT,
                                jasperPrint);
      textExporter.setParameter(JRExporterParameter.OUTPUT_FILE_NAME,
                        REPORT_DIRECTORY + "/" + reportName + ".txt");
      textExporter.setParameter(JRTextExporterParameter.CHARACTER_WIDTH,
                                new Integer(10));
      textExporter.setParameter(JRTextExporterParameter.
                                CHARACTER_HEIGHT, new Integer(10));
      System.out.println("Exporting report...");
      textExporter.exportReport();
      System.out.println("Done!");
   }
   catch (JRException e)
   {
      e.printStackTrace();
   }
}

public static void main(String[] args)
{
   new PlainTextExportDemo().plainTextExport(args[0]);
}
}
```

After compiling and executing the above code with the report generated by the
JRXML template we have just written, we should have a text file with the following
contents in our hard drive:

```
    Text Heavy Report

Exporting to plain text makes more sense when the
report is completely (or mostly) text.
Since tables and graphical elements don't translate to
plain text very well.
We created this report template to demonstrate
exporting to plain text.
Exciting, isn't it?
```

Notice, in this example, we had to set some parameters in addition to the
output file name. The JRTextExporterParameter.CHARACTER_WIDTH and
JRTextExporterParameter.CHARACTER_HEIGHT parameters tell JasperReports how

many pixels in the report to map to a character in the exported text. This is because the exported text is basically a bunch of pixels, and the JasperReports engine does not directly recognize the characters in it. By specifying the CHARACTER_WIDTH and CHARACTER_HEIGHT parameters, the engine can make an educated guess on how to map the pixels to ASCII characters.

An alternative way of helping JasperReports map report pixels to ASCII characters is to specify the page width and page height of the exported report. This can be achieved by setting the JRExportParameter.PAGE_WIDTH and JRExportParameter.PAGE_HEIGHT parameters to appropriate values on JRTextExporter.

Either the page width and height or the character width and height (or both) must be specified when exporting to plain text. If both page and character dimensions are specified, the character dimensions take precedence.

> Since the algorithm JasperReports uses to generate plain text reports maps pixels to ASCII characters, the conversion is not always 100% accurate. In most cases, report templates must be modified in order for them to be successfully exported to text. For these reasons, we recommend avoiding exporting reports to plain text unless absolutely necessary.

# Directing HTML Reports to a Browser

In previous chapters, we have seen examples of generating a PDF report and streaming it to the browser on the fly. Earlier in this chapter, we saw how to export reports to an HTML format and store it in the file system. In this section, we will cover how to export a report to HTML and immediately send it to the user's browser window. The following example is a servlet that exports an already filled JasperPrint object to HTML and displays the resulting exported report to the browser. As can be seen from the code, it takes the base report name as a request parameter. Executing this report using the BarChartDemoReport from Chapter 7 results in the following page displayed in the browser.

```
package net.ensode.jasperbook;

import java.io.File;
import java.io.IOException;
import java.io.PrintWriter;

import javax.servlet.ServletContext;
import javax.servlet.ServletException;
import javax.servlet.http.HttpServlet;
import javax.servlet.http.HttpServletRequest;
import javax.servlet.http.HttpServletResponse;
```

```
import net.sf.jasperreports.engine.JRException;
import net.sf.jasperreports.engine.JRExporterParameter;
import net.sf.jasperreports.engine.JasperPrint;
import net.sf.jasperreports.engine.export.JRHtmlExporter;
import net.sf.jasperreports.engine.export.JRHtmlExporterParameter;
import net.sf.jasperreports.engine.util.JRLoader;
import net.sf.jasperreports.j2ee.servlets.ImageServlet;

public class HtmlReportServlet extends HttpServlet
{
  public static final String REPORT_DIRECTORY = "/reports";

  protected void doGet(HttpServletRequest request,
      HttpServletResponse response) throws ServletException, IOException
  {
    ServletContext context =
                        this.getServletConfig().getServletContext();
    String reportName = request.getParameter("reportName");
    File file = new File(context.getRealPath(REPORT_DIRECTORY + "/"
                                      + reportName + ".jrprint"));
    PrintWriter printWriter = response.getWriter();

    try
    {

      JasperPrint jasperPrint = (JasperPrint) JRLoader.loadObject(file
                                .getPath());
      JRHtmlExporter htmlExporter = new JRHtmlExporter();

      response.setContentType("text/html");
      request.getSession().setAttribute(ImageServlet.DEFAULT_JASPER_
                                PRINT_SESSION_ATTRIBUTE, jasperPrint);

      htmlExporter.setParameter(JRExporterParameter.JASPER_PRINT,
                                jasperPrint);
      htmlExporter.setParameter(JRExporterParameter.OUTPUT_WRITER,
                                printWriter);
      htmlExporter.setParameter(JRHtmlExporterParameter.IMAGES_URI,
                                "image?image=");
      htmlExporter.exportReport();
    }
    catch (JRException e)
    {
      // display stack trace in the browser
      e.printStackTrace(printWriter);
    }
  }
}
```

Directing the browser to the URL for this servlet will result in the report being displayed in the browser in HTML, as can be seen in the following screenshot:

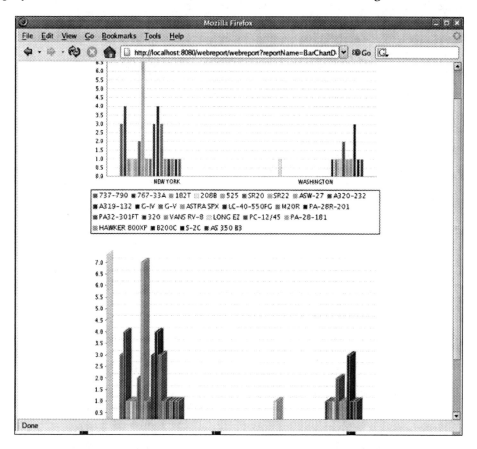

We chose to export this particular report to illustrate that the HTML exporting capability works fine for more complex reports. This report generates charts at fill time, which get translated to image files when exporting to HTML.

In order to stream a report as HTML to the browser, we need to set some parameters as an instance of net.sf.jasperreports.engine.export.JRHtmlExporter. The first parameter name is defined in the net.sf.jasperreports.engine. JRExporterParameter.JASPER_PRINT constant. Its value must be an instance of net.sf.jasperreports.engine.JasperPrint containing the report we wish to stream to the browser. The next parameter we need to set is defined in the net. sf.jasperreports.engine.JRExporterParameter.OUTPUT_WRITER constant, as can be seen in the example. Its corresponding value must be the instance of java.io.PrintWriter obtained by calling the getWriter() method on the HttpServletResponse object.

If the report we are exporting contains images, then there are a couple of extra steps we need to take to make sure the images are displayed correctly in the browser. We must attach the JasperPrint instance to the HTTP session. The session attribute name is defined in the DEFAULT_JASPER_PRINT_SESSION_ATTRIBUTE constant defined in net.sf.jasperreports.j2ee.servlets.ImageServlet.

We also need to set the JRHtmlExporterParameter.IMAGES_URI parameter as an instance of JRHtmlExporter. Its corresponding value must be a string indicating the location of the images. In practice, this value is almost always set to the URL mapped to the net.sf.jasperreports.j2ee.servlets.ImageServlet included with JasperReports. In our example, we set its value to "image?image=", which is a typical value. Of course, the ImageServlet must be included in web.xml for reports with images to render properly. The web.xml corresponding to the previous servlet deployment is as follows:

```
<!DOCTYPE web-app PUBLIC
 "-//Sun Microsystems, Inc.//DTD Web Application 2.3//EN"
 "http://java.sun.com/dtd/web-app_2_3.dtd">
<web-app>
  <servlet>
    <servlet-name>webreport</servlet-name>
    <servlet-class>
      net.ensode.jasperbook.HtmlReportServlet
    </servlet-class>
  </servlet>
  <servlet>
    <servlet-name>ImageServlet</servlet-name>
    <servlet-class>
      net.sf.jasperreports.j2ee.servlets.ImageServlet
    </servlet-class>
  </servlet>
  <servlet-mapping>
    <servlet-name>webreport</servlet-name>
    <url-pattern>/webreport</url-pattern>
  </servlet-mapping>
  <servlet-mapping>
    <servlet-name>ImageServlet</servlet-name>
    <url-pattern>/image</url-pattern>
  </servlet-mapping>
</web-app>
```

Notice that for this example, we loaded an already filled report from the file system and streamed it to the browser as HTML. It is also possible to load a Jasper template, fill it, then export the resulting report to HTML, and stream it to the browser. To accomplish this, we would load the Jasper template from the file system, fill it using the JasperFillManager.fillReport() method, and then export the resulting JasperPrint object to HTML. The following example is a modified version of the previous servlet. This new version illustrates this procedure.

```java
package net.ensode.jasperbook;

import java.io.IOException;
import java.io.InputStream;
import java.io.PrintWriter;
import java.sql.Connection;
import java.sql.DriverManager;
import java.sql.SQLException;
import java.util.HashMap;

import javax.servlet.ServletException;
import javax.servlet.ServletOutputStream;
import javax.servlet.http.HttpServlet;
import javax.servlet.http.HttpServletRequest;
import javax.servlet.http.HttpServletResponse;

import net.sf.jasperreports.engine.JRException;
import net.sf.jasperreports.engine.JRExporterParameter;
import net.sf.jasperreports.engine.JasperFillManager;
import net.sf.jasperreports.engine.JasperPrint;
import net.sf.jasperreports.engine.export.JRHtmlExporter;
import net.sf.jasperreports.engine.export.JRHtmlExporterParameter;
import net.sf.jasperreports.j2ee.servlets.ImageServlet;

public class HtmlReportServlet2 extends HttpServlet
{
  public static final String REPORT_DIRECTORY = "/reports";

  protected void doGet(HttpServletRequest request, HttpServletResponse
                    response) throws ServletException, IOException
  {
    Connection connection;
    String reportName = request.getParameter("reportName");
```

```
      PrintWriter printWriter = response.getWriter();
      InputStream reportStream = getServletConfig().getServletContext()
          .getResourceAsStream("/" + REPORT_DIRECTORY + "/" + reportName
                                                      + ".jasper");

   JasperPrint jasperPrint;

   try
   {
     Class.forName("com.mysql.jdbc.Driver"); connection =
              DriverManager.getConnection("jdbc:mysql://localhost:
              3306/flightstats?user=root&password=password");

    jasperPrint = JasperFillManager.fillReport(reportStream,
              new HashMap(), connection);

    JRHtmlExporter htmlExporter = new JRHtmlExporter();

    response.setContentType("text/html");
    request.getSession().setAttribute(ImageServlet.DEFAULT_JASPER_
                            PRINT_SESSION_ATTRIBUTE, jasperPrint);

    htmlExporter.setParameter(JRExporterParameter.JASPER_PRINT,
                            jasperPrint);
    htmlExporter.setParameter(JRExporterParameter.OUTPUT_WRITER,
                            printWriter);
    htmlExporter.setParameter(JRHtmlExporterParameter.IMAGES_URI,
                            "image?image=");

    htmlExporter.exportReport();

    connection.close();
   }
   catch (Throwable t)
   {
     // display stack trace in the browser
     t.printStackTrace(printWriter);
   }

  }
}
```

The main difference between this example and the previous one is that instead
of loading the JasperPrint object from the file system, we are loading the Jasper
template, filling it, and storing the filled report in a JasperPrint object. This instance
is then used as the value for the JRExporterParameter.JASPER_PRINT parameter.

# Summary

In this chapter, we learned how to export reports to all formats supported by JasperReports. We learned to export reports to PDF by taking advantage of the `JRPdfExporter` class. We also saw how to export reports to RTF/Microsoft Word by taking advantage of the `JRRtfExporter` class.

Similarly, to export reports to Microsoft Excel, HTML, and CSV formats we used the `JExcelApiExporter`, `JRHtmlExporter`, and `JRCsvExporter` classes respectively. The `JRXmlExporter` class of JasperReports provided us with the functionality to export our reports to the XML format.

Finally, we learned to export reports to Plain Text by taking advantage of the `JRTextExporter` class. However, the algorithm JasperReports uses to generate Plain Text reports does not always produce accurate results while mapping the report pixels to ASCII characters. The chapter also gave us an insight on how to direct HTML reports to a browser.

# 10
# Graphical Report Design with iReport

So far we have been creating all our reports by writing JRXML templates by hand. There are several report designers that can help us visually generate JRXML templates. When using report designers, there is little or no need to edit JRXML templates by hand. Some of the existing report designers are standalone applications; others are plug-ins for IDEs or text editors.

The following table lists some of the available IDE/Editor plug-in report designers:

| Name | IDE/Editor | URL |
| --- | --- | --- |
| JasperAssistant | Eclipse | `http://www.jasperassistant.com/` |
| Sunshine Reports | Eclipse | `http://www.sunshinereports.com/` |
| JasperReportsViewer | JEdit | `http://www.sourceillustrated.com/jasperjedit/` |

Some of the standalone report designers include JasperPal (`http://jasperpal.sourceforge.net`) and iReport (`http://ireport.sourceforge.net`). However, **iReport** is the official report designer for JasperReports.

In this chapter, we will be focusing on iReport since covering all of these report designers would no doubt result in shallow coverage of each one of them.

iReport started as an independent project by Giulio Toffoli. JasperSoft recognized the popularity of iReport and in October, 2005 hired Giulio Toffoli, and made iReport the official report designer for JasperSoft. Just like JasperReports, iReport is open source. It is licensed under the **GNU Public License (GPL)**.

By the end of this chapter, you will be able to:

- Obtain and set up iReport
- Quickly create database reports by taking advantage of iReport's Report Wizard
- Graphically, design reports with iReport
- Add multiple columns to a report
- Group report data
- Add images and charts to a report

# Obtaining iReport

iReport can be downloaded from its home page at `http://ireport.sourceforge.net/` by clicking on the **Download** menu item at the top left main menu, then clicking on the link for the latest release, and finally clicking on a mirror. It can be downloaded as a source file, as a ZIP file, as a gzip'ed TAR file, or as a self-extracting Windows executable.

To install iReport, either execute the self-extracting executable, or extract the ZIP, or gzip'ed TAR file to any directory. This will create a directory called `iReport-x.y.z` directory, where `x`, `y`, and `z` represent the major, minor, and point release version of iReport.

To execute iReport, simply execute the `iReport.bat` (for Microsoft Windows systems) or `iReport.sh` (for *nix systems) file from the command line or by double clicking on it from a file manager. The following screenshot illustrates how iReport looks when it is opened for the first time:

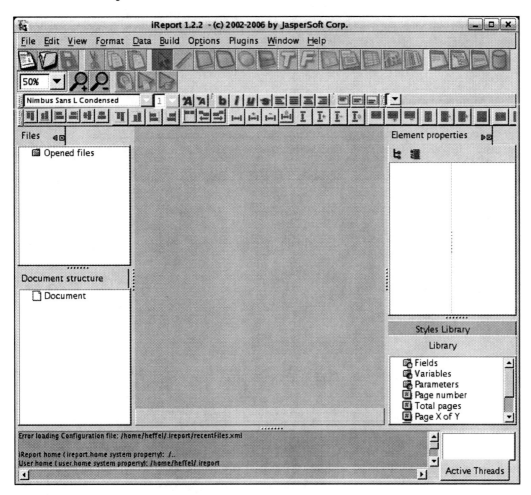

# Setting Up iReport

iReport can help us quickly generate database reports. To do so, we need to provide it with JDBC driver and connection information for our database.

iReport comes bundled with a JDBC driver for MySQL. If we need to connect to a different database, we need to add the JDBC driver to iReport's CLASSPATH. This can be done by clicking on **Options | Classpath**.

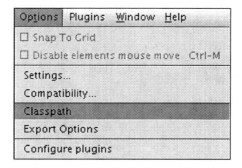

After doing so we should see a window like the following:

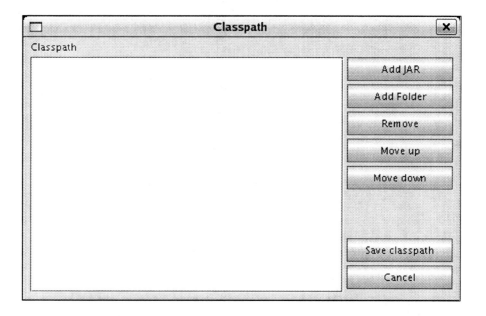

To add our JDBC driver to the CLASSPATH, we need to click on the **Add JAR** button, then navigate to the location of the JAR file containing the JDBC driver, select it, and click on the **Open** button at the bottom of the pop-up window.

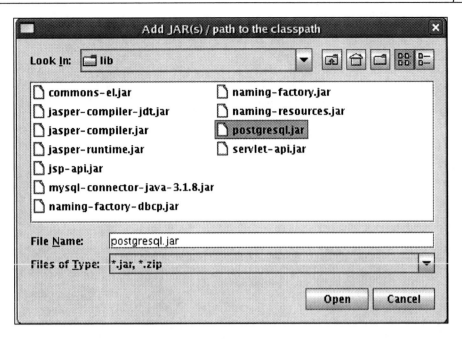

After following these steps, the **Classpath** iReport window should show the newly added JAR file. We then need to click on the **Save classpath** button to make the change permanent.

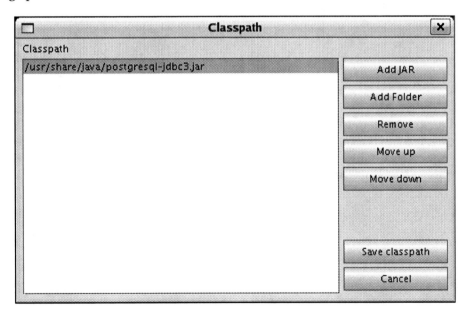

Once we have added the JDBC driver to iReport's CLASSPATH, we need to create a new database connection. To do so, we need to click on **Data | Connections / Datasources**.

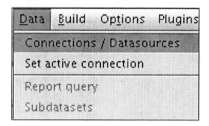

We should then see a pop-up window like the following:

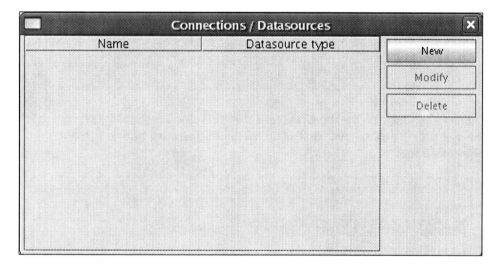

To add the connection, we need to click on the **New** button, select the appropriate JDBC driver, fill in the connection information, and click on the **Save** button. The following screenshot illustrates the information that needs to be entered to access the FlightStats database we have been using throughout the book:

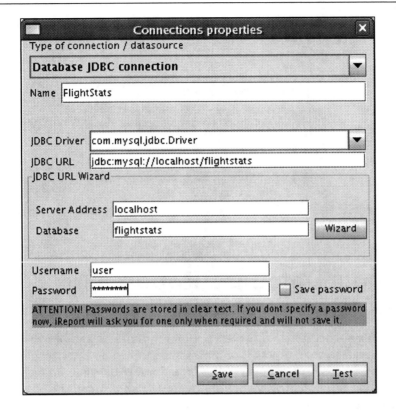

 In the previous section, we added the JDBC driver for PostgreSQL for illustration purposes only since, as we mentioned previously, iReport comes bundled with a JDBC driver for MySQL. Here, we are creating a connection to the MySQL FlightStats database we have been using throughout the book.

 **Easiest Way to Enter the JDBC URL**

The easiest way to enter the JDBC URL is to populate the **Server Address** and **Database** text fields, and then click on the **Wizard** button. This will result in the JDBC URL being automatically populated with a URL in the correct format for the RDBMS we are using.

Before saving the database connection properties, it is a good idea to click on the **Test** button to make sure we can connect to the database. If we can, we should see a pop-up window like the following:

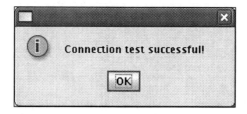

After verifying that we can successfully connect to the database, we are ready to create some database reports.

# Creating a Database Report in Record Time

iReport contains a wizard that allows us to quickly generate database reports (very useful if the boss asks for a report 15 minutes before quitting time on a Friday!). The wizard allows us to use one of several predefined templates that are included with iReport. Included report templates are divided into two groups: templates laid out in a 'Columnar' manner, and templates laid out in a 'Tabular' manner. Columnar templates generate reports that are laid out in columns, and tabular templates generate reports that are laid out like a table.

In this section, we will create a report displaying all aircraft with a horsepower of 1000 HP or more.

To quickly create a database report, we need to select the **Report Wizard** menu item from the **File** menu.

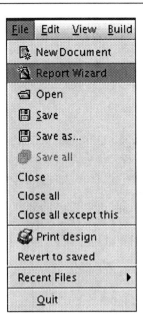

Then enter the database query that will retrieve report data from the database on the resulting pop-up window, and then click on the button labeled **Next**.

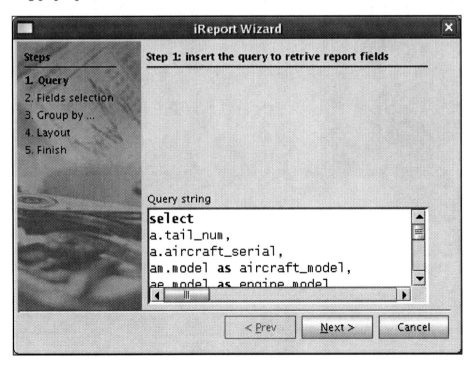

The complete query for the report is:

```
select
a.tail_num,
a.aircraft_serial,
am.model as aircraft_model,
ae.model as engine_model
from aircraft a, aircraft_models am, aircraft_engines ae
where a.aircraft_model_code = am.aircraft_model_code
and a.aircraft_engine_code = ae.aircraft_engine_code
and ae.horsepower >= 1000
```

The following window shows a list of all columns selected in the query, allowing us to select which ones we would like to use as report fields:

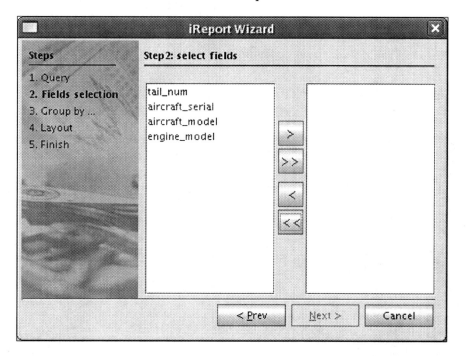

In this case, we want the data for all columns in the query to be displayed in the report. Therefore, we select all columns by clicking on the button labeled >>.

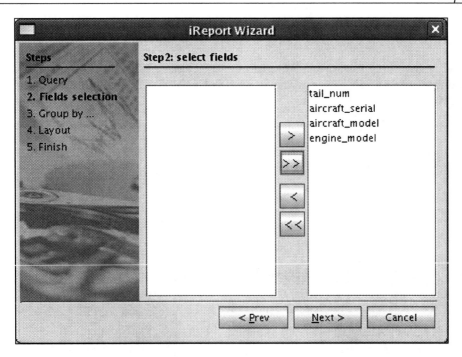

We then select how we want to group the data and click **Next**. This creates a report group (refer to the *Grouping Report Data* section in Chapter 6 for details).

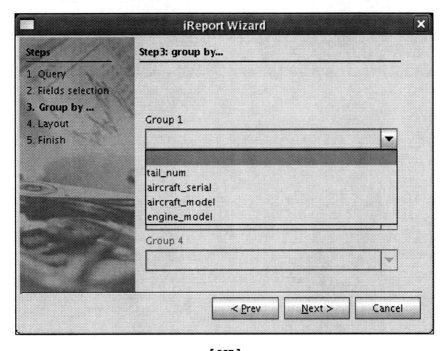

In this example, we will not group the report data. The screenshot illustrates how the drop-down contains the report fields selected in the previous step.

We then select the report layout ('Columnar' or 'Tabular'). Each option results in a different set of predefined templates to use. In this example, we will use the default tabular template, `classicT.xml`.

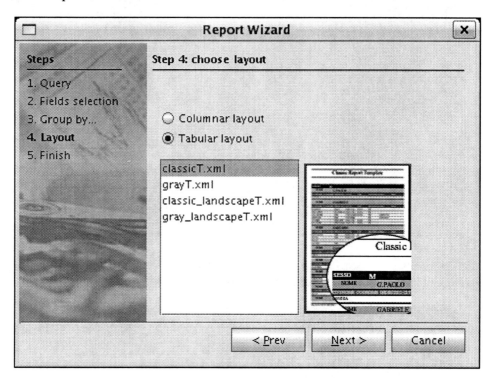

After selecting the layout and template, we click on **Next** to be presented with the last step.

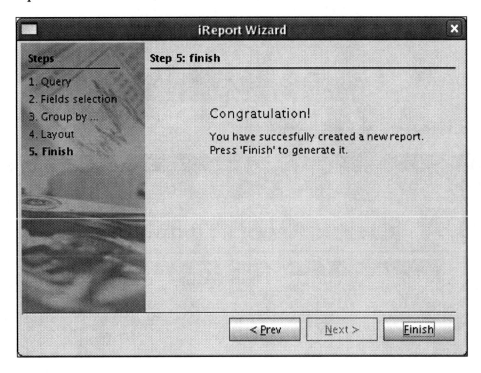

We then click on **Finish** to generate the report's JRXML template.

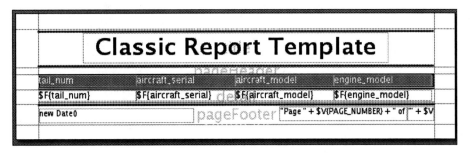

The generated report is not automatically saved. It is a good idea to do so at this point.

We can then compile and execute the report in one step by clicking on the **Build |
Execute report (using active conn.)** menu item.

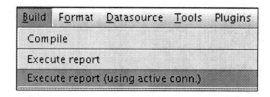

We can now see the generated report.

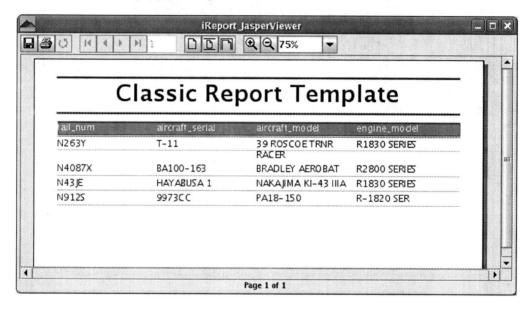

Admittedly, the report title and column headers need some tweaking. To modify the report title so that it actually reflects the report contents, we can either double-click on the report title on iReport's main window and type an appropriate report title, or right-click on the title and select **properties** from the resulting pop-up menu.

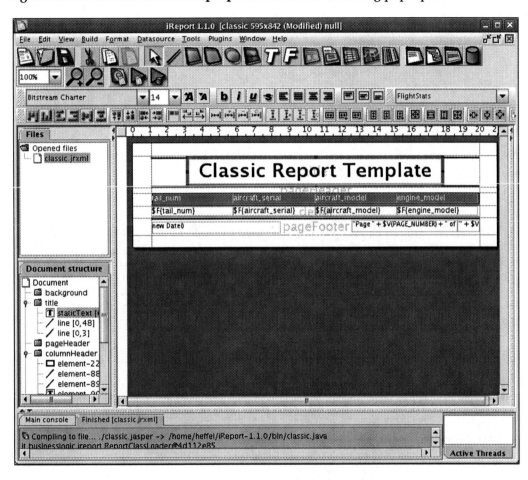

Double-clicking on the title is certainly the fastest way to modify it. However, the **properties** pop-up window allows us to modify not only the text, but also the font, borders, and several other properties.The following screenshot illustrates how to change the text through the **properties** pop-up window:

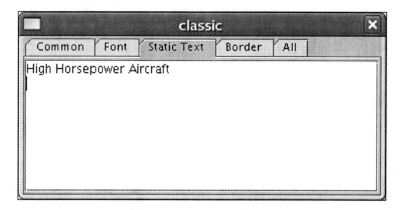

We repeat the procedure for each header. The following screenshot shows the resulting template as displayed in iReport's main window:

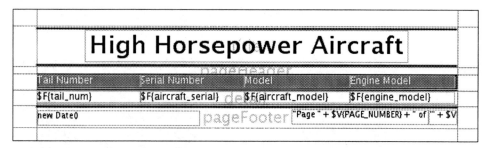

We compile and execute the report one more time to obtain the final version.

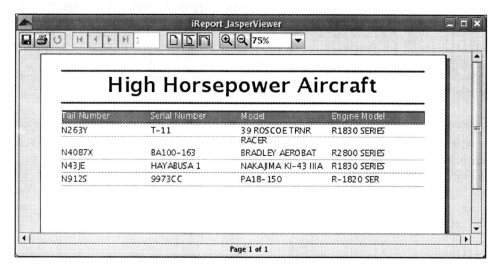

There you have it, the boss can have his report, and we can leave work and enjoy the weekend.

# Creating a Report "From Scratch"

In the previous section, we discussed how to quickly generate a database report by using iReport's **Report Wizard**. The wizard is very convenient since it allows us to create a report very quickly. However, its disadvantage is that it is not very flexible. In this section, we will cover how to create a report from scratch in iReport. Our report will show the tail number, serial number, and model of every aircraft in the FlightStats database.

To create a new report, click on the **File | New Document** menu item.

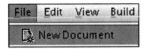

We should get a pop-up window like the following:

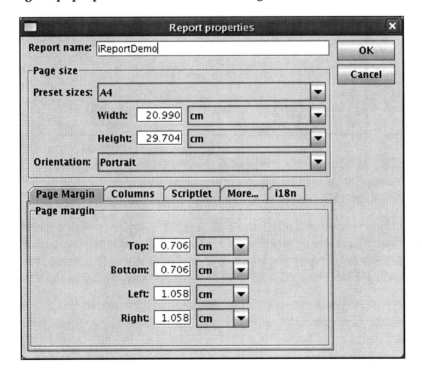

As can be seen in the screenshot, we can select the report's **width** and **height**, **orientation**, and **Page margin**. From the **Columns** tab, we can select **columns** (number), **width**, and **spacing** of the columns. From the **Scriptlet** tab, we can indicate what class to use as a scriptlet (if any). The **More** tab allows us to set the option of having the report title and/or summary in a new page and other miscellaneous settings. The **i18n** tab allows us to specify a resource bundle base name (the 'root' file name for a property file containing localized messages) for report localization, specify the report's behavior when a resource bundle is missing a value for a specific key in the report's locale, and set the report's XML encoding.

In this example, we will set the report name to **iReportDemo** and take all the other defaults. After clicking on the **OK** button, iReport's main window should look like this:

```
                        title

                     pageHeader
                    columnHeader


                       detail


                    columnFooter
                     pageFooter

                   lastPageFooter

                     summary
```

The horizontal lines divide the different report sections. Any item we insert between any two horizontal lines will be placed in the appropriate report section's band. Horizontal lines can be dragged to resize the appropriate section(s).

The vertical lines represent the left and right report margins. It is not possible to drag the vertical lines. To modify the left and right margins, we need to click on **Edit | Report Properties** to bring up the report properties window (the same one that pops up when creating a new report), and modifying the report margins from there.

Now that we have an empty report template, let us add a report title. For this, we will use the static text **Aircraft Report**. To add the static text, we need to click on the static text tool icon.

We then need to outline the area where the static text will be located.

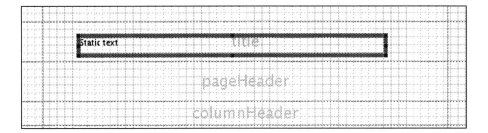

iReport, by default, inserts the text **Static text** inside the outline. To modify this default text, we need to double-click anywhere inside the static text area. We can then overwrite the default text with an appropriate title. Alternatively, we can right-click on the static text area and select the **Properties** menu item from the resulting pop-up window. Doing so, we will see the following pop-up window:

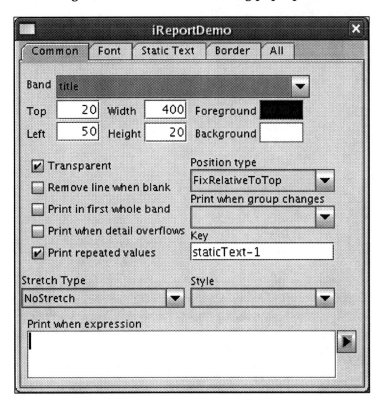

To modify the static text, we need to click on the **Static Text** tab, and enter the desired text in the text area.

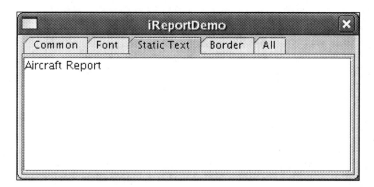

Our report should now look like this:

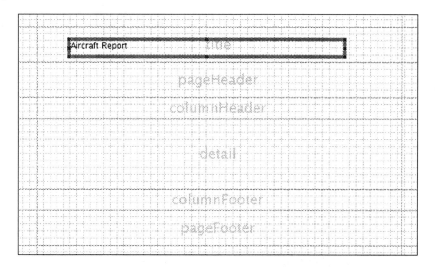

We can increase the size of the text by clicking on **Static Text** and selecting a new size from the font size combo box, make the font bold by clicking on the **b** icon, and center it by clicking on the icon to center text. These two icons and the combo box are outlined in the following screenshot:

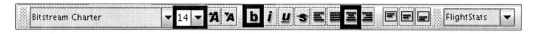

After setting the font size to 18, making it bold, and centering it, our report now looks like this:

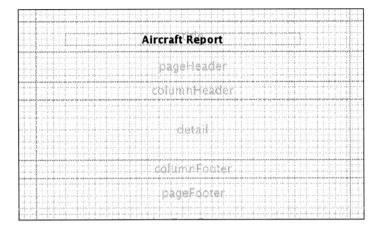

As we can see, the text is centered within its outline; but the outline itself is not quite centered. To center the outline, we need to click on the ▨ icon. This icon will center the selection both vertically and horizontally. The ▨ icon will center horizontally, and the ▨ icon will align vertically.

Using the same techniques used for adding the report title, we can add some more static text fields for the page header. After adding the page header, our report now looks like this:

We modified the vertical alignment of all three text fields in the page header (and the horizontal alignment of the leftmost text field) by selecting the appropriate values on the static text properties pop-up window that comes up when right-clicking on any text field and selecting **properties** from the resulting pop-up menu. The drop-down components used to modify static text alignment can be found under the **Font** tab, as can be seen in the following screenshot:

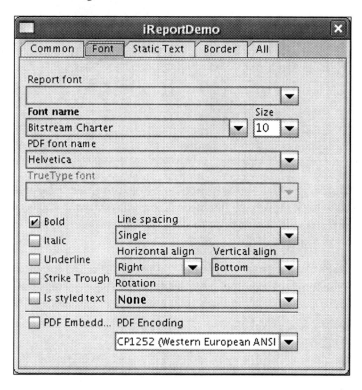

Now it is time to add some dynamic data to the report. We can enter a report query by clicking on the **Edit | Report query** menu item or by clicking on the database icon.

Clicking on the icon or on the **Edit | Report query** menu item will take us to the
following pop-up window:

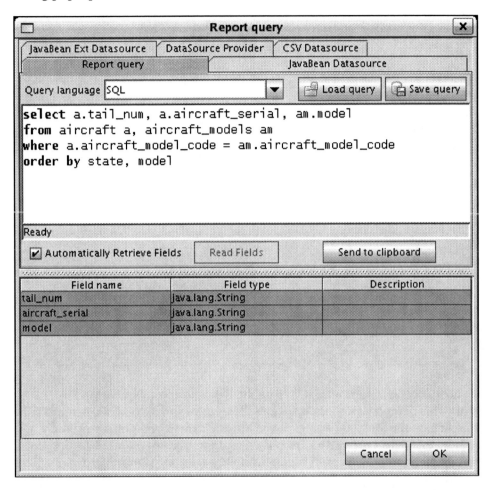

As we type the report query, by default iReport retrieves report fields from it. This
query will retrieve the tail number, serial number, and model of every aircraft in
the database.

Now that we have a query and report fields, we can add text fields to the report. We
can do so by clicking on the text field tool icon.

Then by outlining the location of the text field on the report, it should look like this now:

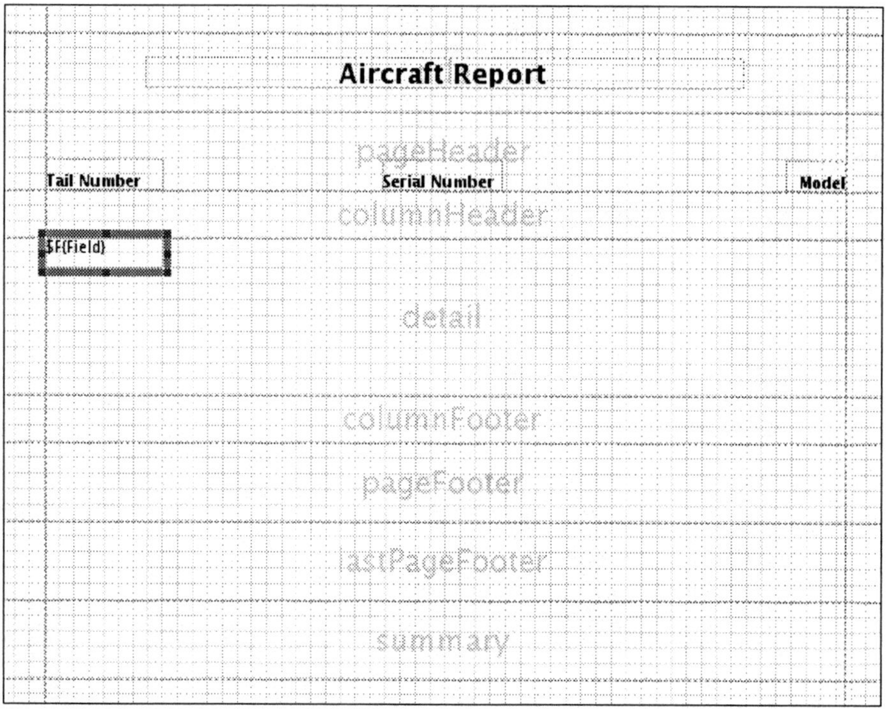

Notice how iReport inserts a fake field as the default report expression. To substitute this default report expression with an appropriate one, we need to either double-click on the text field and type the appropriate expression, or right-click on the field and select **properties** from the resulting pop-up menu. Selecting the **properties** menu item will result in the following window popping up:

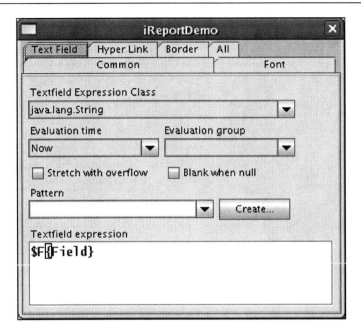

Here, we can substitute the default text field expression with an appropriate one. iReport turns the text field expression *green* to indicate that the expression is valid. As can be seen in the screenshot, this window allows us to change the text field expression class, evaluation time, and other properties.

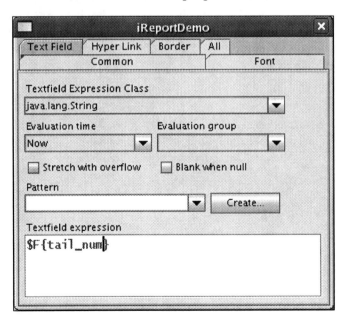

We repeat the process for the other two fields in the report. After doing so, our report now looks like this:

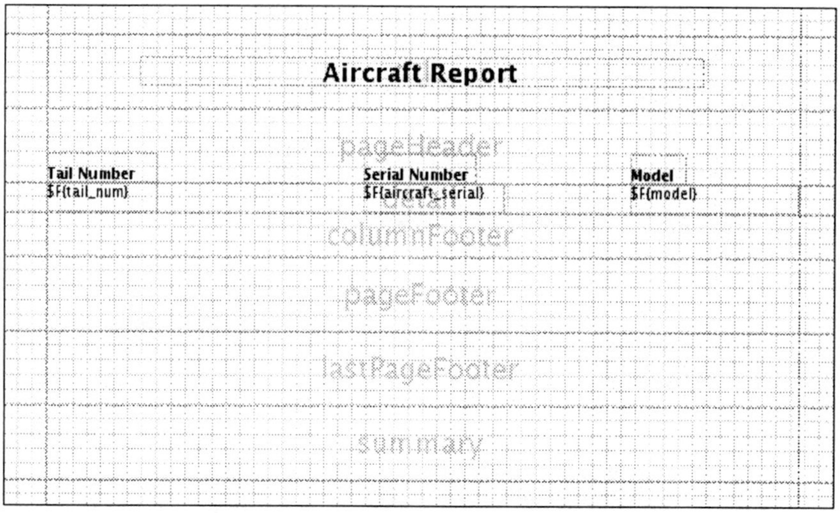

We decided to change the alignment of the **Model** static text to right, and to right-align it with its corresponding text field.

To avoid extra vertical space between records, we resized the detail band by dragging its bottom margin up. Also, to avoid having empty space between the page header and the detail band, we set the column header band height to 0. We now have a simple but complete report. We can execute it by clicking on the **Build | Execute report (using active conn.)** menu item. This will compile, fill, and display our report, which should look like this:

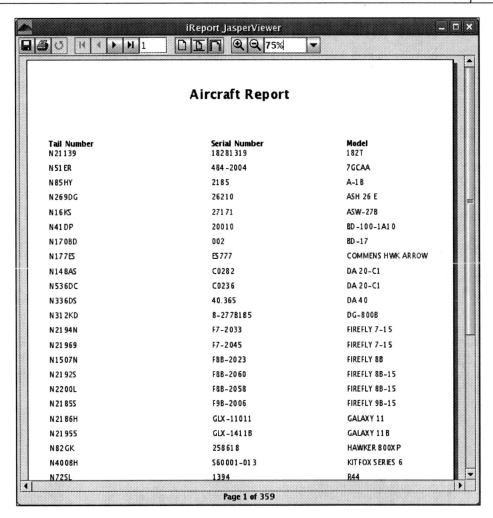

That's it! We have created a simple report graphically with iReport.

# Creating More Elaborate Reports

In the previous section, we created a fairly simple database report. In this section, we will modify that report to illustrate how to add images, charts, and multiple columns to a report. We will also see how to group report data. We will cover how to do all these tasks graphically with iReport.

# Adding Images to a Report

Adding static images to a report is very simple with iReport. All that is needed is to click on the image tool icon.

Then outline the area where the image will be placed on the report. In this example, we will add a company logo to our report.

As we can see, iReport puts a placeholder image inside its outline. To enter the image expression (recall from Chapter 7 that an image expression is an expression that resolves into the location of the image, which can be a URL or a location in the file system), we double-click on the image to obtain the following window:

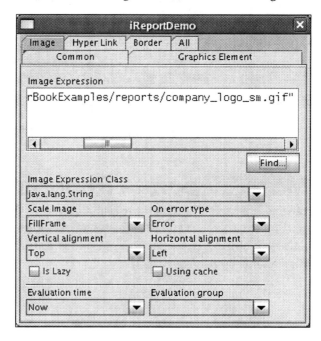

We can either type in the image expression or, if the image is in a local or network drive, we can click on the **Find** button and select the image file from the resulting file selector window. After entering the image expression our report now looks like this:

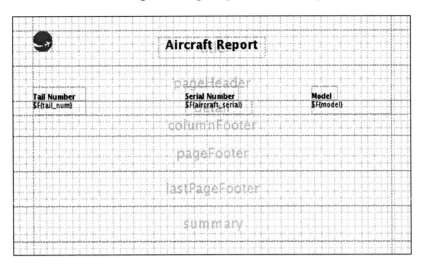

That is all it takes to add an image to a report.

# Adding Multiple Columns to a Report

The report we've been creating so far in this chapter contains over 11,000 records. It spans over 300 pages. As we can see, there is a lot of space between the text fields. Perhaps it would be a good idea to place the text fields closer together and add an additional column. This would cut the number of pages in the report by half.

To change the number of columns in the report, we need to click on **Edit | Report properties**, and then click on the **Columns** tab around the middle of the window.

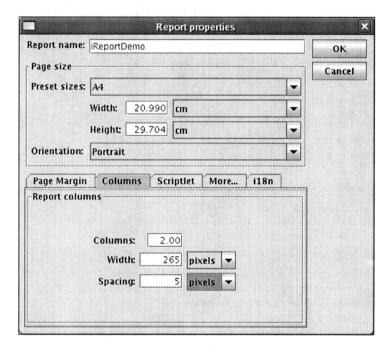

For this example, we will modify the report so that it has two columns, 265 pixels in width, with 5 pixels spacing between them. By using this layout, each column would take approximately half of the page, which should be enough for our needs.

Next, we need to move the static text in the page header to the column header band, and resize the fields so that they fit in the new, narrower width of the columns. Since we resized the column header band to a height of 0 earlier, we can't expand it graphically. We can only expand it by modifying the generated JRXML template directly. This can be accomplished by clicking on **Edit | XML Source** and editing the value of the **height** attribute of the <band> element inside the <columnHeader> element.

**Selecting an Appropriate XML Editor**

By default, iReport comes configured to use notepad as its XML editor. Notepad is not the best editor to use for XML editing, and it is only available on Windows workstations. To modify the default XML editor, we need to go to **Options | Settings**, then click on the **External programs** tab, and then type or select an editor to use in the **External editor** field.

After applying these changes, our report preview in iReport looks like this:

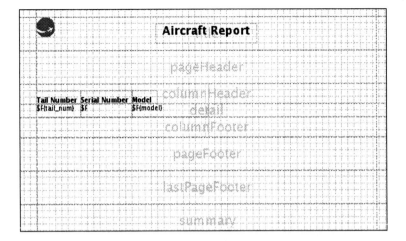

We can see the resulting report by clicking on **Build | Execute report (using active conn.)**.

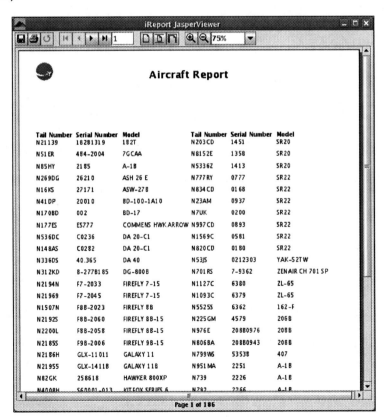

# Grouping Report Data

Suppose, we are asked to generate a report that provides aircraft data for aircraft registered in the United States, and we are required to divide the data by state. This is a perfect situation to apply report groups. Recall from Chapter 6 that report groups allow us to divide report data when a report expression changes.

Since our new requirement involves limiting the report data to aircraft registered in the United States, and dividing the data by state, we need to modify the report query. This can be accomplished by clicking on **Data | Report query** and entering the new query in the **Report SQL query** tab.

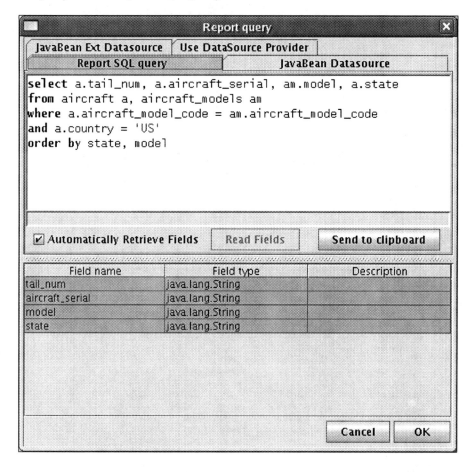

The new query limits the result set to aircraft registered in the United States. To define report groups, we need to click on **View | Report Groups**, and then click on the **New** button.

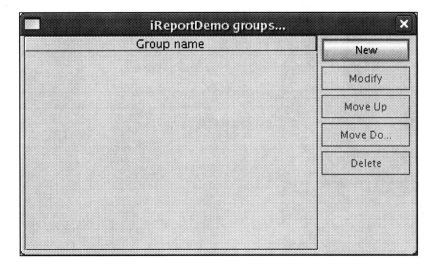

We then enter the report group, the group expression, and the desired group options.

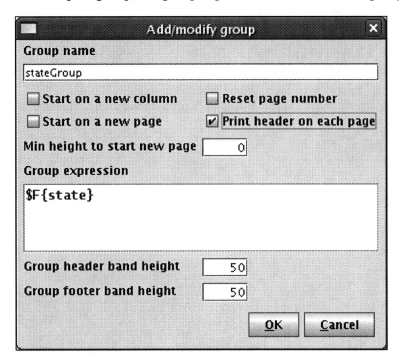

In this case, we will name the group **stateGroup**. We want to print the group header on each page, and we want the **state** field to be the group expression.

For aesthetic purposes, we move the static text fields in the column header band to the group header band, remove the column and page header bands by changing their height to zero, and add additional information to the group header band. After making all these changes, our report preview looks like this:

We execute the report by clicking on **Build | Execute report (using active conn.)** to see the generated report.

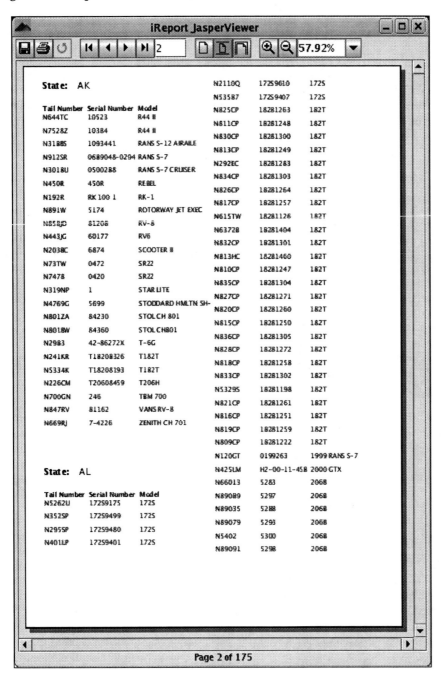

# Adding Charts to a Report

To add a chart to a report, we need to click on the chart tool icon.

We then need to outline the area where the chart will be placed in the report. After we are done outlining, the following window will pop-up, allowing us to select the type of chart we want to add to the report:

For this example, we will add a 3-D bar chart to the report. All that needs to be done is to click on the appropriate chart type, and then click on the **OK** button. Our chart will graphically illustrate the number of aircraft registered in each state in the United States (we will explain how to have the chart display the appropriate data later in this section). We will place it in the summary section at the end of the report. Since the chart will illustrate a lot of data, we need to resize the summary section so that our chart can fit. After resizing the summary section, outlining the area of the report to be covered by the chart, and selecting the chart type, the summary section of our report preview now looks like this:

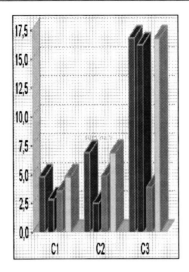

To fine-tune the appearance of the chart, we can right-click on it and select **Chart properties** from the pop-up menu.

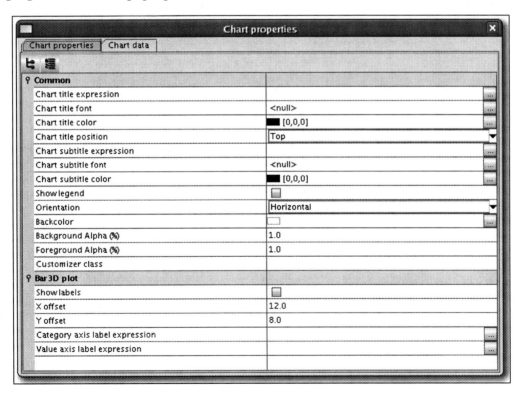

Since our chart will illustrate the total number of aircraft registered in each state, we need to create a new report variable to hold this information (refer to Chapter 6 for an explanation of report variables).

To add a report variable, we need to click on **View | Variables**, the following window will pop up:

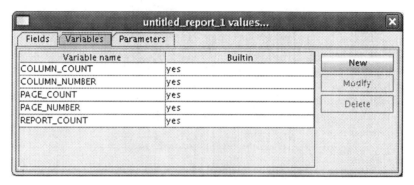

We click on the **New** button to create a new report variable.

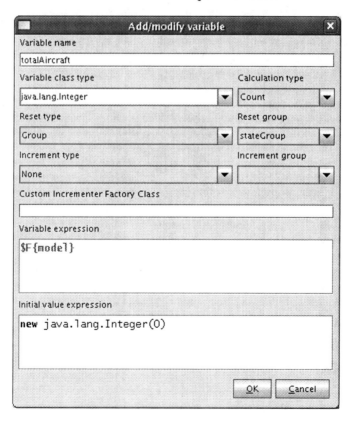

Since this variable's purpose is to count the number of aircraft in each state, it makes sense to make it an integer, with an initial value of zero and set it to reset its value for each state (remember **stateGroup** is a report group we created earlier, dividing the report by states). Now that we have created the report variable, we can use it as the value expression for our chart. Next, we right-click on the 3-D bar chart and select the **Chart properties** tab and then **Chart data** tab.

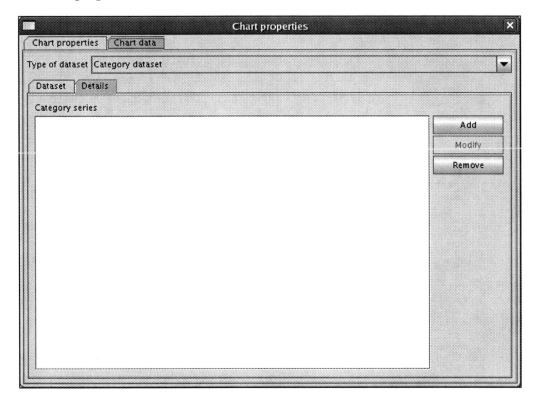

We add a new category dataset to the chart by clicking on the **Add** button. The following window pops up:

We fill out the series, category, and value expressions, and click on the **Ok** button. The **Label expression** text field allows us to customize the labels for the items (categories) in the chart. In our case, the state abbreviation (the default label) is appropriate. Therefore, we choose to leave it blank. We are now ready to run the report (by clicking on **Build | Execute report (using active conn.)**) to see our newly created chart.

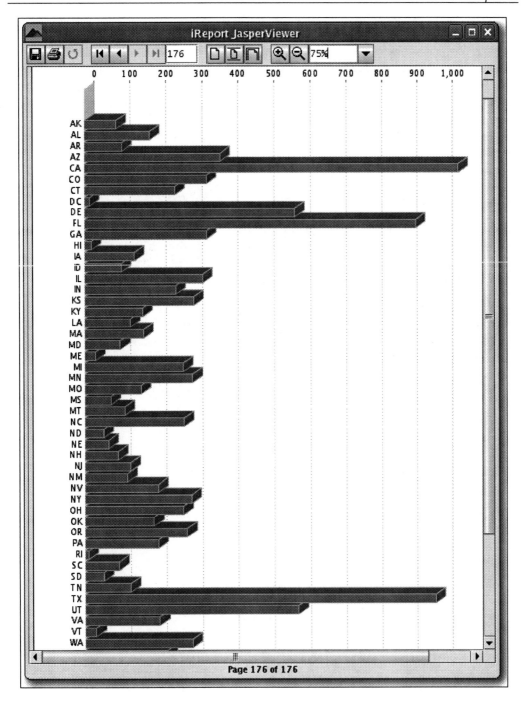

# Help and Support

Although this chapter didn't cover every iReport feature, we are confident that iReport is intuitive enough after you get comfortable with it. Some of the iReport features not covered in this chapter include subreport creation, adding crosstabs to a report, and adding lines, ellipses, and rectangles to a report. However, if additional help is needed, JasperSoft provides additional documentation for iReport, and lots of knowledgeable people frequent the iReport forums at
`http://sourceforge.net/forum/?group_id=64348`.

# Summary

This chapter taught us how to install and set up iReport, use iReport's report wizard to quickly generate a report, and graphically design custom reports with iReport. Moreover, we also learned how to group report data graphically with iReport, to add multiple columns to a report, and finally to add images and charts to a report graphically with iReport.

iReport is a very capable tool that can significantly reduce report design time. However, to use all features of iReport effectively, an iReport user must be familiar with basic JasperReports concepts like bands, report variables, report fields, and others.

# 11
# Integrating JasperReports with other Frameworks

In previous chapters, we have seen several examples of web-based applications generating reports and streaming them to the browser. In those examples, we have been using 'raw' servlets to generate reports. Most modern Java web-based applications are written using one of several web application frameworks. In this chapter, we will discuss how to integrate JasperReports with three of the most popular Java web application frameworks, **Spring Web MVC**, **JavaServer Faces**, and **Struts**.

In addition to using a web application framework, most modern Java projects use an Object-Relational Mapping tool for database access. In this chapter, we will cover how to generate reports with database data obtained using Hibernate, the most popular Java Object-Relational Mapping tool.

Please note that this chapter assumes some familiarity with the above frameworks. Feel free to skip to the sections that apply to frameworks used in your project.

## Integrating JasperReports with Hibernate

Hibernate (`http://www.hibernate.org`) is a very popular Object-Relational Mapping tool. JasperReports (version 1.2 and newer) includes native support for Hibernate integration. This integration consists of allowing embedded report queries to be written in the **Hibernate Query Language (HQL)**. The following JRXML template illustrates how to do this:

```
<?xml version="1.0" encoding="UTF-8"?>
<!DOCTYPE jasperReport PUBLIC "//JasperReports//DTD Report Design//EN"
  "http://jasperreports.sourceforge.net/dtds/jasperreport.dtd">
<jasperReport name="HibernateQueryDemoReport">
```

```xml
<parameter name="countryCode" class="java.lang.String"/>
<queryString language="hql">
  <![CDATA[from Aircraft aircraft where country = $P{countryCode}
           order by aircraft.id]]>
</queryString>
<field name="id" class="java.lang.String"/>
<field name="aircraftSerial" class="java.lang.String"/>
<field name="yearBuilt" class="java.lang.String"/>
<title>
  <band height="30">
    <textField>
      <reportElement width="555" height="30" x="0" y="0"/>
      <textFieldExpression>
        <![CDATA["Aircraft Registered in Country Code: " +
                 $P{countryCode}]]>
      </textFieldExpression>
    </textField>
  </band>
</title>
<pageHeader>
  <band height="30">
    <staticText>
      <reportElement width="100" height="30" x="0" y="0"/>
      <text>
        <![CDATA[Tail Number]]>
      </text>
    </staticText>
    <staticText>
      <reportElement width="100" height="30" x="100" y="0" />
      <text>
        <![CDATA[Serial Number]]>
      </text>
    </staticText>
    <staticText>
      <reportElement width="100" height="30" x="200" y="0"/>
      <text>
        <![CDATA[Year Built]]>
      </text>
    </staticText>
  </band>
</pageHeader>
<detail>
  <band height="30">
    <textField>
      <reportElement width="100" height="30" x="0" y="0"/>
```

```
        <textFieldExpression>
          <![CDATA[$F{id}]]>
        </textFieldExpression>
      </textField>
      <textField>
        <reportElement width="100" height="30" x="100" y="0"/>
        <textFieldExpression>
          <![CDATA[$F{aircraftSerial}]]>
        </textFieldExpression>
      </textField>
      <textField>
        <reportElement width="100" height="30" x="200" y="0"/>
        <textFieldExpression>
          <![CDATA[$F{yearBuilt}]]>
        </textFieldExpression>
      </textField>
    </band>
  </detail>
</jasperReport>
```

This JRXML template does not look much different from other JRXML templates we have seen before. The only difference is that its embedded report query is written in HQL. To let JasperReports know that it should interpret the query as HQL (as opposed to SQL), the `language` attribute of the `<queryString>` element must be set to `hql`.

There is nothing special we need to do to compile a report using HQL as its query language. We can use standard ANT tasks or compile it programmatically, just like any other JRXML template.

The HQL query in this template retrieves data in the `aircraft` table for all aircraft registered in the country specified by the `countryCode` parameter. Hibernate uses *Value Objects* that map to database tables. In order for the HQL query in the JRXML template to work, we need to create a Value Object that maps to the `aircraft` table.

> To develop the example for this section, we used an Eclipse plug-in called **Hibernate Synchronizer**. Hibernate Synchronizer generates Hibernate Java source code and XML configuration from the database schema. It greatly speeds up development of the Data Access Layer of an application using Hibernate for database access. Hibernate Synchronizer can be downloaded from http://hibernatesynch.sourceforge.net.

The code for this Value Object is as follows:

```java
package net.ensode.jasperbook.dbaccess;
import net.ensode.jasperbook.dbaccess.base.BaseAircraft;
public class Aircraft extends BaseAircraft
{
  private static final long serialVersionUID = 1L;
  /* [CONSTRUCTOR MARKER BEGIN] */
  public Aircraft()
  {
    super();
  }
  /**
   * Constructor for primary key
   */
  public Aircraft(java.lang.String id)
  {
    super(id);
  }
  /**
   * Constructor for required fields
   */
  public Aircraft(java.lang.String id, java.lang.String
      aircraftSerial, java.lang.String aircraftModelCode,
      java.lang.String aircraftEngineCode, java.lang.String
      yearBuilt, java.lang.String aircraftTypeId, java.lang.String
      aircraftEngineTypeId, java.lang.String registrantTypeId,
      java.lang.String name, java.lang.String address1,
      java.lang.String address2, java.lang.String city, java.lang
      String state, java.lang.String zip, java.lang.String region,
      java.lang.String county, java.lang.String country, java.lang
      String certification, java.lang.String statusCode, java.lang
      String modeSCode, java.lang.String fractOwner, java.util.Date
      lastActionDate, java.util.Date certIssueDate, java.util.Date
      airWorthDate)
  {

    super(id, aircraftSerial, aircraftModelCode, aircraftEngineCode,
    yearBuilt, aircraftTypeId, aircraftEngineTypeId, registrantTypeId,
    name, address1, address2, city, state, zip, region, county,
    country, certification, statusCode, modeSCode, fractOwner,
    lastActionDate, certIssueDate, airWorthDate);
  }

  /* [CONSTRUCTOR MARKER END] */

}
```

Notice that the above class extends a class called `BaseAircraft`, and its source code is as follows:

```
package net.ensode.jasperbook.dbaccess.base;

import java.lang.Comparable;

public abstract class BaseAircraft implements Comparable, Serializable
{
  public static String REF = "Aircraft";
  public static String PROP_AIRCRAFT_SERIAL = "AircraftSerial";
  public static String PROP_AIRCRAFT_TYPE_ID = "AircraftTypeId";
  public static String PROP_STATE = "State";
  public static String PROP_REGISTRANT_TYPE_ID = "RegistrantTypeId";
  public static String PROP_ADDRESS1 = "Address1";

  //remaining property constants removed for brevity

  //constructors
  public BaseAircraft()
  {
    initialize();
  }

  /**
   * Constructor for primary key
   */
  public BaseAircraft(java.lang.String id)
  {
    this.setId(id);
    initialize();
  }

  /**
   * Constructor for required fields
   */
  public BaseAircraft(java.lang.String id, java.lang.String
          aircraftSerial, java.lang.String aircraftModelCode,
          java.lang.String aircraftEngineCode, java.lang.String
          yearBuilt, java.lang.String aircraftTypeId, java.lang.String
          aircraftEngineTypeId, java.lang.String registrantTypeId,
          java.lang.String name, java.lang.String address1, java.lang.
          String address2, java.lang.String city, java.lang.String
          state, java.lang.String zip, java.lang.String region, java.
          lang.String county, java.lang.String country, java.lang.
          String certification, java.lang.String statusCode, java.lang.
          String modeSCode, java.lang.String fractOwner, java.util.Date
```

```
            lastActionDate, java.util.Date certIssueDate, java.util.Date
            airWorthDate)
  {
    this.setId(id);
    this.setAircraftSerial(aircraftSerial);
    this.setAircraftModelCode(aircraftModelCode);
    this.setAircraftEngineCode(aircraftEngineCode);
    this.setYearBuilt(yearBuilt);
    this.setAircraftTypeId(aircraftTypeId);
    this.setAircraftEngineTypeId(aircraftEngineTypeId);
    this.setRegistrantTypeId(registrantTypeId);
    this.setName(name);
    this.setAddress1(address1);
    this.setAddress2(address2);
    this.setCity(city);
    this.setState(state);
    this.setZip(zip);
    this.setRegion(region);
    this.setCounty(county);
    this.setCountry(country);
    this.setCertification(certification);
    this.setStatusCode(statusCode);
    this.setModeSCode(modeSCode);
    this.setFractOwner(fractOwner);
    this.setLastActionDate(lastActionDate);
    this.setCertIssueDate(certIssueDate);
    this.setAirWorthDate(airWorthDate);
    initialize();
  }

  protected void initialize()
  {
  }

  private int hashCode = Integer.MIN_VALUE;

  // primary key
  private java.lang.String id;

  // fields
  private java.lang.String aircraftSerial;
  private java.lang.String aircraftModelCode;
  private java.lang.String aircraftEngineCode;
  private java.lang.String yearBuilt;
  private java.lang.String aircraftTypeId;
```

```
private java.lang.String aircraftEngineTypeId;
private java.lang.String registrantTypeId;
private java.lang.String name;
private java.lang.String address1;
private java.lang.String address2;
private java.lang.String city;
private java.lang.String state;
private java.lang.String zip;
private java.lang.String region;
private java.lang.String county;
private java.lang.String country;
private java.lang.String certification;
private java.lang.String statusCode;
private java.lang.String modeSCode;
private java.lang.String fractOwner;
private java.util.Date lastActionDate;
private java.util.Date certIssueDate;
private java.util.Date airWorthDate;

//Setters and getters omitted for brevity

public boolean equals(Object obj)
{
  if (null == obj)
    return false;
  if (!(obj instanceof net.ensode.jasperbook.dbaccess.Aircraft))
    return false;
  else
  {
    net.ensode.jasperbook.dbaccess.Aircraft aircraft =
                    (net.ensode.jasperbook.dbaccess.Aircraft) obj;
    if (null == this.getId() || null == aircraft.getId())
      return false;
    else
      return (this.getId().equals(aircraft.getId()));
  }
}

public int hashCode()
{
  if (Integer.MIN_VALUE == this.hashCode)
  {
    if (null == this.getId())
      return super.hashCode();
    else........
```

```
        {
          String hashStr = this.getClass().getName() + ":"
                                          + this.getId().hashCode();
          this.hashCode = hashStr.hashCode();
        }
      }
      return this.hashCode;
  }

  public int compareTo(Object obj)
  {
    if (obj.hashCode() > hashCode())
      return 1;
    else if (obj.hashCode() < hashCode())
      return -1;
    else
      return 0;
  }

  public String toString()
  {
    return super.toString();
  }
}
```

In order to let Hibernate know that the preceeding class maps to the `aircraft` table, we need to write an XML configuration file.

```
<?xml version="1.0"?>
<!DOCTYPE hibernate-mapping PUBLIC
  "-//Hibernate/Hibernate Mapping DTD//EN"
  "http://hibernate.sourceforge.net/hibernate-mapping-3.0.dtd">

<hibernate-mapping package="net.ensode.jasperbook.dbaccess">
  <class name="Aircraft"
        table="aircraft">
    <id name="Id"
        type="string"
        column="tail_num">
    </id>

    <property name="AircraftSerial"
              column="aircraft_serial"
              type="string"
              not-null="true"
              length="20"/>
```

```
<property name="AircraftModelCode"
         column="aircraft_model_code"
         type="string"
         not-null="true"
         length="7"/>
<property name="AircraftEngineCode"
         column="aircraft_engine_code"
         type="string"
         not-null="true"
         length="5"/>
<property name="YearBuilt"
         column="year_built"
         type="java.lang.String"
         not-null="true"
         length="4"/>
<property name="AircraftTypeId"
         column="aircraft_type_id"
         type="java.lang.String"
         not-null="true"
         length="3"/>
<property name="AircraftEngineTypeId"
         column="aircraft_engine_type_id"
         type="java.lang.String"
         not-null="true"
         length="3"/>
<property name="RegistrantTypeId"
         column="registrant_type_id"
         type="java.lang.String"
         not-null="true"
         length="3"/>
<property name="Name"
         column="name"
         type="string"
         not-null="true"
         length="50"/>
<property name="Address1"
         column="address1"
         type="string"
         not-null="true"
         length="33"/>
```

```
        <property name="Address2"
                 column="address2"
                 type="string"
                 not-null="true"
                 length="33"/>
        <property name="City"
                 column="city"
                 type="string"
                 not-null="true"
                 length="18"/>
        <property name="State"
                 column="state"
                 type="string"
                 not-null="true"
                 length="2"/>
        <property name="Zip"
                 column="zip"
                 type="string"
                 not-null="true"
                 length="10"/>
        <property name="Region"
                 column="region"
                 type="string"
                 not-null="true"
                 length="1"/>
        <property name="County"
                 column="county"
                 type="string"
                 not-null="true"
                 length="3"/>
        <property name="Country"
                 column="country"
                 type="string"
                 not-null="true"
                 length="2"/>
        <property name="Certification"
                 column="certification"
                 type="string"
                 not-null="true"
                 length="10"/>
```

```
        <property name="StatusCode"
                column="status_code"
                type="string"
                not-null="true"
                length="1"/>
        <property name="ModeSCode"
                column="mode_s_code"
                type="string"
                not-null="true"
                length="8"/>
        <property name="FractOwner"
                column="fract_owner"
                type="string"
                not-null="true"
                length="1"/>
        <property name="LastActionDate"
                column="last_action_date"
                type="date"
                not-null="true"
                length="10"/>
        <property name="AirWorthDate"
                column="air_worth_date"
                type="date"
                not-null="true"
                length="10"/>
    </class>
</hibernate-mapping>
```

This XML file lets Hibernate know that the `Aircraft` class maps to the `aircraft` table, and also defines the mapping between the table's columns and the class fields.

Hibernate needs another XML configuration file, which allows it to know the database connection information and what XML files to use to map database tables to Java classes. This XML configuration file is called `hibernate.cfg.xml`.

```
<?xml version='1.0' encoding='UTF-8'?>
<!DOCTYPE hibernate-configuration PUBLIC
  "-//Hibernate/Hibernate Configuration DTD 3.0//EN"
  "http://hibernate.sourceforge.net/hibernate-configuration-3.0.dtd">
<hibernate-configuration>
  <session-factory>
    <!-- local connection properties -->
    <property name="hibernate.connection.url">
      jdbc:mysql://localhost:3306/flightstats
    </property>
```

```
      <property name="hibernate.connection.driver_class">
        com.mysql.jdbc.Driver
      </property>
      <property name="hibernate.connection.username">user</property>
      <property name="hibernate.connection.password">password</property>
      <!-- property name="hibernate.connection.pool_size"></property -->
      <!-- dialect for MySQL -->
      <property name="dialect">
        org.hibernate.dialect.MySQLDialect
      </property>
      <property name="hibernate.show_sql">false</property>
      <property name="hibernate.transaction.factory_class">
        org.hibernate.transaction.JDBCTransactionFactory
      </property>
      <mapping resource="Aircraft.hbm.xml" />
      <mapping resource="AircraftEngines.hbm.xml"/>
      <mapping resource="AircraftEngineTypes.hbm.xml"/>
      <mapping resource="AircraftModels.hbm.xml"/>
      <mapping resource="AircraftTypes.hbm.xml"/>
    </session-factory>
  </hibernate-configuration>
```

The following code fragment illustrates how to fill a report using HQL as its query language:

```
package net.ensode.jasperbook;

import java.util.HashMap;
import java.util.Map;

import net.sf.jasperreports.engine.JRException;
import net.sf.jasperreports.engine.JasperFillManager;
import net.sf.jasperreports.engine.query.
JRHibernateQueryExecuterFactory;

import org.hibernate.Session;
import org.hibernate.SessionFactory;
import org.hibernate.cfg.Configuration;

public class HibernateQueryDemo
{
  Session session;
  SessionFactory sessionFactory;

  public static void main(String[] args)
  {
```

```
      new HibernateQueryDemo().fillReport(args[0]);
   }
   public void fillReport(String countryCode)
   {
      String reportDirectory = "reports";
      session = createSession();

      Map parameterMap = new HashMap();
      parameterMap.put(JRHibernateQueryExecuterFactory.PARAMETER_
                    HIBERNATE_SESSION, session);
      parameterMap.put("countryCode", countryCode);

      try
      {
         System.out.println("Filling report...");
         JasperFillManager.fillReportToFile(reportDirectory
                    + "/HibernateQueryDemoReport.jasper", parameterMap);
         System.out.println("Done!");
      }
      catch (JRException e)
      {
         System.out.println("There was an error filling the report.");
         e.printStackTrace();
      }
   }

   private Session createSession()
   {
      SessionFactory sessionFactory = new Configuration().configure().
                                buildSessionFactory();
      return sessionFactory.openSession();
   }
}
```

Once again there is not much difference between filling a report using an embedded HQL query and filling a report using an embedded SQL query or a report using a datasource. The main difference is that an instance of org.hibernate.Session must be passed to the report via a parameter named

`JRHibernateQueryExecuterFactory.PARAMETER_HIBERNATE_SESSION`. Executing this code will generate a report like the following:

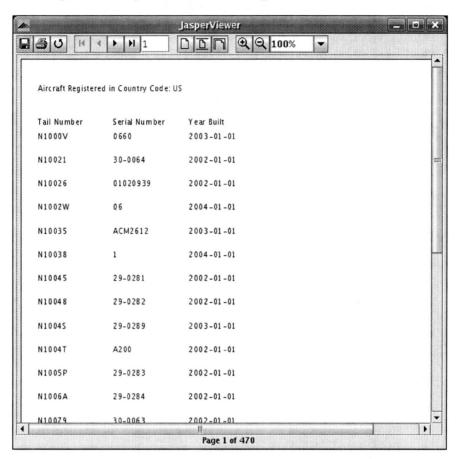

Of course, in order for this procedure to work, Hibernate must be properly configured to connect to the database where the report will be retrieving data from. Refer to the online Hibernate documentation at `http://hibernate.org/5.html` for details.

JasperReports versions prior to 1.2 lack direct integration with Hibernate. A technique commonly used before this integration was to use Hibernate to populate a collection of data objects and use these data objects to create a `JRBeanCollectionDataSource` instance. Then, use this instance of `JRBeanCollectionDataSource` to populate the report. This technique is explained in detail in the Hibernate website at `http://www.hibernate.org/79.html`.

As we can see, integrating JasperReports and Hibernate is trivial. Since Hibernate is a very popular Object-Relational Mapping tool, this integration was a welcome addition to JasperReports 1.2.

# Integrating JasperReports with Spring

Spring (http://www.springframework.org) is a very popular framework that helps simplify development of Java EE applications. The Spring Framework integrates nicely with JasperReports. In this section, we will develop a simple web application using Spring Web MVC, which is Spring's native web application framework.

The web.xml for our simple application is as follows:

```xml
<?xml version="1.0" encoding="ISO-8859-1"?>

<!DOCTYPE web-app PUBLIC
  "-//Sun Microsystems, Inc.//DTD Web Application 2.3//EN"
  "http://java.sun.com/dtd/web-app_2_3.dtd">
<web-app>
  <servlet>
    <servlet-name>jasperSpring</servlet-name>
    <servlet-class>
      org.springframework.web.servlet.DispatcherServlet
    </servlet-class>
    <load-on-startup>1</load-on-startup>
  </servlet>

  <servlet-mapping>
    <servlet-name>jasperSpring</servlet-name>
    <url-pattern>/jasperSpring/*</url-pattern>
  </servlet-mapping>
</web-app>
```

As can be seen in this web.xml code, there is only one servlet in our application. This servlet, called the DispatcherServlet, is provided by the springframework. Please note that we named our servlet jasperSpring to make it clear that this instance of DispatcherServlet will be used to generate reports. However, DispatcherServlet is not specific to JasperReports functionality.

Each application developed with the springframework must contain an application context, which is usually an XML file containing additional configuration. For Spring Web MVC applications, the application context is named after the servlet, following the servletname-servlet.xml pattern. For our application, the application context file is named as jasperSpring-servlet.xml.

```xml
<?xml version="1.0" encoding="UTF-8"?>
<!DOCTYPE beans PUBLIC "-//SPRING//DTD BEAN//EN" "http://www.
 springframework.org/dtd/spring-beans.dtd">

<beans>
  <bean id="dataSource"
        class="org.springframework.jdbc.datasource.
               DriverManagerDataSource" destroy-method="close">
    <property name="driverClassName">
      <value>com.mysql.jdbc.Driver</value>
    </property>
    <property name="url">
      <value>jdbc:mysql://localhost:3306/flightstats</value>
    </property>
    <property name="username">
      <value>user</value>
    </property>
    <property name="password">
      <value>secret</value>
    </property>
  </bean>
  <bean id="publicUrlMapping"
        class="org.springframework.web.servlet.handler.
               SimpleUrlHandlerMapping">
    <property name="mappings">
      <props>
        <prop key="report">jasperController</prop>
      </props>
    </property>
  </bean>

  <bean id="jasperController"
        class="net.ensode.jasperbook.spring.JasperSpringController">
    <property name="dataSource">
      <ref local="dataSource"/>
    </property>
  </bean>
  <bean id="viewResolver"
        class="org.springframework.web.servlet.view.
               ResourceBundleViewResolver">
    <property name="basename" value="views"/>
  </bean>
</beans>
```

One of the main features of the `springframework` is that it allows applications to be very loosely coupled by allowing dependencies to be defined in XML configuration files. This allows changing dependencies without having to change a single line of code.

In the `jasperSpring-servlet.xml` file, we define a dependency on the database datasource by declaring the bean with an `id` of `datasource` and setting it up as a property of the `jasperController` bean. The bean with the `id` of `publicUrlMapping` maps the `report` URL to our controller. The bean with the `id` of `viewResolver` is an instance of `org.springframework.web.servlet.view.ResourceBundleViewResolver`.

Its purpose is to look up values in a resource bundle to determine what view to use. Its `basename` property defines the name of the property file containing the keys to look up. In this case, the property file must be named `views.properties`.

```
report.class=org.springframework.web.servlet.view.jasperreports.
JasperReportsPdfView
report.url=reports/DbReportDS.jasper
```

Notice that the base name of the keys (`report`, in this case) must match the name of the controller property defined in the application context for `SimpleUrlHandlerMapping`. It is in this property file that we actually declare that JasperReports will be used to render the data.

In this example, we are using the `JasperReportsPdfView` class to export to PDF. The Spring framework also supports exporting to CSV, HTML, and Excel. To export to one of these formats, the classes to use would be `JasperReportsCsvView`, `JasperReportsHtmlView`, and `JasperReportsXlsView`, respectively. All of these classes are in the `org.springframework.web.servlet.view.jasperreports` package.

The `report.url` property defines where to find the compiled report template. In order for the `JasperReportsPdfView` class to find the compiled report template, it must be located in a directory matching the value of this property. The report template we will use for this example is the one discussed in the *Database Reporting via a Datasource* section of Chapter 4.

Just as with most MVC frameworks, we never code our servlets directly when writing web applications using Spring MVC; instead, we write controller classes. In this example, our controller class implements the `org.springframework.web.servlet.mvc.Controller` interface. This interface defines a single method called `handleRequest()`.

```
package net.ensode.jasperbook.spring;

import java.io.IOException;
```

```
import java.sql.Connection;
import java.sql.ResultSet;
import java.sql.SQLException;
import java.sql.Statement;
import java.util.HashMap;
import java.util.Map;

import javax.servlet.ServletException;
import javax.servlet.http.HttpServletRequest;
import javax.servlet.http.HttpServletResponse;
import javax.sql.DataSource;

import net.sf.jasperreports.engine.JRResultSetDataSource;

import org.springframework.web.servlet.ModelAndView;
import org.springframework.web.servlet.mvc.Controller;

public class JasperSpringController implements Controller
{
  private DataSource dataSource;

  public ModelAndView handleRequest(HttpServletRequest request,
      HttpServletResponse response) throws ServletException,
      IOException, ClassNotFoundException, SQLException
  {
    return new ModelAndView("report", getModel());
  }

  private Map getModel() throws ClassNotFoundException, SQLException
  {
    Connection connection;
    Statement statement;
    ResultSet resultSet;
    HashMap model = new HashMap();

    String query = "select a.tail_num, a.aircraft_serial, "
      + "am.model as aircraft_model, ae.model as engine_model from
          aircraft a, "
      + "aircraft_models am, aircraft_engines ae where "
      + "a.aircraft_engine_code in ("
      + "select aircraft_engine_code from aircraft_engines "
      + "where horsepower >= 1000) and am.aircraft_model_code = "
      + "a.aircraft_model_code "
      + "and ae.aircraft_engine_code = a.aircraft_engine_code";

    connection = dataSource.getConnection();
    statement = connection.createStatement();
```

```
    resultSet = statement.executeQuery(query);

    JRResultSetDataSource resultSetDataSource =
                                new JRResultSetDataSource(resultSet);

    model.put("datasource", resultSetDataSource);

    return model;
  }

  public void setDataSource (DataSource dataSource)
  {
    this.dataSource=dataSource;
  }
}
```

Note that our implementation of the `handleRequest()` method is very simple. It returns a new instance of `org.springframework.web.servlet.ModelAndView`. We pass the view name (defined in the application context) and a map containing the data to be displayed to the constructor of `ModelAndView`, and return it.

The `getModel()` method of `JasperSpringController` executes an SQL query in the database and populates an instance of `JRResultSetDataSource` with the results.

Finally, we need to write a JSP that will invoke `JasperSpringController`.

```
<%@ page language="java" contentType="text/html; charset=UTF-8"
 pageEncoding="UTF-8"%>
<!DOCTYPE HTML PUBLIC "-//W3C//DTD HTML 4.01 Transitional//EN">
<html>
  <head>
    <meta http-equiv="Content-Type" content="text/html; charset=UTF-8">
    <title>Generate Report</title>
  </head>
  <body>
    Click on the button to generate the report.
    <form name="reportForm" action="jasperSpring/report" method="post">
      <input type="submit" name="submitButton" value="Submit"/>
    </form>
  </body>
</html>
```

Notice that no special JSP tag libraries are needed to integrate with Spring. After we deploy our web application and direct our browser to `http://localhost:8080/jasperspring/generate_report.jsp`, we should see a web page like the following:

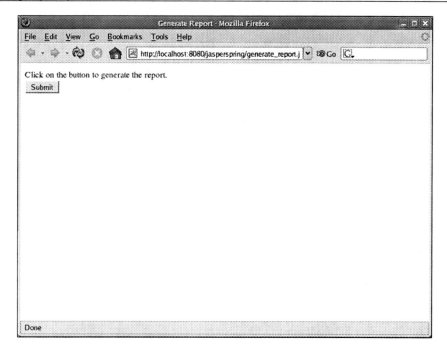

After clicking the **Submit** button, the report will be generated and displayed in the browser in PDF format.

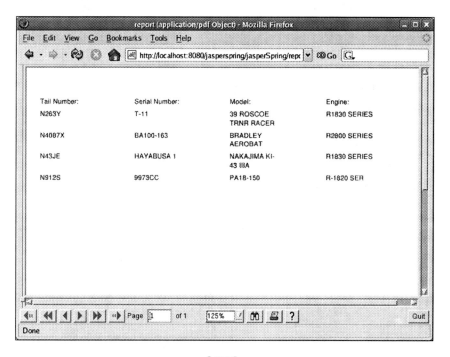

# Integrating JasperReports with JavaServer Faces

**JavaServer Faces (JSF)** is the standard technology for developing user interfaces for Java server applications. In theory, JavaServer Faces is view technology agnostic (that is, it can be used to develop user interfaces for a variety of technologies). However, in practice, JSF is almost always used to develop web applications.

JSF applications typically consist of JSP and backing beans, with the latter serving as controllers for the former. JSF and JasperReports integration can be accomplished by creating a backing bean that will generate a report. The following example illustrates this technique:

```
package net.ensode.jsf;

import java.io.IOException;
import java.io.InputStream;
import java.sql.Connection;
import java.sql.DriverManager;
import java.sql.SQLException;
import java.util.HashMap;

import javax.faces.context.FacesContext;
import javax.faces.event.ActionEvent;
import javax.servlet.ServletOutputStream;
import javax.servlet.http.HttpServletResponse;

import net.sf.jasperreports.engine.JRException;
import net.sf.jasperreports.engine.JasperRunManager;

public class ReportGenerator
{
  public void generateReport(ActionEvent actionEvent)
      throws ClassNotFoundException, SQLException, IOException,
      JRException
  {
    Connection connection;
    FacesContext context = FacesContext.getCurrentInstance();
    HttpServletResponse response = (HttpServletResponse)
                      context.getExternalContext().getResponse();
    InputStream reportStream = context.getExternalContext().
                   getResourceAsStream("/reports/DbReport.jasper");
    ServletOutputStream servletOutputStream =
                          response.getOutputStream();
```

```
        Class.forName("com.mysql.jdbc.Driver");

        connection = DriverManager.getConnection("jdbc:mysql://localhost:
                3306/flightstats?user=user&password=secret");

JasperRunManager.runReportToPdfStream(reportStream,
                servletOutputStream, new HashMap(), connection);

        connection.close();

        response.setContentType("application/pdf");
        servletOutputStream.flush();
        servletOutputStream.close();

    }
}
```

JasperReports does not natively integrate with JSF. Therefore, the trick to getting them to work together is to use the JSF API to obtain objects from the servlet API, since JasperReports integrates nicely with these objects. The HttpServletResponse object is of particular interest.

As can be seen in the preceding example, we can obtain the HttpServletResponse object by calling the FacesContext.getExternalContext().getResponse() method. We can then obtain an instance of ServletOutputStream from the response object as usual, by calling the HttpServletResponse.getOutputStream() method.

In order to know what report to compile, we need to load the compiled report template as a stream. This is accomplished by a call to the FacesContext.getExternalContext().getResourceAsStream() method, as illustrated in the code. For this example, we will use the report template discussed in the *Embedding SQL Queries into a Report Template* section of Chapter 4.

Once we have obtained the HttpServletResponse object and the ServletOutputStream object, and loaded the report template into memory, then all we need to do to generate the report is execute the JasperRunManager.runReportToPdfStream() method, passing the appropriate parameters. This, of course, assumes that we want to render the report as a PDF; to render in other formats, we need to substitute with the appropriate call.

In order to execute the `generateReport()` method in the backing bean, we need to bind it to a JSP action. The following JSP illustrates how to do this:

```
<%@ page language="java" contentType="text/html; charset=UTF-8"
 pageEncoding="UTF-8"%>
<%@ taglib uri="http://java.sun.com/jsf/html" prefix="h"%>
<%@ taglib uri="http://java.sun.com/jsf/core" prefix="f"%>
<!DOCTYPE HTML PUBLIC "-//W3C//DTD HTML 4.01 Transitional//EN">
<html>
<head>
<meta http-equiv="Content-Type" content="text/html; charset=UTF-8">
<title>Generate Report</title>
</head>
<body>
<f:view>
   <h:outputText value="Click on the link below to generate the
                        report."/>
   <h:form>
     <h:commandLink action="generate_report"
       actionListener="#{reportGenerator.generateReport}">
       <h:outputText value="Generate Report"/>
     </h:commandLink>
   </h:form>
</f:view>
</body>
</html>
```

This JSP links the action of clicking on a `commandLink` component (basically an HTML link) to the `generateReport()` method on the `ReportGenerator` backing bean. This JSP file is rendered as follows:

Clicking on the **Generate Report** link results in the report template being filled, exported to PDF, and displayed to the user.

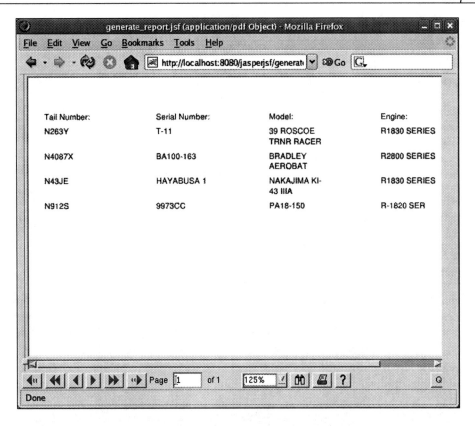

In order for this to work as expected, some configuration needs to be done behind the scenes. The `faces-config.xml` file must be configured properly to let JSF know that `ReportGenerator` is a backing bean.

```
<?xml version="1.0" encoding="UTF-8"?>
<!DOCTYPE faces-config PUBLIC
  "-//Sun Microsystems, Inc.//DTD JavaServer Faces Config 1.0//EN"
  "http://java.sun.com/dtd/web-facesconfig_1_0.dtd">
<faces-config>
  <managed-bean>
    <managed-bean-name>reportGenerator</managed-bean-name>
    <managed-bean-class>
      net.ensode.jsf.ReportGenerator
    </managed-bean-class>
    <managed-bean-scope>request</managed-bean-scope>
  </managed-bean>
</faces-config>
```

This file must be placed in the WEB-INF directory inside the war file used to deploy the application.

The last step needed to make this technique work properly is to set up the `web.xml` file to use JSF.

```
<?xml version="1.0" encoding="ISO-8859-1"?>
<!DOCTYPE web-app PUBLIC
  "-//Sun Microsystems, Inc.//DTD Web Application 2.3//EN"
  "http://java.sun.com/dtd/web-app_2_3.dtd">
<web-app>
  <servlet>
    <servlet-name>Faces Servlet</servlet-name>
    <servlet-class>javax.faces.webapp.FacesServlet</servlet-class>
    <load-on-startup>1</load-on-startup>
  </servlet>
  <servlet-mapping>
    <servlet-name>Faces Servlet</servlet-name>
    <url-pattern>*.jsf</url-pattern>
  </servlet-mapping>
</web-app>
```

This tells the web container to use the `javax.faces.webapp.FacesServlet` servlet to process any requests for file names ending in `.jsf`. Of course, in order for this to work, a JAR file containing an implementation of the JavaServer Faces specification must be in the CLASSPATH. For this example, we used the Apache licensed MyFaces implementation.

# Integrating JasperReports with Struts

The **Struts** framework is the most popular Java web application framework. Typically, Struts applications consist of JSP, Action classes that serve as the controller component of MVC, form beans that map HTML form elements, and an XML configuration file. For more information on the Struts framework take a look at *Learning Jakarta Struts 1.2* (ISBN: 1-904811-54-X) by Packt Publishing. JasperReports Struts integration consists of writing a controller that will generate a report when executed.

The following action class demonstrates this technique:

```
package net.ensode.jasperbook.struts;

import java.io.InputStream;
import java.sql.Connection;
import java.sql.DriverManager;
import java.util.HashMap;

import javax.servlet.ServletOutputStream;
import javax.servlet.http.HttpServletRequest;
import javax.servlet.http.HttpServletResponse;
import net.sf.jasperreports.engine.JasperRunManager;
```

```
import org.apache.struts.action.Action;
import org.apache.struts.action.ActionForm;
import org.apache.struts.action.ActionForward;
import org.apache.struts.action.ActionMapping;

public class GenerateReportAction extends Action
{
  public ActionForward execute(ActionMapping mapping, ActionForm form,
      HttpServletRequest request, HttpServletResponse response)
      throws Exception
  {

    Connection connection;
    ServletOutputStream servletOutputStream =
                                        response.getOutputStream();
    InputStream reportStream = getServlet().getServletConfig()
                          .getServletContext().getResourceAsStream(
                          "/reports/DbReport.jasper");
    response.setContentType("application/pdf");

    Class.forName("com.mysql.jdbc.Driver");

    connection = DriverManager.getConnection("jdbc:mysql://localhost:
              3306/flightstats?user=user&password=secret");

    JasperRunManager.runReportToPdfStream(reportStream,
                    servletOutputStream, new HashMap(), connection);

    connection.close();

    servletOutputStream.flush();
    servletOutputStream.close();

    return mapping.getInputForward();
  }
}
```

All action classes must extend the class `org.apache.struts.action.Action`. Typically, the `execute()` method is overridden to implement custom logic for servicing a request. As can be seen in the code above, the `execute()` method takes an instance of `HttpServletResponse` as one of its parameters. This makes it easy to write Action classes that generate reports.

The technique illustrated in the preceding example is not much different from what we have seen in various earlier examples throughout the book. In most examples, we used standard Java Servlets to generate web reports, implementing the report logic in the servlet's `doGet()` method. Since both the `HttpServlet.doGet()` and `Action.execute()` methods take an instance of `HttpServletResponse` as one of their parameters, the technique to generate a report from an Action class is virtually identical to the technique used when using a servlet.

Let us take a look at the JSP that will invoke the `GenerateReportAction.execute()` method.

```
<%@ taglib uri="/tags/struts-logic" prefix="logic"%>
<%@ taglib uri="/tags/struts-html" prefix="html"%>
<%@ taglib uri="/tags/struts-bean" prefix="bean"%>
<!DOCTYPE HTML PUBLIC "-//W3C//DTD HTML 4.01 Transitional//EN">
<html>
  <head>
    <title>Generate Report</title>
  </head>
  <body>
    <p>Click on the button to generate the report.</p>
    <html:form action="/generate_report">
      <html:submit/>
    </html:form>
  </body>
</html>
```

This JSP will generate a very simple HTML form with a **submit** button as its only input field.

Next, let us take a look at the form bean for this JSP.

```
package net.ensode.jasperbook.struts;

import org.apache.struts.action.ActionForm;

public class GenerateReportForm extends ActionForm
{

}
```

Since the HTML form generated by the preceding JSP has no input fields other than a **submit** button, its corresponding form bean has no fields. We still need to write it because when writing Struts applications, each JSP must have a corresponding form bean.

To wire the Action class, the form bean, and the JSP together, we need to create a `struts-config.xml` file and deploy it in the `WEB-INF` directory of the application's war file.

```
<?xml version="1.0" encoding="ISO-8859-1"?>

<!DOCTYPE struts-config PUBLIC
 "-//Apache Software Foundation//DTD Struts Configuration 1.2//EN"
 "http://jakarta.apache.org/struts/dtds/struts-config_1_2.dtd">

<struts-config>
  <!-- ====================================== Form Bean Definitions -->

  <form-beans>
    <form-bean name="generateReportForm"
               type="net.ensode.jasperbook.struts.GenerateReportForm">
    </form-bean>
  </form-beans>
  <!-- ================================ Action Mapping Definitions -->
  <action-mappings>
    <action path="/generate_report"
            type="net.ensode.jasperbook.struts.GenerateReportAction"
            name="generateReportForm"
            scope="request"
            input="generate_report.jsp">
    </action>
  </action-mappings>
</struts-config>
```

The `<form-bean>` tag defines the GenerateReportForm class as a form bean and assigns the generateReportForm logical name to it.

The `<action>` tag maps the GenerateReportAction action class to the /generate_report path. It also specifies that the GenerateReportForm form bean will be associated with this action. Finally, it links the generate_report.jsp JSP file via the input attribute.

Like all server-side Java web applications, Struts applications must contain a web.xml file in the WEB-INF directory inside the application's war file.

```
<?xml version="1.0" encoding="ISO-8859-1"?>

<!DOCTYPE web-app PUBLIC
 "-//Sun Microsystems, Inc.//DTD Web Application 2.2//EN"
 "http://java.sun.com/j2ee/dtds/web-app_2_2.dtd">

<web-app>
  <display-name>Struts JasperReports Application</display-name>
```

```xml
<!-- Standard Action Servlet Configuration (with debugging) -->
<servlet>
  <servlet-name>action</servlet-name>
  <servlet-class>org.apache.struts.action.ActionServlet
  </servlet-class>
  <init-param>
    <param-name>config</param-name>
    <param-value>/WEB-INF/struts-config.xml</param-value>
  </init-param>
  <init-param>
    <param-name>debug</param-name>
    <param-value>2</param-value>
  </init-param>
  <init-param>
    <param-name>detail</param-name>
    <param-value>2</param-value>
  </init-param>
  <load-on-startup>2</load-on-startup>
</servlet>
<!-- Standard Action Servlet Mapping -->
<servlet-mapping>
  <servlet-name>action</servlet-name>
  <url-pattern>*.do</url-pattern>
</servlet-mapping>
<!-- The Usual Welcome File List -->
<welcome-file-list>
  <welcome-file>index.jsp</welcome-file>
</welcome-file-list>
<!-- Struts Tag Library Descriptors -->
<taglib>
  <taglib-uri>/tags/struts-bean</taglib-uri>
  <taglib-location>/WEB-INF/struts-bean.tld</taglib-location>
</taglib>

<taglib>
  <taglib-uri>/tags/struts-html</taglib-uri>
  <taglib-location>/WEB-INF/struts-html.tld</taglib-location>
</taglib>

<taglib>
  <taglib-uri>/tags/struts-logic</taglib-uri>
  <taglib-location>/WEB-INF/struts-logic.tld</taglib-location>
</taglib>
</web-app>
```

This `web.xml` file simply defines the Struts `ActionServlet` to process all URLs ending in `.do`. The Struts `ActionServlet` calls the appropriate JSP and Action class behind the scenes for the appropriate URL.

Following the standard procedure for deploying web applications, we create a WAR file with the preceding files and required dependencies, deploy it to a servlet container, and point the browser to the corresponding URL. We should then see a web page like the following:

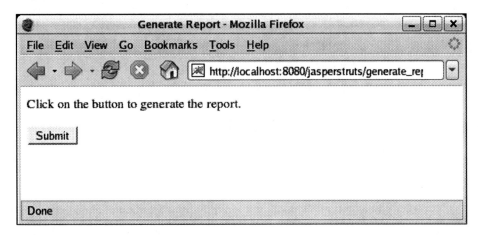

Clicking on the **Submit** button generates the report, exports it to PDF, and displays it on the browser.

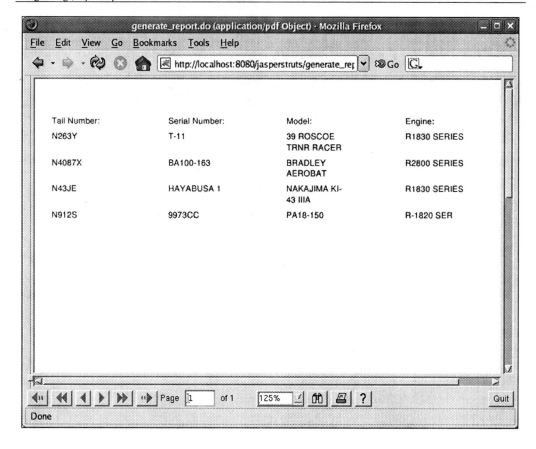

# Summary

The chapter starts with integrating JasperReports with Hibernate by writing embedded report queries in the Hibernate Query Language (HQL). JasperReports with HQL queries is similar to reports containing SQL queries except that the language attribute of the `<queryString>` element must be set to `hql`. Next, we saw how to integrate JasperReports with the Spring framework by taking advantage of Spring's built-in JasperReports integration.

The chapter also dealt with JavaServer Faces and JasperReports integration and illustrated how to write backing beans that fill a report and display it in the browser. Finally, the chapter illustrated the integration of JasperReports with Struts by explaining how to write action classes that fill a report and display it in the browser.

# Index

pie3DChart element 183
pieChart element 183
plot element 180
queryString element 39, 59
rectangle element 171
reportElement 30
report parameters, retrieving 83
staticText element 30
text element 30
textField attribute 59
variable element 139
**JRXML report template**
background element 48
Binary report template, creating 33
columnFooter element 50
columnHeader element 49
compiled report template, previewing 34, 35
compiling, programmatically 33
compiling through ANT 36, 37
creating 29
detail element 45, 50
fieldDescription element 108
field element 47
group element 48, 131
group element, attributes 133
import element 46
jasperReport root element 116
jasperReport root element, attributes 116
lastPageFooter element 51
modified 93, 95
multiple columns logic, encapsulating 126, 128
output 37
pageFooter element 51
pageHeader element 49, 65
parameter element 47
parameters, sending to report template 83, 85
property element 46
queryString element 47
reportFont element 46
report parameters, declaring 83
sub-elements, subreport element 167
subreport element 167
summary element 52
title element 48
variable element 47

with static data 80
XML report previewing 30
**JSF 309**

# M

**map datasource**
about 87
JRDataSource class used 90, 91
JRMapArrayDataSource class 89
JRMapArrayDataSource class used 87, 89

# O

**optional libraries, Jasper Reports**
about 25
Apache ANT 25
iText 27
Jakarta POI 27
JFreeChart 27
**optional tools, Jasper Reports**
JDBC driver 26
JDT compiler 26
**OutOfMemoryException 218**

# P

**PDF documents**
bookmarks 215
**pie charts**
creating 181
JRXML template 181, 183
pie3DChart element 183
pieChart element 183
**plot element**
about 180
attributes 180
backcolor attribute 180
backgroundAlpha attribute 180
foregroundAlpha attribute 180
orientation attribute 180
**POJOs.** *See* **java objects as datasource**

# R

**RDBMS.** *See* **relational database systems**
**relational database systems**
JAR files required 26

# [PACKT] Thank you for buying
PUBLISHING **JasperReports for Java Developers**

## Packt Open Source Project Royalties

When we sell a book written on an Open Source project, we pay a royalty directly to that project. Therefore by purchasing JasperReports for Java Developers, Packt will have given some of the money received to the JasperReports project.

In the long term, we see ourselves and you—customers and readers of our books—as part of the Open Source ecosystem, providing sustainable revenue for the projects we publish on. Our aim at Packt is to establish publishing royalties as an essential part of the service and support a business model that sustains Open Source.

If you're working with an Open Source project that you would like us to publish on, and subsequently pay royalties to, please get in touch with us.

## Writing for Packt

We welcome all inquiries from people who are interested in authoring. Book proposals should be sent to authors@packtpub.com. If your book idea is still at an early stage and you would like to discuss it first before writing a formal book proposal, contact us; one of our commissioning editors will get in touch with you.

We're not just looking for published authors; if you have strong technical skills but no writing experience, our experienced editors can help you develop a writing career, or simply get some additional reward for your expertise.

## About Packt Publishing

Packt, pronounced 'packed', published its first book "Mastering phpMyAdmin for Effective MySQL Management" in April 2004 and subsequently continued to specialize in publishing highly focused books on specific technologies and solutions.

Our books and publications share the experiences of your fellow IT professionals in adapting and customizing today's systems, applications, and frameworks. Our solution-based books give you the knowledge and power to customize the software and technologies you're using to get the job done. Packt books are more specific and less general than the IT books you have seen in the past. Our unique business model allows us to bring you more focused information, giving you more of what you need to know, and less of what you don't.

Packt is a modern, yet unique publishing company, which focuses on producing quality, cutting-edge books for communities of developers, administrators, and newbies alike. For more information, please visit our website: www.PacktPub.com.

PUBLISHING

Managing and Customizing
OpenCms 6

**Managing and Customizing OpenCms 6 Websites**

ISBN: 1-904811-76-0          Paperback: 240 pages

A complete guide to set up, configuration and administration.

1. Understand the OpenCms web publishing process

2. Learn how to create your own, complex, OpenCms website

3. Develop the skills to implement, customize and maintain an OpenCms website

Learning Jakarta Struts 1.2
A concise and practical tutorial

A step-by-step introduction to building Struts web applications for Java developers

Stephan Wiesner          PACKT

# Learning Jakarta Struts 1.2: a concise and practical tutorial

ISBN: 1-904811-80-9          Paperback: 204 pages

A step-by-step introduction to building Struts web applications for Java developers.

1. Learn to build Struts applications right away

2. Build an ecommerce store step-by-step using Struts

3. Well-structured and logical progression through the essentials

Please check **www.PacktPub.com** for information on our titles

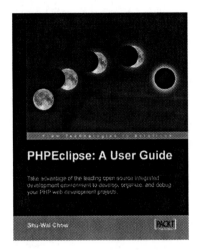

## PHPEclipse: A User Guide

ISBN: 1-904811-44-2          Paperback: 206 pages

Take advantage of the leading open source integrated development environment to develop, organize, and debug your PHP web development projects.

1. Compact guide to using Eclipse and PHPEclipse for web development

2. Slash development time by improving the efficiency of your PHP coding and organizing your projects in the PHPEclipse environment

3. Learn to use Eclipse for debugging PHP applications, interfacing with databases, and managing source code

4. No previous knowledge of Eclipse required

## Building Websites with Joomla!

ISBN: 1-904811-94-9          Paperback: 340 pages

A step-by-step tutorial to getting your Joomla! CMS website up fast.

1. Walk through each step in a friendly and accessible way

2. Customize and extend your Joomla! site

3. Get your Joomla! website up fast

Please check **www.PacktPub.com** for information on our titles

Printed in the United States
103889LV00002B/79-80/A

9 781904 811909